Advance Praise for
EARLY BUDDHIST TEACHINGS

"In my assessment, this is the best answer to the questions 'How did Buddhism begin and how best can we describe it?'"

—G. A. Somaratne, assistant professor in Buddhist studies, the University of Hong Kong

"An excellent introduction to early Buddhist teachings. The author has meticulously analyzed the key Buddhist doctrines and presented them in an equally meticulous manner."

—Guang Xing, chair of the master of Buddhist studies program and deputy director of the Centre for Buddhist Studies, the University of Hong Kong

"By the foremost scholar on early Buddhism and Abhidhamma, this brilliant yet simply presented explication of the first principles of Buddhist philosophy analyses the unique contributions of Buddhism against the backdrop of other traditions current at the time of its origins. It explains how the radically new doctrine of nonself, its 'middleness' between spiritual eternalism and materialist annihilationism, unfolds in terms of philosophy, psychology, and practical ethics. The teachings are made accessible with finely nuanced translations of Buddhist texts and the astute rendering of Buddhist technical terms into modern English equivalents. The appendix on Buddhist pluralism is an insightful, important, and timely reminder of the Buddha's rejection of ultraorthodoxy, exclusivism, and fanaticism."

—Kate Crosby, professor of Buddhist studies, King's College, London

EARLY BUDDHIST TEACHINGS

The Middle Position in Theory and Practice

Y. Karunadasa

Wisdom

Wisdom Publications
199 Elm Street
Somerville, MA 02144 USA
wisdompubs.org

First published by the Centre of Buddhist Studies, the University of Hong Kong, 2013

Library of Congress Cataloging-in-Publication Data
Names: Karunadasa, Y., author.
Title: Early Buddhist teachings: the middle position in theory and practice / Y. Karunadasa.
Description: Somerville, MA: Wisdom Publications, 2018. | "First published by the Centre of Buddhist Studies, the University of Hong Kong, 2013." | Includes bibliographical references and index. |
Identifiers: LCCN 2017026914 (print) | LCCN 2017028139 (ebook) | ISBN 9781614294689 (ebook) | ISBN 1614294682 (ebook) | ISBN 9781614294528 (pbk.: alk. paper) | ISBN 1614294526 (pbk.: alk. paper)
Subjects: LCSH: Middle Way (Buddhism)
Classification: LCC BQ4280 (ebook) | LCC BQ4280 .K37 2018 (print) | DDC 294.3—dc23
LC record available at https://lccn.loc.gov/2017026914

ISBN 978-1-61429-452-8 ebook ISBN 978-1-61429-468-9

22 21 20 19 18 5 4 3 2 1

Cover design by Graciela Galup. Cover art: Head of the Buddha; Afghanistan, 300-400 AD; Stucco / Universal History Archive/UIG / Bridgeman Images
Interior design by James D. Skatges. Set in Diacritical Garamond Pro 11.25/14.

Wisdom Publications' books are printed on acid-free paper and meet the guidelines for permanence and durability of the Production Guidelines for Book Longevity of the Council on Library Resources.

Printed in the United States of America.

CONTENTS

PREFACE

Early Buddhist teachings are the subject of an increasingly impressive body of scholarship in the form of monographs, book chapters, scholarly articles, and encyclopedia entries. The present volume takes up the position that the best way to understand early Buddhist teachings is as a critical response to the binary opposition between two perennial worldviews: spiritual eternalism (*sassatavāda*) and materialist annihilationism (*ucchedavāda*). The first is the theory of the metaphysical self, a self that is distinct from the physical body. The second is the theory of the physical self, a self that is identical with the physical body. These two theoretical views, as the Buddha clearly indicates, have a tendency to persist throughout the history of human thought. It is by keeping itself equally aloof from both of these views of the self that early Buddhism becomes a middle position. If the doctrine of dependent arising is called the "middle doctrine," this is because it transcends the mutual conflict between spiritual eternalism and materialist annihilationism. If the noble eightfold path is called the "middle path," this is because, in the selfsame manner, it transcends the two extremist practices associated with the two theoretical views, namely, self-mortification and sensual indulgence. Thus both in theory (dependent arising) and practice (noble eightfold path), early Buddhism follows a middle position.

For early Buddhism, "middleness" does not mean moderation. Nor does it mean a compromise of the two extremes or a synthesis that embraces the two extremes. As defined by the Buddha himself, middleness is to be understood as "not entering either of the two extremes" (*ubho ante anupagamma*). In other words, middleness is the transcendence of the mutual opposition between the two extremes.

There are many other extremes in relation to which Buddhism adopts the middle position, namely, extreme realism (*sabbaṃ atthi*) and extreme nihilism (*sabbaṃ natthi*), extreme monism (*sabbaṃ ekattaṃ*) and extreme pluralism (*sabbaṃ puthuttaṃ*), determinism (both theistic and karmic) and indeterminism, self-causation (*sayaṃ-kata*) and external causation (*paraṃ-kata*), and so on. However, as we shall see in the course of this work, these other extremes can be subsumed under the two main headings: spiritual eternalism and materialist annihilationism.

In the context of what we have observed above, the question arises: Is it logically necessary that the truth should lie in the middle rather than in one of the two extremes? In answering this question, we would like to make two observations. The first observation is that nowhere in the early Buddhist discourses is it claimed that truth should necessarily occupy the middle position. The other observation is that if Buddhism adopts the middle position, this is not merely because it is the middle, but because it is the true position.

Then in which sense should we understand the middle position as true? As mentioned above, Buddhism does not postulate the "self" notion either in its spiritual or its materialist version. It is by steering clear of these two versions of the "self" notion that Buddhism becomes a middle position, and not for any other reason. What the middle position clearly amounts to is that whereas others took for granted the reality of the subject as a self-entity, the Buddha challenged its very reality and reduced both subject and object, perceiver and perceived, to dynamic processes without, of course, abrogating the duality between the subject and the object. The subject-object abrogation is part of mystical experience. It has no place in the teachings of the Buddha.

We believe that it is only when one takes this middle context into consideration that one can properly understand not only what led to the birth of Buddhism but also the significance of its basic teachings, such as, for instance, dependent arising and the doctrine of nonself, or the theory and practice of moral life, the diagnosis of the human condition, the unanswered questions, the Buddhist critique of theoretical views, or the nature of *nibbāna*, the final goal of Buddhism. These Buddhist doctrines, as we have shown in the course of this work, assume their significance in distancing themselves from the two worldviews of spiritual eternalism and annihilationist materialism. It is this factor that provides synthetic unity and thematic coherence to all Buddhist teachings.

The present work is mainly based on the Sutta Piṭaka, the Basket of Discourses of the Pāli Buddhist canon. However, where necessary, it will consult the postcanonical commentarial exegesis in interpreting the early Buddhist teachings.

Y. Karunadasa
Centre of Buddhist Studies
The University of Hong Kong

ACKNOWLEDGMENTS

Two chapters in this book, one on dependent arising and the other on nonself, are based on two articles I contributed to *The Sri Lanka Journal of Buddhist Studies*, whose editor in chief is the Venerable Dr. K. L. Dhammajoti, the Glorious Sun Professor of Buddhist Studies at the University of Hong Kong. I am most grateful to him for his consent to reproduce them here.

I am equally grateful to the Venerable Dr. Guang Xing, assistant professor at the Centre of Buddhist Studies of the University of Hong Kong, for suggesting that I prepare a book on early Buddhist teachings and for the deep and abiding interest he has evinced in this work ever since I began it some years ago.

I express my grateful thanks to Dr. Asoka Welitota for helping me in word-processing the manuscript when he was a PhD student at the University of Hong Kong.

I owe a special debt of gratitude to Mr. Anthony Robert Scott, my friend and erstwhile student, for carefully going through the manuscript and making many valuable suggestions to improve the quality of the book. I benefited much from his critical mind and sound sense.

I must express my grateful thanks to Aosi Mak, teaching assistant at the Centre of Buddhist Studies, for devoting much of her precious time to the arduous task of formatting the manuscript and proofreading and generating the index, thus preparing the manuscript for publication.

Finally, I would like to express my grateful thanks to Professor C. F.

Lee, to the Venerable Hin Hung, director of the Centre of Buddhist Studies, and to other members of the Li Chong Yuet Ming Buddhist Studies Fund of the Li Ka Shing Foundation for accepting this book to be included in The University of Hong Kong Centre of Buddhist Studies Publication Series.

Y. Karunadasa
Centre of Buddhist Studies
The University of Hong Kong
August 1, 2013

I

SOME PRELIMINARY OBSERVATIONS

IN THE BUDDHA'S teachings as we find them presented in the early Buddhist discourses, we can identify two noteworthy characteristics. One is that they are not claimed to be a divine revelation. As the founder of a religion, the Buddha did not attribute the authorship of what he had discovered through supreme human effort to a higher source, to a personal God, or to an impersonal godhead. The other is that the Buddha's teachings are not claimed to be a reformed version of a previous doctrine, a doctrine that had prevailed earlier but that had been forgotten or misunderstood later. What these two characteristics clearly demonstrate is that the Buddha took full responsibility for what he taught.[1]

The best way to understand what the Buddha taught is to describe it as a discovery. Thus with reference to the doctrine of dependent arising, which is the most fundamental teaching in Buddhism, the Buddha says:

> Whether tathāgatas arise or not, this order exists, namely, the fixed nature of phenomena, the regular pattern of phenomena or conditionality. This the tathāgata discovers and comprehends. Having discovered and comprehended it, he points it out, teaches it, lays it down, establishes, reveals, analyzes, clarifies it, and says "look."[2]

If the Dhamma is a discovery, then it is the pivotal role of the Dhamma that comes into more prominence. From the Buddhist perspective, therefore, what is more important is not the historicity of the discoverer (Buddha) but the veracity and the validity of the discovery (Dhamma). As a matter of fact, as recorded in one Buddhist discourse, the Buddha himself says that he depends on the Dhamma, honors the Dhamma, is respectful and deferential to the Dhamma, and considers the Dhamma as his banner and standard, his overlord.[3] Equally significant in this connection is what the Buddha told Ānanda, his close disciple, a few days before his *parinibbāna*: "Ānanda, the doctrine and discipline, which I have taught and enjoined, is to be your teacher after my passing."[4]

Because of the pivotal role assigned to the Dhamma, the Buddha himself recognizes that others, too, can present the Dhamma and elaborate on it. Many are the occasions recorded in the Buddhist discourses when the Buddha appreciates his own disciples' expositions of the Dhamma.[5]

Among the most preeminent expounders of the Dhamma are both monastic members and lay disciples. As recognized by the Buddha himself, these include Puṇṇa Mantāniputta, a Buddhist monk; Dhammadinnā, a Buddhist nun; and Citta and Hatthaka, two disciples among the laity.

Furthermore, the Buddha encourages his disciples to elaborate on the Dhamma. Accordingly, the Buddha tells Māra that he will not attain *parinibbāna* until he has monks, nuns, and male and female lay disciples "who are wise, disciplined, confident, secure from bondage, learned, upholders of the Dhamma, practicing in accordance with the Dhamma, practicing in the proper way, conducting themselves accordingly; who have learned their own teacher's doctrine and can explain it, teach it, proclaim it, establish it, disclose it, analyze it, and elucidate it; and who can refute thoroughly with reasons any prevailing misinterpretations of the Dhamma."[6]

There are two things that merit our attention here. One is that the Buddha refers not only to monks and nuns but also to male and female lay disciples. The other is that the Buddha expects his disciples to not only correctly understand and disseminate the Dhamma but also refute with good reasons any doctrinal misinterpretations.

One noteworthy feature of the early Buddhist discourses is that they themselves tell us how the teachings contained in them are presented and how they should be understood accordingly. In his well-known discourse on the Parable of the Raft, the Buddha compared his doctrine to a raft. It is for the purpose of crossing over and not to be grasped as a theory. As a means to an end the Dhamma has only relative value, relative to the realization of the goal. We find this idea beautifully illustrated in the Chinese Buddhist saying that the Dhamma is like a finger pointing to the moon. If we concentrate our attention only on the finger, we cannot see the moon. Nor can we see the moon without looking at the finger.

As a further extension of this idea, it came to be recognized that the Dhamma as a means can be presented in many different ways, from many different perspectives. As recorded in one discourse, when two disciples of the Buddha, a monk and a carpenter, had an unstoppable argument as to the number of feelings, one recognizing two feelings and the other three, Ānanda reported this matter to the Buddha. Then the Buddha told Ānanda that both of them were correct, because they looked at the issue from two different perspectives.

As to the number of feelings, the Buddha told Ānanda that he had presented them not only as two or three, but also as five, six, eighteen, thirty-six, and one hundred and eight in different presentations.[7]

It was on this occasion that the Buddha made the statement that has crucial implications for correctly interpreting the Buddha's teachings: "In this way, Ānanda, this Dhamma has been stated by me in [different] presentations."[8] The clear message conveyed here is that what accords with actuality and, therefore, what is true need not be repeated in the same way as a holy hymn or a sacred mantra. Rather, what is true can be restated in many ways, from many different perspectives. As elsewhere, here too Buddhism avoids absolutism and dogmatism: there is no one absolutist way of presenting the Dhamma that must be dogmatically adhered to.

What is equally important is that the Buddha goes on to say that when the Dhamma has thus been presented in many different ways, one should not tenaciously adhere to one particular presentation, then argue and quarrel with others who base themselves on other presentations.[9]

That the Dhamma has been presented from many different perspectives can be seen from other Buddhist discourses as well. To give some examples: The well-known five mental hindrances (*nīvaraṇa*) are from another perspective presented as ten, and the seven factors of enlightenment (*bojjhaṅga*) are from another perspective presented as fourteen.[10] In one and the same collection of discourses, we find a person who has entered the stream of the noble eightfold path (*sotāpanna*) being described in more than one way, and the path leading to the unconditioned (*nibbāna*) described in eleven different ways.[11] Even the noble truth of suffering (*dukkha*) has been *formally* defined in three different ways, adopting three different perspectives.[12]

One purpose of our referring to some instances of the Dhamma being presented in many different ways is this: By taking these and other similar cases into consideration we should not hasten to conclude that they represent different historical stages in the development of Buddhist thought, unless of course there is clear evidence to the contrary. Rather, they should be understood in light of the Buddha's statement that the Dhamma has been shown in different presentations.

If the Dhamma can be presented from many different perspectives, this is because the Dhamma is not actuality as such but a description of the nature of actuality. The Dhamma is a conceptual, theoretical model that describes the nature of actuality through a series of propositions. We find this idea formally expressed in an Abhidhamma compendium when it says: "It is by not going beyond concepts (*paññatti*) that the nature of actuality has been presented."[13] Here the term "concept" denotes both concept-as-naming (*nāma-paññatti*) and concept-as-meaning (*attha-paññatti*).[14] Therefore what this means is that the nature of actuality has been presented within a conceptual, theoretical framework through the symbolic medium of language.

As a matter of fact, there can be more than one conceptual or theoretical model encapsulating the nature of actuality. The validity of each will be determined by its ability to take us to the goal, that is, from bondage to freedom, from ignorance to wisdom, from our present predicament to final emancipation.

If the Dhamma can be presented as different conceptual models, it can also be communicated through a variety of languages. Buddhism does not have a holy language. When it was reported to the Buddha that his Dhamma should be rendered into the elitist language of Sanskrit, the Buddha did not endorse it but allowed the Dhamma to be understood by each through his or her own language.[15] The Dhamma as well as the language through which it is presented are, as such, a means to an end and not the end in itself.

Another critical guideline mentioned in the Buddhist discourses for correctly understanding the teachings contained in them is the distinction drawn between two kinds of discourses: a discourse "whose meaning is already drawn out" (*nītattha*) and a discourse "whose meaning has to be drawn out" (*neyyattha*).[16] The former refers to those statements to be understood as they stand, as explicit and definitive, and the latter to those statements that should be interpreted to fall in line with the explicit and the definitive. "Whose meaning is already drawn out" is an expression for philosophical language, the use of impersonal technical terms to bring out the true nature of actuality. "Whose meaning is to be drawn out" is an expression for the usc of conventional and transactional terms in ordinary parlance in presenting the Buddhist teachings. This distinction between the two kinds of discourses is so crucial that to overlook it is to misrepresent the teachings of the Buddha. Hence the Buddha says:

> Whoever declares a discourse with a meaning already drawn out as a discourse with a meaning to be drawn out, and [conversely] whoever declares a discourse with a meaning to be drawn out as a discourse with a meaning already drawn out, such a one makes a false statement with regard to the Blessed One.[17]

In order to understand the significance of the above quotation, it is necessary to note that Buddhist philosophy is a dynamic-process philosophy. When others took for granted the reality of the subject as a self-entity, the Buddha challenged its reality and reduced both subject and object, perceiver and perceived, to dynamic processes. The Buddhist teachings on impermanence, nonself, and dependent arising mean that in the final analysis there are no agents, entities, and substances. There are only mental and material phenomena that arise in dependence on other mental and material phenomena, with no self-subsisting noumena as the ground of their being.

From the Buddhist perspective, therefore, wrongly hypostatized entities and objects of reification are nothing but conceptual constructs, logical abstractions, or pure denominations with no corresponding objective counterparts. Even the principle of dependent arising in its abstract sense, as the commentarial exegesis clarifies it, turns out to be a conceptual construct with no objective reality. In this connection, it is observed that whether the *tathāgatas* appear or not, it is with ignorance as a condition that volitional activities arise, and it is with volitional activities as a condition that consciousness arises. The occurrence of several factors in this manner by way of dependent arising is an objective occurrence. Nevertheless, there is no independently existing abstract principle called "dependent arising," besides or in addition to the objective occurrence of the dependently arising factors. What led to this commentarial clarification is the attempt made by some other Buddhist schools to reify the principle of dependent arising.[18]

The same situation is true of impermanence (*anicca*), suffering (*dukkha*), and selflessness (*anatta*), the three main characteristics of all sentient existence. In addition to what is subject to these three characteristics, there are no corresponding characteristics existing as independent entities. If the characteristic of impermanence, for instance, were to be postulated as a real entity, then it would be necessary to postulate a secondary characteristic of impermanence to account for its own impermanence. And this secondary characteristic of impermanence would in turn require a secondary-secondary characteristic of impermanence to account for its own impermanence. In this way—so runs the argument—it would inevitably involve what the commentarial exegesis calls a process of interminability (*anupaccheda*), or infinite regress (*anavaṭṭhāna*).[19]

Since the Buddhist view of actuality is free from entities and substances, in presenting it through the medium of language difficulties can certainly arise, for the structure of language is such that sometimes it can falsify the view of actuality as presented by Buddhism. For example, the subject-predicate sentence, "the nominative expression" (*kattu-sādhana*) in Buddhist exegesis, gives rise to the false notion that corresponding to the grammatical subject there is an ontological subject as well. An example is: "cognition cognizes" (*viññāṇaṃ vijānāti*). This kind of definition is made by superimposing a distinction where there is no such distinction (*abhede bheda-parikappanā*). The distinction thus created is that between the agent and the action. For this very reason, the definition based on "the nominative expression" is said to be tentative and provisional, not valid in an ultimate sense.[20]

Accordingly, all such innocent-looking sentences as "I see," "my eyes see," "I see with my eyes," and "the eye-consciousness sees" are not valid in an ultimate sense. And why? For they all assume a distinction between the agent and its action. To make them valid, we need to rephrase them in the language of causality (dependent arising). When so rephrased, they all mean: "depending on the eye and the eye-object arises eye-consciousness."

Again, the use of the genitive expression (*sāmi-vacana*), as, for example, "the color of the rainbow," creates "the distinction between the support and the supported" (*ādhāra-ādheya*), that is, the distinction between substance and quality.[21] Such a distinction Buddhism does not recognize. It is only a product of our imagination. Its recognition leaves the door open for the intrusion of the notion of a "substantial self" (*attavāda*) with all that it entails.

What the above observations amount to is that the structure of language does not exactly correspond to the structure of actuality. It is this philosophical notion that lies behind the two kinds of statement mentioned above, the technical-philosophical (*nītattha*) and the consensual-transactional (*neyyattha*). What is important to remember here is that if we use only technical philosophical language, just because it is the right language, it will fail to communicate what we want to communicate. Convention requires the use of such expressions as "I see," "I hear," and so on, but as long as one does not imagine independent agents corresponding to them, such expressions are valid.

On the other hand, as the Buddhist commentarial exegesis observes, if, for the sake of conforming to the actual situation, one were to say "the five aggregates eat" (*khandhā bhuñjanti*) or "the five aggregates walk" (*khandhā gacchanti*), instead of saying "a person eats" or "a person walks," such a situation would result in "breach of convention (*vohāra-bheda*), leading to a breakdown in meaningful communication."[22] Hence in presenting the Dhamma the Buddha does not exceed linguistic conventions but uses such terms as "person" without being led astray by their superficial implications.[23] Language is certainly necessary as a means of communicating the Dhamma. Nevertheless, on the use of language there is this well-known saying of the Buddha: Addressing Citta the householder, the Buddha says, "These, Citta, are names (*samaññā*), expressions (*nirutti*), turns of speech (*vohāra*), and designations (*paññatti*) in common use in the world. And of these the tathāgata makes use indeed, but is not led astray by them."[24] Neither clinging to language nor overstepping it is the golden mean.

The two kinds of statement, referred to above, are equally valid, provided they are understood in the proper context. The Buddha does not say that one kind of statement is higher or lower than the other. What he says instead is that the two statements should not be confused, because they need to be understood in two different contexts. We make a mistake only if we interpret one as if it were the other.

In the early Buddhist discourses we also find constant reference to some six specific characteristics of the Dhamma taught by the Buddha:

1. The Dhamma is well-expounded (*svākkhāta*).
2. It is visible here and now (*sandiṭṭhika*).
3. It does not involve time (*akālika*).
4. It invites one to come and see it (*ehi-passika*).
5. It leads onward to the goal (*opanayika*).
6. It is to be realized for themselves by the wise (*paccattaṃ veditabbo viññūhi*).[25]

The first, which is the quality of being well expounded, can easily be seen in the Buddha's discourses. Here we do not come across esotericism or mysticism, either in the language used or in the ideas expressed. The view that the Buddha communicated his doctrine through silence, a silence that is more "thunderous" than communication through language, finds no place in the early Buddhist discourses.

Furthermore, the Buddha says that he does not have "the closed fist of the teachers" (*ācariya-muṭṭhi*),[26] teachers who make distinctions between esoteric and exoteric aspects of their teachings. The more one elaborates the Buddha's doctrine and discipline, the more it shines, and not when it is concealed.[27] The Dhamma is not confined to an elitist class, but "is for the benefit and happiness of the many."

Hence it is that addressing his first sixty disciples who became arahants, the Buddha exhorted them to spread the Dhamma "for the blessing of the many-folk, for the happiness of the many-folk, out of compassion for the world, for the welfare, the blessing, the happiness of devas and men. Let not two of you go by one way."[28] There is no adequate evidence to show that any religious teacher, during or before the time of the Buddha, resorted to missionary activity. Buddhism could, therefore, be considered as the first missionary religion in the world.

The next three specific characteristics of the Dhamma are three ways of looking at it as teachings that can be personally verified, here and now. "Visible here and now" means that the Dhamma can be experientially validated and authenticated here and now. "Does not involve time" means that the Dhamma can be understood in living immediacy without going to the past or to the future. "Come and see" means that the Dhamma invites us not to come and accept it, but to come and examine it before we decide to follow it: the Dhamma does not encourage our accepting and following it on blind faith. "Leading onward" refers to the fact that when practiced, the Dhamma takes us toward the goal, that is, toward the realization of nibbāna, the complete emancipation from all suffering. The last characteristic of the Dhamma, that is, "to be realized for themselves by the wise," means that the Dhamma is to be directly and personally experienced and realized through wisdom, not through knowledge, which is accumulated memory.

We find these specific characteristics of the Dhamma clearly illustrated in a dialogue between Bhadraka the headman and the Buddha. Bhadraka wanted to know how he could understand the origin and the passing away of suffering. The Buddha said to him:

> If, headman, I were to teach you about the origin and the passing away of suffering with reference to the past, saying, "So it was in the past," perplexity and uncertainty about that might arise in you. And if I were to teach you about the origin and the passing away of suffering with reference to the future, saying, "So it will be in the future," perplexity and uncertainty about that might arise in you. Instead, headman, while I am sitting right here, and you are sitting right there, I will teach you about the origin and the passing away of suffering.

Then the Buddha explained to the headman, with many examples, how all suffering arises with self-centered desire as its cause, and how all suffering ceases with the cessation of its cause, which is self-centered desire. The Buddha asked the headman to apply this principle, which he has seen here and now, which he has fathomed immediately, to the past and the future as well.[29]

Here we find an instance of inferential (inductive) knowledge (*anvaye ñāṇa*), which is one of the means of knowledge recognized in early Buddhist epistemology.[30] Having first understood the fact of suffering and its cause, in the immediate present, through personal verification, one draws an inference (*nayaṃ neti*) with regard to the past and the future as follows:

> Whatever suffering arose in the past, all that arose rooted in desire with desire as its source; for desire is the root of suffering.

> Whatever suffering will arise in the future, all that will arise rooted in desire with desire as its source, for desire is the root of suffering.[31]

Now it is necessary to note here that all the teachings of the Buddha, as the Buddha himself declares, are related to two themes: suffering and cessation of suffering. It is these two themes that we find in the four noble truths, which represent the essence of the Buddha's teachings. And it is by penetrating the four noble truths that one realizes complete emancipation from all suffering. So what the dialogue between Bhadraka and the Buddha clearly demonstrates is that the four noble truths can be penetrated here and now, without direct knowledge of the fact of rebecoming (*punabbhava*).[32] It is of course true that rebecoming is a fundamental doctrine in the teachings of the Buddha. Nevertheless, as clearly shown above, if suffering arose in the past (in past births), and if suffering will arise in the future (in future births), in both cases, it is entirely due to self-centered desire—which fact can be understood and penetrated here and now, in living immediacy, without going to the past and to the future.

What comes into relief from the six specific characteristics of the Dhamma, as illustrated in the dialogue between Bhadraka the headman and the Buddha, is the authority of self-experience, which we find further elaborated in the Buddha's discourse to the Kālāmas as well. As recorded in this discourse, when the Buddha visited a small town called Kesaputta, the inhabitants of this town, known as Kālāmas, told the Buddha that religious teachers of different persuasions had presented them with a variety of doctrines, one different from another, and therefore they "have doubt and perplexity as to who among these venerable teachers spoke the truth." Then, addressing the Kālāmas, the Buddha said:

> Yes, Kālāmas, it is proper that you have doubt, that you have perplexity, for a doubt has arisen in a matter that is doubtful. Now look, you Kālāmas, do not be led by reports, or tradition, or hearsay. Be not led by the authority of religious texts, nor by mere logic or inference, nor by considering appearances, nor by the delight in speculative opinions, nor by seeming possibilities, nor by the idea "this is our teacher." But, O Kālāmas, when you know for yourselves that certain things are unwholesome and bad, then give them up . . . And when you know for yourselves that certain

things are wholesome and good, then accept them and follow them.

Then the Buddha told the Kālāmas how they themselves could decide on what is bad and unwholesome and what is good and wholesome:

> "Now what do you think, Kālāmas? When greed arises within a man, does it arise to his profit or to his loss?"
>
> "To his loss, Sir."
>
> "Now, Kālāmas, does not this man, thus become greedy, being overcome by greed and losing control of his mind, does he not kill a living creature, take what is not given, go after another's wife, tell lies and lead another into such a state as causes his loss and sorrow for a long time?"
>
> "He does, Sir."[33]

The Buddha made similar observations with respect to aversion and delusion and was thus able to convince the Kālāmas of the undesirability of doing what is bad and unwholesome.

Then the Buddha told the Kālāmas that when a person is free from greed, aversion, and delusion, what he does is beneficial to him as well as others. And in this way the Buddha was able to convince them of the desirability of doing what is good and wholesome.

If the Kālāma discourse begins by enumerating the epistemological grounds that cannot be fully relied on, it concludes by establishing the authority of self-experience (*paccattaṃ veditabba*) as the most reliable ground for deciding on what is morally unwholesome and what is morally wholesome.

In concluding this introductory chapter, we would like to focus on another important issue: How can we identify the Dhamma? How can we separate it from what it is not?

We believe that the best way to answer this question is to approach it from the perspective of the final goal of the Buddha's teachings. Their final goal, as we all know, is nibbāna. Nibbāna has been described in many ways, from many perspectives. But its most standard definition is "the cessation of passion, aversion, and delusion."[34] These are the three basic causes of all moral evil because all forms of moral evil are traceable to them. Therefore, when these three morally unwholesome factors are eliminated, all moral defilements come to an end. What we need to remember here is that when passion, aversion, and delusion cease, the corresponding positive counterparts emerge: the absence of passion, aversion, and delusion positively means the presence of generosity, loving kindness, and wisdom.[35]

Now, as recorded in one Buddhist discourse, even followers of other religions will have to agree that there cannot be many final goals (*puthu niṭṭhā*). There has to be only one final goal (*ekā niṭṭhā*) as the highest spirituality, and this highest spirituality cannot be anything other than the elimination of passion, aversion, and delusion, or the presence, in their highest levels, of generosity, loving kindness, and wisdom.[36] This gives us a clear indication as to how we should separate the Dhamma from what it is not: whatever leads to the cessation of passion, aversion, and delusion is the Dhamma; whatever leads away from it is not the Dhamma. This criterion is, in fact, clearly indicated in several Buddhist discourses. The criterion of what is or what is not the Dhamma is ultimately pragmatic, not textual, although of course it occurs in Buddhist texts.

2

THE BIRTH OF BUDDHISM

A Critical Response to the Binary Opposition between Two Worldviews

THE BUDDHA often refers to the binary opposition between two worldviews and sees his own teaching as one that sets itself equally aloof from both of them. Thus, addressing Kaccāna, the Buddha says:

> This world, Kaccāna, for the most part depends on a duality—on the notion of "existence" and the notion of "nonexistence." But for one who sees the origin of the world as it really is with correct wisdom, there is no notion of "nonexistence" in regard to the world. And for one who sees the cessation of the world as it really is with correct wisdom, there is no notion of "existence" in regard to the world. "All exists," Kaccāna, this is one extreme. "All does not exist," this is the second extreme. Without veering toward either of these extremes, the tathāgata teaches the Dhamma by the middle.[1]

It is against these two worldviews that Buddhist polemics are continually directed, and it is by demolishing them that Buddhism seeks to construct its own view of the world. This should explain why most Buddhist teachings are presented in such a way as to unfold themselves, or to follow as a necessary corollary from a criticism of the two theoretical views of existence and nonexistence. This particular context is sometimes clearly stated and sometimes taken for granted. It is within the framework of the Buddhist critique of these two worldviews, therefore, that we need to understand not only the birth of Buddhism but also the significance of its basic doctrines.

The two theoretical views of existence and nonexistence, it may be noted, are sometimes presented as the view of being (*bhava-diṭṭhi*) and the view of nonbeing (*vibhava-diṭṭhi*),[2] but more often as eternalism (*sassatavāda*) and annihilationism (*ucchedavāda*), respectively.[3] What exactly does Buddhism mean by the two views? More important, why does it see itself as a critical response to their binary opposition?

For this purpose, we need to examine, at least in bare outline, the religious and philosophical background against which Buddhism arose. The prevailing mood of the time is very well reflected in the Buddhist discourses. The very first discourse in the entire Sutta Piṭaka of the Pāli canon, known as "The All-Embracing Net of Views," is an appraisal, from the Buddhist perspective, of some sixty-two religious and philosophical views, which are said to represent all possible theoretical speculations on the nature of the self and the world. This is the only discourse to which the Buddha himself has given several titles, among which one is "The Incomparable Victory in the Battle against Theoretical Views."[4]

All these theoretical views, despite their wide variety, can be divided into three main groups. The first group includes religious beliefs, the second, materialist theories that arose in direct opposition to religion, and the third, many forms of skepticism that arose as a reaction against both religious beliefs and materialist theories.

As to religion, there were two main movements. One is Brahmanism and the other, Samanism. Brahmanism was a linear development of ancient Vedic thought; it embraced both traditional religious views as well as elitist doctrines confined to a few. Samanism, on the other hand, embraced a broader spectrum of religious teachings and practices, and they all seem to have arisen either in isolation from or in direct opposition to Brahmanism. In Brahmanism, the trend was more toward theism, monism, and orthodoxy. In Samanism, it was more toward nontheism, pluralism, and heterodoxy.

There was, however, one basic idea that was commonly accepted by all religions belonging to both Brahmanism and Samanism. This basic idea, as presented in the Buddhist discourses, is as follows: "The self is one thing and the body another" (*Aññaṃ jīvaṃ aññaṃ sarīraṃ*).[5] This view assumes a duality between two basic principles, one spiritual and the other material: a permanent metaphysical self, on the one hand, and the temporary physical body, on the other. Accordingly, one's true essence is to be found not in the perishable physical body but in the permanent metaphysical self. Hence this view came to be described in the Buddhist discourses as eternalism (*sassatavāda*), or the eternalist theory of the self. Let us call it the theory of the metaphysical self, while noting at the same time that all religions and philosophies, both past and present, that subscribe to it are, from the Buddhist perspective, different versions of eternalism.

The theoretical view of annihilationism arose in direct opposition to all religion. It took its stand on the epistemological ground that sense perception was the only valid means of knowledge and, therefore, it questioned the validity of theological and metaphysical theories that did not come within the ambit of sense experience. As such, annihilationism rejected the religious version of the self and introduced its own version of the self. As presented in the Buddhist discourses, it is as follows: "The self is the same as the body" (*Taṃ jīvaṃ taṃ sarīraṃ*).[6] Here the emphasis is not on the duality but on the identity of the self and the physical body. For annihilationism, therefore, "the self is something material and a product of the four primary elements of matter."[7] Accordingly, one's true essence is to be found not in an elusive metaphysical principle but in the empirically observable physical body. If the self and the physical body are identical, it logically and necessarily follows that at death, with the breakup of the body, the self too comes to annihilation with no possibility for its postmortem survival. Hence this theory of the self came to be described in the Buddhist discourses as annihilationism, or the annihilationist theory of the self. Let us call it the theory of the physical self, while noting at the same time that all materialist ideologies, both past and present, that subscribe to it are, from the Buddhist perspective, different versions of annihilationism.

The best example of a philosopher who espoused materialism during the time of the Buddha was Ajita Kesakambilin. In his view:

> This human being is built up of the four great elements of matter. When he dies the earthy in him returns and relapses to the earth, the fluid to the water, the heat to the fire, the windy to the air, and his faculties pass into space. Four bearers, with the bier as a

> fifth, take his dead body away; till they reach the burning-ground men utter forth eulogies, but there his bones are bleached, and his offerings end in ashes. It is a doctrine of fools, this talk of gifts. It is an empty lie, mere idle talk, when men say there is profit therein. Fools and wise alike, on the dissolution of the body, are cut off, annihilated, and after death they are not.[8]

Materialism, as assumed by some, rejects what is called *ātmavāda*, or the belief in a self or soul. Generally speaking, this may be true. Nonetheless, from the Buddhist perspective, this assumption is not tenable. According to Buddhism's understanding of the "self" theory, any kind of entity, whether it is material, mental, or spiritual, can become a soul or self-entity (*ātman*) if it becomes an object of self-appropriation. This process of self-appropriation is said to manifest in three ways: "this is mine (*etaṃ mama*), this I am (*eso'ham asmi*), and this is my self (*eso me attā*)."[9] As materialism takes the physical body to be an object of self-appropriation, to that extent it is also a variety of the "self" or "soul" theory. One could then contend that what the materialists appropriate as the self or soul is not a metaphysical entity but the empirically observable, perishable physical body. In the context of Buddhist teachings, however, what matters is not the permanence or impermanence of the object of self-appropriation but the very fact of self-appropriation.

Accordingly, Buddhism sees both eternalism and annihilationism as two versions of the "self" or "soul" theory. The first is its metaphysical version and the second its physical version—a position of mutual exclusion to which the Buddha refers thus:

> Monks, there are these two views, the view of being [eternalism] and the view of nonbeing [annihilationism]. Any recluses or brahmins who rely on the view of being, adopt the view of being, accept the view of being, are opposed to the view of nonbeing. Any recluses or brahmins who rely on the view of nonbeing, adopt the view of nonbeing, accept the view of nonbeing, are opposed to the view of being.[10]

There is a close connection between spiritual eternalism and the practice of self-mortification. The polarity between two principles, one spiritual and the other physical, implies a mutual conflict between the two. Between the soul and the body, it is the soul that is in bondage. What prevents its upward journey is the gravitational pull of the body. To redeem the soul and to ensure its perpetuation in a state of eternal bliss it is necessary, therefore, to mortify the flesh. It is this idea that seems to be the rationale for all forms of asceticism and self-denial, what Buddhism calls the practice of self-mortification (*attakilamathānuyoga*).[11] It is very likely that it was this belief that the body is a bondage to the self that led to many forms of ascetic practices during the time of the Buddha. A case in point was Jainism, which advocated rigid austerities to liberate the soul. Ascetic practices could assume varying degrees of intensity and visibility depending on how in each religion the relationship between the soul and the physical body is sought to be defined. Nevertheless, the duality principle on which the eternalist view is based logically leads to the justification of ascetic practices as a means to salvation.

On the other hand, the materialist version of the "self" or "soul" theory naturally veers toward the opposite direction, what Buddhism calls the practice of sensual indulgence (*kāmasukhallikānuyoga*).[12] As materialism believes in the identity of the self or soul and the physical body, it sees no reason why one should eschew immediate sense pleasures for the sake of an elusive bliss in a dubious future.

It is very likely that it was this polarization of intellectual thought into spiritual eternalism and materialist annihilationism that paved the way for the birth of skepticism. Skepticism too was not one uniform intellectual movement, as it embraced a number of schools.

A prototypical example of a skeptic philosopher who lived during the time of the Buddha was Sañjaya Belaṭṭhiputta. His position was that he could rationally argue for or against any speculative theory, as, for instance, a theory pertaining to postmortem survival:[13] where one is not sure, the healthiest attitude is to suspend judgment.

In the Indian context, however, skepticism does not necessarily mean a purely intellectual exercise. There is evidence to suggest that some adopted skepticism on the grounds that knowledge was not only impossible but also a danger to moral development and salvation.[14]

If the polarization of intellectual thought into the two ideologies paved the way for the birth of skepticism, it is very likely that it led to the emergence of Buddhism as well. In fact, this is very much suggested by the

Buddha's first sermon, known as the "Setting in Motion of the Wheel of the Dhamma." It begins thus:

> Monks, there are these two extremes that should not be practiced by one who has gone forth. One is addiction to sensual pleasure, which is low, vulgar, secular, ignoble, and leading to no good. The other is addiction to self-mortification, which is painful, ignoble, and leading to no good. Now, monks, without entering either of these two extremes, there is a middle way, fully awakened to by the tathāgata, making for vision, making for knowledge, which conduces to calming, to super knowledge, to awakening, to nibbāna. And what, monks, is this middle way? It is this noble eight-factored path itself, that is to say: right view, right intention, right speech, right action, right mode of living, right endeavor, right mindfulness, and right concentration.[15]

It will be seen that the two extremist practices referred to by the Buddha in this discourse are the practical manifestations of eternalism and annihilationism. If the Buddha's path to emancipation is called "the middle path" it is because it sets itself equally aloof from both of them. From the Buddhist perspective, "middleness" does not mean moderation or a compromise between the two extremes. As defined by the Buddha himself, it means "without entering either of the two extremes" (*ubho ante anupagamma*).[16]

Avoidance of the two extremist practices also means the avoidance of both eternalism and annihilationism, which serve as their theoretical background. As we shall see in chapter 3, it is through the Buddhist doctrine of dependent arising that Buddhism avoids both spiritual eternalism and materialist annihilationism. Therefore "dependent arising" came to be rightly introduced as "the doctrine of the middle."

Thus, in the early Buddhist discourses, the term "middle" came to be used in two different contexts: "middle way" to mean the noble eightfold path, and "middle doctrine" to mean dependent arising. Both in theory and practice, therefore, Buddhism follows a middle position.

The use of the term "middle" in this twofold sense brings into focus the intellectual milieu in which Buddhism arose. A middle position becomes meaningful only in the context of two extremes. As we have noted, the pair of extremes in relation to which Buddhism speaks of a middle position prevailed in pre-Buddhist India. This fact should show how pre-Buddhist religious and philosophical views served as a background to the birth of Buddhism. However, Buddhism arose not as a linear progression of either spiritual eternalism or materialist annihilationism. Rather, it arose as a critical response to their binary opposition.

It will be noticed that three of the words used by the Buddha in assessing sensual indulgence, namely, inferior (*hina*), rustic (*gamma*), and profane (*pothujjanika*), are conspicuously absent in his assessment of self-mortification. The implication seems to be that although spiritual eternalism does not lead to the right goal, nevertheless it does not lead to a collapse of the moral life. Spiritual eternalism is not subversive of the moral foundation of human society. It recognizes a spiritual source in the human being, and in so doing it also recognizes moral distinctions. In fact, according to the Buddha's assessment, all religions are different forms of *kammavāda*, since they all advocate the supremacy of the moral life. For this very reason, as we shall see in chapter 11, the Buddha does not say that any of the religions that come under eternalism are necessarily false. What he says instead is that they are "not satisfactory" (*anassāsika*).[17]

On the other hand, hedonistic materialism encourages a pattern of life that takes gratification in sensuality as the ultimate purpose of life. It takes for granted that our present existence is entirely due to fortuitous circumstances (*adhicca-samuppanna*), which in turn leads to the conclusion that we are not morally responsible for what we do during our temporary sojourn in this world. Therefore, hedonistic materialism is evaluated by the Buddha as a "false view" (*micchā-diṭṭhi*), for it does not provide a proper foundation for the practice of any religion, not necessarily Buddhism alone.[18]

Evaluating the two extremes in this way, as the Buddha says in another discourse, is neither to disparage those who practice them nor to extol those who avoid them. Disparaging and extolling occur only when one expresses one's own views with persons in mind. When one teaches only the Dhamma, one avoids any reference to persons. Therefore, as the Buddha says, what the above quoted words mean, in brief, is this: "The pursuit of either extreme does not lead to the right goal and is therefore not the right way. The practice of the middle path leads to the right goal and is therefore the right way."[19]

The Buddha biography itself delineates the mutual conflict between the two practices of sensual indulgence and self-mortification. If the

Buddha-to-be's lay life of luxury as a royal prince exemplifies one extreme, his life as an ascetic practicing austerities exemplifies the other. His attainment of enlightenment by giving up both extremes shows the efficacy of the middle path for deliverance from all suffering.

Early Buddhism's critique of theoretical views, it may be noted, takes into consideration their psychological motivation as well, that is, the mental dispositions that serve as their causative factors. The idea is that our desires and expectations have an impact on what we choose to believe in. According to the Buddhist diagnosis of the "psychology of eternalism," the belief in an eternal self is due to the craving for being (*bhava-taṇhā*), the craving for the eternalization of the self, the desire to perpetuate individuality into eternity. As per the Buddhist diagnosis of the "psychology of annihilationism," the belief in a temporary self is due to the craving for nonbeing (*vibhava-taṇhā*), the desire for complete annihilation at death.[20] If the former is due to the craving for eternal life, the latter is due to the craving for eternal death. Since materialist annihilationism rejects the possibility of postmortem survival, it tends to encourage a person to lead a life without a sense of moral responsibility. Therefore, it abhors any prospect of after-death existence, as that implies the possibility of moral accountability. It is this psychological resistance on the part of one who believes in materialism that leads to the desire to be completely annihilated at death.

Thus, the mutual conflict between spiritual and materialist theories represents not only the mutual conflict between two perennial ideologies but also the human mind's oscillation between two deep-seated desires.

> These one-sided views may also spring from *emotional* reasons, expressive of the basic attitudes to life. They may reflect the moods of optimism and pessimism, hope and despair, the wish to feel secure through metaphysical support, or the desire to live without inhibitions in a materialistically conceived universe. The theoretical views of eternalism or annihilationism held by an individual may well change during his lifetime, together with the corresponding moods of emotional needs.[21]

Our intellectual needs could also have an impact on their prevalence and proliferation.

> There is also an *intellectual* root: the speculative and theorizing propensity of the mind. Certain thinkers, people of the theorizing type (*diṭṭhicarita*) in Buddhist psychology, are prone to create various elaborate philosophical systems in which, with great ingenuity, they play off against each other the pairs of conceptual opposites. The great satisfaction this gives to those engaged in such thought-constructions further reinforces the adherence to them.[22]

If Buddhism dissociates itself from spiritual eternalism, this means that it does not recognize some spiritual substance within us that relates us to a transcendental reality, a reality that serves as the ultimate ground of existence. It is the soul or the self in its spiritual sense that connects the individual existence to a purported higher metaphysical reality. Since Buddhism does not recognize the "soul" idea, the notion of a "higher metaphysical reality" finds no place in Buddhist teachings. It is only the world of sensory experience that Buddhism recognizes, the world that we experience through our six sense faculties. This is perhaps where Buddhism parts company from all religions that come under the category of "eternalism," the religions that believe in an immortal soul and a higher reality, whether this higher reality is called God in a personal sense or the godhead in an impersonal sense.

If Buddhism dissociates itself from materialist annihilationism, this means that from the Buddhist perspective the human personality is not a pure product of matter. It is an uninterrupted and interconnected process of psychophysical phenomena that does not have a fortuitous beginning (*adhicca-samuppanna*) nor an abrupt ending (*uccheda*).[23] In common with all other religions, Buddhism too recognizes survival and the validity of the moral order (*kamma-niyāma*). It is the belief in a hereafter, in whichever way it is interpreted in each religion, and the recognition of the moral order that serve as the uniting factor of all religions.

In concluding this chapter on the birth of Buddhism as a middle position, it is interesting to notice that the term "middle" assumes a geographical dimension as well. Buddhism arose in what was then called the "middle region" (*majjhima-desa*) in North India, and not in its adjacent regions (*paccanta-desa*).

We could even add a cosmological dimension to the term "middle." In the hierarchy of the Buddhist cosmos we humans are like a middle class. Above us are the denizens of the celestial worlds, who are all the time immersed in their own divine pleasures. Below us are the lower levels of living beings, who are ignorant and perpetually engrossed in attending to their elementary needs for food and shelter. So it is only we humans who have the salutary atmosphere and the necessary wherewithal to follow the teachings of the Buddha, only we humans who can thus realize the final goal of Buddhism. It is not surprising, therefore, that as the Buddha himself says, the heavenly beings themselves fancy that to be born as human beings is to go to heaven (*Manussattaṃ kho, bhikkhu, devānaṃ sugati-gamana-saṅkhātaṃ*).[24] For Buddhism, the true heaven is not up above but here below in this terrestrial world of human beings.

3

DEPENDENT ARISING

The Definition of Dependent Arising

DEPENDENT ARISING, as we noted in the preceding chapter, is called the "doctrine of the middle," since it transcends the binary opposition between spiritual eternalism and materialist annihilationism. The abstract structural form of this doctrine, as defined by the Buddha, is as follows: "This being present, that comes to be; on this arising, that arises. This being absent, that does not come to be; on this ceasing, that ceases."[1]

This definition shows that whatever arises is arising in dependence on conditions; whatever ceases is ceasing because of the cessation of those conditions that made it arise. It gives us a clear idea of the nature of the relation that subsists between the cause and the effect. If we call the cause and the effect A and B, respectively, then it is not correct to say that B comes from A, or that B is an evolved stage of A. If it were so, then the language should have changed from "this being present, that comes to be" to "from this, that comes to be."[2]

Dependent arising, in other words, is not some kind of evolutionary change, an idea mainly associated with Sāṃkhya philosophy. According to Sāṃkhya philosophy, the effect remains in the cause in a latent, unmanifest form and becomes actualized as the result of an evolutionary process called *pariṇāma*. Thus for the Sāṃkhya the causal operation consists in rendering manifest (*āvibhūta*) what has remained unmanifest (*tirobhūta*).

As a matter of fact, *pariṇāma*, in the sense of "evolution," is never used either in the Pāli discourses or in the Theravāda Buddhist exegesis in order to explain dependent arising. It is of course true that the term occurs in other contexts,[3] yet it is conspicuously absent in contexts where dependent arising is explained. Interestingly enough, the term used in the Buddhist texts in describing the notion of "change" is not *pariṇāma*, but *vi-pariṇāma*. Hence we have the oft-recurring sentence, "All conditioned phenomena are of the nature of *vipariṇāma*."[4] Another case in point is *vipariṇāma-dukkha*, that is, "suffering that occurs from reversal of circumstances."[5] If the verbal form *pariṇamati* means "to become samewise," the verbal form *vipariṇamati* means "to become otherwise" (*aññathā hoti*).[6] What *vipariṇāma* brings into focus is not evolutionary change, but change with no unchanging substance behind the process of change.

The Theravādin exegetes were well acquainted with the Sāṃkhya theory,[7] from which they wanted to dissociate the Buddhist teaching on dependent arising. Hence they observe that according to Buddhism: (1) The cause "does not have the effect in its womb," that is, the effect is not in the cause in a latent form. (2) "The cause is not in the effect," that is, the cause is not in the effect in an actualized form. (3) "The effect is empty of the cause," that is, the cause is not immanent in the effect.[8] These are three different ways of rejecting the evolutionary theory of change.

This same idea seems to be expressed by the use of the term "nonperversion" (*abyāpāra*) to describe the relationship that subsists between the cause and the effect. Nonperversion means: "When the condition exists, there is the arising of the effect; when the condition does not exist, the effect ceases to be."[9] The force of this statement is that nothing passes from the cause to the effect, or that the cause "does not pervade the effect." What this clearly amounts to is that "dependent arising" is not based on the dichotomy between substance and quality.

According to Buddhism the cause is neither a substantial entity nor an active agent. This means that Buddhism also keeps equally aloof from such theories as that of the Pūrva Mīmāṃsā school of Indian philosophy. The latter causal theory is called "the theory of force" (*śaktivāda*) because here the cause is defined as some kind of force (*śakti*) that brings about the effect. It is perhaps with this theory in mind that the Pāli exegesis observes that the cause does not have its "own sway/own power" (*vasavattitā*) to produce the effect.[10] In a cognitive process, for example, all mental phenomena, such as attention and perception, take place naturally according to the principles of psychological order (*cittaniyāma*), each stage in the continuum being conditioned by the immediately preceding one, with no substance passing from one stage to another.[11]

The Scope of Dependent Arising

One question often raised in modern scholarship on Buddhism relates to the range of application of dependent arising. Does it apply to the whole of animate and inanimate existence, or to something less? From the Buddhist perspective, the answer will depend on what Buddhism means by "world" (*loka*) and "the all" (*sabba*). For this purpose, we would like to cite two quotations from the Pāli discourses.

> "The world, the world," they call it, venerable sir. In what sense is there a world? In what sense is there a concept of the world?
>
> To this question raised by Samiddhi, the Buddha replies:
>
> Wherever, Samiddhi, there is the eye, the visible forms, the visual consciousness, and the things perceptible with the visual consciousness, there lies the world, there lies the concept of the world. Wherever there is the ear, . . . the nose, . . . the tongue, . . . the body, . . . the mind, there lies the world, there lies the concept of the world.[12]

The Buddha's reply shows that there have to be three kinds of phenomena present for the world to be realized, namely, the six sense faculties, the corresponding six sense objects, and the six respective sense consciousnesses.

Since the entirety of our conscious experience depends on the twelve sense bases (the six sense faculties and the six sense objects), these twelve sense bases are also defined as "the basic data" of what constitutes "the all" or "totality" (*sabba*):

> And what, bhikkhus, is "the all"? The eye and forms, the ear and sounds, the nose and odors, the tongue and tastes, the body and tactile objects, the mind and mental phenomena. This is called "the all." And there is no other "all" besides this "all."
>
> If anyone, bhikkhus, should speak thus: "Having rejected this all, I shall make known another all"—that would be a mere empty boast on his part. If he were questioned he would not be able to reply and, further, he would meet with vexation. For what reason? Because, bhikkhus, that would not be within his domain.[13]

Thus the Buddha does not deny the objective reality of the world. What he denies is that which transcends the bounds of possible experience.

In other words, for early Buddhism "world" means "individual existence" in relation to the external world. It is, in fact, only through the activity of our physical and mental sense faculties that a world can be experienced and known at all. What is seen, heard, smelled, tasted, and touched by the physical sense faculties and our various mental functions, both conscious and unconscious—this is the world in which we live. It is precisely this world, the world as given in experience, comprising both knowledge and the known in the widest sense, that Buddhism analyzes into several basic factors, such as the five aggregates, the twelve sense bases, and the eighteen elements of cognition. It is also precisely this world that Buddhism seeks to explain on the basis of its doctrine of dependent arising.

Dependent Arising as the Middle Doctrine

Dependent arising is presented as "the middle doctrine" because it steers clear of the mutual conflict between spiritual eternalism and materialist annihilationism. These two theoretical views are also called the "view of being" and the "view of nonbeing," or the "view of existence" and the "view of nonexistence," respectively.

Another two mutually exclusive views are "all exists" (*sabbaṃ atthi*) and "all does not exist" (*sabbaṃ natthi*).[14] The first view represents an extreme form of realism that asserts that everything exists absolutely, whereas the second posits an extreme form of nihilism that asserts that absolutely nothing exists. According to dependent arising, it is not a question of existing or nonexisting, but of dependent arising.

Then follows another pair of views: "all are a unity" (*sabbaṃ ekattaṃ*) and "all are a plurality" (*sabbaṃ puthuttaṃ*).[15] The first is to be understood as a monistic view that everything is reducible to a common ground, some sort of self-substance, whereas the second encompasses the opposite radically pluralistic view that the whole of existence is resolvable into a concatenation of discrete entities with no interconnection and interdependence.

It is true that Buddhism analyzes individual existence into a number of factors, such as the five aggregates, the twelve sense bases, and the eighteen elements of cognition. However, the factors that obtain through analysis are not discrete, independently existing entities, since they arise in dependence on many other factors. The factors into which a thing is analyzed are synthesized according to the principle of dependent arising. Analysis, when not supplemented by synthesis, leads to pluralism. Synthesis, when not supplemented by analysis, leads to monism. What one finds in Buddhism is a combined use of both methods. This results in a philosophical vision that beautifully transcends the dialectical opposition between monism and pluralism.

Another pair of theoretical views that dependent arising transcends is self-causation (*sayaṃ-kata*) and external causation (*paraṃ-kata*).[16] The first view conjectures a complete identity between the agent/doer and the one who experiences: *A* does (something) and *A* himself experiences (its result). This is based on the recognition of an unchanging self-entity that persists throughout time. According to the second view, there is complete otherness between the agent/doer and the one who experiences: *A* does (something) but *B* experiences (its result).

When the Buddha was asked which of these alternatives is valid, he did not approve either, because he teaches the doctrine by adopting the middle position. The Buddhist position is neither one of complete oneness (absolute identity) nor one of complete otherness (absolute diversity). If, as the first theory says, the same self-entity does and the same self-entity experiences, this will result in a situation where the process of doing and experiencing will not come to an end. The self-entity, as both agent/doer and experiencer, will get trapped in eternity (*sassataṃ etaṃ pareti*). On the other hand, as the second theory says, if someone does and someone else experiences, this will result in a situation where consequences of moral actions will come to complete annihilation (*ucchedaṃ etaṃ pareti*).[17] The latter view fails to establish a causal correlation between the act and its consequences.

From the Buddhist perspective, rigid concepts of absolute identity and absolute diversity cannot do justice to the dynamic stream of becoming (*bhava-sota*), a process of dependent arising and ceasing. As the *Visuddhimagga* clarifies: "And with a stream of continuity, there is neither identity nor otherness. For if there were absolute identity in a stream of continuity, there would be no forming of curd from milk. And yet if there were absolute otherness, the curd would not be derived from the milk. And so too with all causally arisen things."[18]

Strict determinism and strict indeterminism represent another pair of mutually exclusive positions. The first is of two kinds: One is theistic determinism, which says that everything is due to creation on the part of God (*sabbaṃ issara-nimmāṇa-hetu*). The other is karmic determinism, which says that everything is due to past *kamma* (*sabbaṃ pubbekata-hetu*). In direct opposition to both is strict indeterminism or the theory of fortuitous origination.[19] As we shall see in chapter 7 on the theory of moral life, it is again through dependent arising that Buddhism keeps itself equally aloof from both strict determinism and strict indeterminism.

Dependent arising also provides a "middle position" answer to the very natural question posed as to why a human being experiences what he or she experiences: Is it due to self-causation or to external causation, or to both or neither? From the Buddhist perspective, human experience—whether it is pleasant or painful—is neither self-caused, nor other-caused, nor both-caused, nor due to accidental circumstances (*adhicca-samuppanna*), but is of dependent arising (*paṭiccasamuppannaṃ*).[20]

Another aspect of dependent arising as the "middle doctrine" can be seen in relation to the two cosmogonycal theories that seek to explain the absolute beginning of the universe (*pubbanta-kappika*) along with the ultimate direction it is heading for (*aparanta-kappika*).[21] According to the Buddha, no temporal beginning of the universe is conceivable. For Buddhism, therefore, questions relating to the uncaused first cause and the consummation of the universe in its ultimate destiny do not arise. Buddhism concentrates not on the origin or end of the order, but on the order itself. As such, the purpose of dependent arising is not to explain how it all began, nor to explain how it will finally end, but to show how things occur.

The Application of Dependent Arising

We have already clarified the structural principle of dependent arising in the abstract. As to its concrete application we can distinguish between two types: one is general and the other special. The general application can be seen in such instances where causal explanations are given for the arising of consciousness, the sequence of the cognitive process, the operation of the moral order, and so on. Dependent arising has also been used to understand the gradual evolution of society and the origins of social disorder, which, from the Buddhist perspective, stem ultimately from craving, as does individual suffering. We shall have the occasion to examine these causal explanations where appropriate in the chapters that follow.

It is on the special application of dependent arising that we propose to focus here. This can be seen in a twelve-factored formula whose purpose is to explain the causal structure of individual existence in its saṃsāric dimension. For Buddhism, individual existence means the causally organized five aggregates of grasping. Therefore we can also say that the purpose of the twelve-factored formula is to explain the dependent arising of the five aggregates of grasping.

The five aggregates of grasping are not five static entities. Rather, they are five constantly changing aspects of individual existence that always interact with the external world. It is not correct to say that they exist, nor is it correct to say that they do not exist. What is dependently arisen is not definable either by way of existence (*atthitā*) or by way of nonexistence (*natthitā*). There is only a continuum of arising and ceasing.

The Twelve-Factored Formula of Dependent Arising

With ignorance (*avijjā*) as condition are volitional constructions (*saṅkhāra*).
With volitional constructions as condition is consciousness (*viññāṇa*).
With consciousness as condition is mentality-materiality (*nāma-rūpa*).
With mentality-materiality as condition is the sixfold sense base (*saḷāyatana*).
With the sixfold sense base as condition is contact (*phassa*).
With contact as condition is feeling (*vedanā*).

With feeling as condition is craving (*taṇhā*).
With craving as condition is clinging (*upādāna*).
With clinging as condition is becoming (*bhava*).
With becoming as condition is birth (*jāti*).
With birth as condition are aging and death, grief, lamentation, pain, sorrow, and despair (*jarā-maraṇa-soka-parideva-dukkha-domanassa-upāyāsa*).[22]

In understanding this dependently arising process, what is of crucial importance to remember is that, as the Buddha says, the five aggregates of grasping are not separable from one another,[23] although of course they can be distinguished. Considered in this context, what this really means is that at every stage of the causal process, the five aggregates of grasping, or at least their main constituents, are present. Then the question arises as to why at each stage only one factor is mentioned as the condition and only one factor is mentioned as what is conditioned.

Here the Theravāda Buddhist exegesis comes to our support. In this connection, it makes three main observations:

1. Dependent arising means the arising of effects evenly in dependence on a conjunction of conditions.
2. Arising means "arising together and equally, not piecemeal and successively."
3. If only one factor is mentioned as the condition for another, it is in order to single out the chief condition among many conditions and relate it to the most important conditioned factor among many other conditioned factors.[24]

What these three observations amount to is that from a plurality of conditions arise a plurality of conditioned factors. Stated otherwise: nothing arises from nothing, nothing arises from a single condition, nothing arises as a single conditioned factor. It is always the case that from a multiplicity of conditions arise a multiplicity of conditioned factors. Therefore, strictly speaking, "dependent" means "codependent" (dependence on many factors), and "arising" means "coarising, (arising together with many other factors).

These observations, which we cited from the Buddhist exegesis, are fully in line with the above-mentioned saying of the Buddha, namely, that the five aggregates of grasping are never separable, one from another, and that therefore they all occur together. Therefore, at every stage of the process of dependent arising all the five aggregates of grasping are present. Let us take as an example ignorance, which is listed first. Can ignorance exist in splendid isolation from the five aggregates of grasping? For ignorance to exist, there must be an individual being, which according to Buddhism is the five aggregates of grasping. Therefore, when ignorance functions as a condition, it is one condition among many other conditions. Here "many other conditions" means the five aggregates of grasping without counting ignorance. If only ignorance is mentioned, this, as the Buddhist exegesis says, "is in order to single out the chief condition among a collection of conditions."

In the same way, when volitional constructions arise with ignorance as their condition, there are many other factors that arise together with them, namely, all the five aggregates of grasping excluding volitional constructions. If only volitional constructions are mentioned, this, as the Buddhist exegesis says, "is in order to relate the most important conditioned factor among a collection of conditioned factors." This situation, it must be emphasized here, is true of all other stages in the twelve-factored process of dependent arising.

What we have clarified above provides an answer to an important question raised in modern scholarship on this subject. The question concerns mentality-materiality (*nāma-rūpa*), which is the third conditioned factor in the above-mentioned list of twelve factors.

"Mentality" in the compound "mentality-materiality" denotes five mental factors, namely, feeling, perception, volition, sensory contact, and mental advertence. Now the question is this: If mentality includes, among other factors, both sensory contact and feeling, why are sensory contact and feeling mentioned again in the sequence? It will be noticed that both sensory contact and feeling are mentioned again as the fourth and the fifth conditioned factors. The repetition is certainly not due to a mistake, textual or otherwise. It is perfectly in conformity with what we have observed above, that at every stage of the process, all the five aggregates of grasping are present. What we need to remember here is that when sensory contact arises, it cannot arise as a single factor. It necessarily arises together with all the five aggregates of grasping, excluding sensory contact. If only sensory contact is mentioned, this is in order to relate the most important conditioned factor among a collection of conditioned factors. The same situation is true of feeling as well.

Now we are in a better position to understand the twelve factors involved in the process of dependent arising. The Buddha says:

> In the belief that the person who acts is the same as the person who experiences, . . . one posits eternalism; in the belief that the person who acts is not the same as the person who experiences, . . . one posits materialism. Without veering toward either of these extremes the tathāgata teaches the doctrine by the middle: with ignorance (*avijjā*) as condition, volitional constructions (*saṅkhāra*) come to be.[25]

Here ignorance means the ignorance of the four truths: the fact of suffering, its cause, its cessation, and the way leading to its cessation.[26] It is not-knowingness of things as they actually are. Ignorance of the four truths means that a person acts like a robot, not knowing what he really is and what his true freedom is. Though ignorance is listed first, it is not the first cause. "The first beginning of ignorance is not known [such that we may say], before this there was no ignorance, at this point there arose ignorance. However, that ignorance [itself] is causally conditioned can be known" (*Atha ca pana paññāyati 'idappaccayā avijjā*).[27]

The purpose of the causal process, as noted earlier, is not to explain the absolute origin of the saṃsāric process nor to explain the ultimate end to which it is destined. Hence, after enumerating the twelve-factored causal process, the Buddha says: "Would you, O monks, knowing and seeing thus probe (lit., run behind) the prior end of things . . . or pursue (lit., run after) the final end of things?"[28]

After ignorance come volitional activities. They signify morally wholesome (*puñña*), morally unwholesome (*apuñña*), and unshakable (*āneñja*) volitions that constitute kamma. It will be seen that even wholesome actions are also motivated by ignorance, for all kammic activities are due to self-interest or self-expectation. They are not spontaneous acts of wholesomeness. With volitional activities as condition arises consciousness (*viññāṇa*). The reference is to relinking or rebirth consciousness in the subsequent birth. It is the initial consciousness that arises at the moment of conception. Since it arises as a result of kamma, it is kammically indeterminate, for it is not motivated by the three roots of moral evil or the three roots of moral wholesomeness. Simultaneous with the arising of consciousness, there arises mentality-materiality (*nāma-rūpa*). The latter denotes five mental factors and the organic matter that enters into the composition of an individual being. Both consciousness and mentality-materiality are reciprocally dependent in the sense that while the former is dependent on the latter, the latter too is dependent on the former at one and the same time. It will thus be seen that even at the moment of conception, the main constituents of the five aggregates of clinging are there, for consciousness and mentality-materiality represent the basic data of the five aggregates of clinging. On the inseparable nexus between consciousness and mentality-materiality, we shall have more to say in chapter 5 on the analysis of mind.

With mentality-materiality (psychophysical phenomena) as condition arise the six sense bases, the eye, ear, nose, tongue, body, and mind (*saḷāyatana*), for the psychophysical phenomena in mentality-materiality have latent potentialities to gradually bring about the sixfold sensory apparatus. With the six sense bases as condition arises sensory contact (*phassa*). Sensory contact is defined as the "union of the three," the union between the sense organ, the sense object, and the sensory consciousness.[29] With sensory contact as condition arise feelings (*vedanā*). It is the feelings that experience an object as pleasant, unpleasant, or neutral. With feelings as condition arises craving (*taṇhā*). Craving is threefold: craving for sense pleasures (*kāma-taṇhā*), craving for existence (*bhava-taṇhā*), and craving for nonexistence (*vibhava-taṇhā*). With craving as condition arise four kinds of clinging. The first is clinging to sense pleasures, which is an intensified form of craving. The second is clinging to views, metaphysical views as to the nature of the self and the world. The third is clinging to rites and observances in the belief that they lead to emancipation from suffering. The fourth is clinging to the notion of the "self." It will be noticed that craving is the condition not only for clinging to sense pleasures but also for clinging to views: (a) metaphysical views, (b) views relating to the efficacy of rites and observances, and (c) the belief in an individualized self-entity. These four kinds of grasping induce motivated action and thus become a condition for (future) existence (*bhava*). Since rebirth into one of the three planes of existence is brought about by kamma, in the Buddhist exegesis, existence is distinguished into two, namely, kamma-existence (*kamma-bhava*) and rebirth-existence (*uppatti-bhava*).[30] Kamma-existence is the kammic activities of the previous life that serve as a condition for the succeeding birth (*jāti*). It is the active process of existence (becoming). Rebirth-existence is birth into one of the three planes of existence recognized in Buddhist cosmology: the sense sphere, the fine-material sphere, and the immaterial sphere. This is the passive process of existence (becoming). Finally, with birth as condition there arise decay (*jarā*), death (*maraṇa*), sorrow (*soka*), lamentation (*parideva*), pain (*dukkha*), grief (*domanassa*), and despair (*upāyāsa*).

As noted above, among the twelve causal factors, only two are reciprocally dependent, namely, consciousness (*viññāṇa*) on the one hand and mentality-materiality (*nāma rūpa*) on the other. This shows that it is on the reciprocal interplay between consciousness and mentality-materiality that the whole saṃsāric process of births and deaths revolves. In this sense, their mutual dependence constitutes the irreducible ground of saṃsāric existence. This situation remains the same whether the dependently arising series is traced back to the remote past or traced forward to the distant future. The philosophical implications of this situation we shall discuss in chapter 5 on the analysis of mind.

4

NONSELF AND THE PUTATIVE OVERSELF

THE NOTION of the "self" has many forms, such as the monistic form found in the Upaniṣads, the pluralistic form as evidenced by Sāṃkhya and Jainism, and the materialistic form found in Ucchedavāda. Despite these many permutations, the notion of the "self" can be subsumed under two main headings: the spiritual metaphysical self and the annihilationist physical self. The first version is based on the duality principle—the duality between the self and the body—and the second, on the identity principle—the identity of the self and the body. The Buddhist idea of "nonself" is based on a denial of both versions. Accordingly, Buddhism does not admit either an abiding metaphysical self or a temporary physical self in the psychosomatic complex of the empiric individuality. However, scholars with a Vedantic orientation, along with those who believe in a perennial philosophy based on the supposed transcendental unity of all religions, think otherwise. In their view, Buddhism believes in a Self (the "s" capitalized) that is not identical with any of the components (*khandhas*) of the empiric individuality taken selectively or collectively, but that transcends them at both levels.[1] This is what we have introduced in the title of this chapter as the putative overself. Here we propose to discuss the early Buddhist teaching on nonself and to examine, in light of the ensuing discussion, whether the latter interpretation is tenable.

Is the Notion of "Nonself" Only for Pragmatic Reasons?

Certain modern writings on Buddhism give the impression that if the Buddha rejected the theory of the self, it was purely for a pragmatic reason, that is, to provide a rational foundation for a selfless ethics. It is contended that if the self is not assumed, how can the possibility of man's perfection and emancipation from suffering be explained? The Buddha's answer to this question is that it is the very assumption of a self, both in its materialist and spiritual versions, that makes both possibilities impossible:

> Verily, if one holds the view that the self is identical with the body [materialist annihilationism], in that case there can be no holy life. If one holds the view that the self is one thing and the body another [spiritual eternalism], in that case, too, there can be no holy life. Avoiding both extremes, the Perfect One teaches the doctrine that lies in the middle.[2]

If the self is identical with the physical body (absolute oneness), then there is no possibility for the practice of moral life. Why? If the physical body is the self, then the physical body will completely determine the behavior of the mind. On the other hand, if the self is different from the physical body (absolute otherness), then the need for the practice of moral life does not arise, for the self always remains in its pristine purity.

In this regard, the Buddha says that even if there were to be a portion as small as a pinch of dust that defies change in the psychophysical personality of the human being, then practicing the higher life (*brahmacariya*) would be of no avail.[3] What is meant is that there is no such permanent part and that the higher life can successfully bring about a complete transformation of the human personality. What we need to remember here is that only when there is change is there the possibility for changeability.

If Buddhism denies both versions of the "self" notion, this means that, according to the Buddha, the human personality is plastic and pliable, and therefore wieldable and amenable to change. It has the necessary wherewithal either to elevate itself to a higher level of moral perfection or to descend down to the lowest levels of moral depravity. Strong individuality based on the "self" notion is not the same as indomitable strength of mind.

The Notion of "Nonself"

The characteristic of nonself (*anatta*) is often presented together with two other characteristics, namely, impermanence (*anicca*) and suffering (*dukkha*). Taken together, these are the three hallmarks or the universal properties of all that is sentient. To perceive permanence in impermanence, satisfactoriness in unsatisfactoriness, and self-existence in nonself-existence—this is a perversion of perception, a perversion of thought, and a perversion of the ideological perspective.[4]

Fundamental to Buddhist teaching is the emphatic assertion of impermanence: "Whatever has the nature of arising, all that has the nature of ceasing."[5] As one Buddhist discourse stresses: "There is no moment, no instant, no particle of time when the river stops flowing."[6] This is the simile used to illustrate the eternal flow of happening, the unbroken continuity of change.

As the first (logically, but not chronologically) of the three characteristics of sentient existence, it is in fact impermanence that provides the rational basis for the other two characteristics: what is impermanent is suffering (*yad aniccaṃ taṃ dukkhaṃ*); what is suffering is nonself (*yaṃ dukkhaṃ tad anattā*).[7] Thus the concept of "nonself" is a necessary corollary of the fact of suffering.

The characteristic of nonself is sometimes directly derived from the verifiable characteristic of impermanence:

> If anyone regards the eye (i.e., seeing) as the self, that does not hold, for the arising and passing away of the eye is (clear from experience). With regard to that which arises and passes away, if anyone were to think "my self is arising and passing away," (such a thought) would be contradicted by the person himself. Therefore, it does not hold to regard the eye as the self. Thus the eye (or seeing) is (proved to be) nonself. (The same goes for the other sense faculties.)[8]

Let us take another example. Can feeling, for instance, be considered the self? If it could be so considered, then when a pleasant feeling gives place to an unpleasant feeling, one would have to admit that one's self has changed—if it has not vanished completely.

The two examples clearly demonstrate that it is from the verifiable premise of impermanence that the principle of "nonself" is derived.

Yet another aspect of what nonself means can be elicited from a debate between the Buddha and Saccaka on the idea of "self." Saccaka argues on the premise that just as any kind of seed or vegetable grows and comes to maturity depending on the earth, whatever act a person does, whether it is good or bad, depends entirely on the five aggregates (*khandhas*). He concludes, therefore, that the five aggregates constitute an individual's self.

In response to this, the Buddha says: "When you assert that the five aggregates constitute your self, have you power over them, have you control over them, so that you can say: 'Let my five aggregates be thus, let my five aggregates be not thus'?" Saccaka fails to give a satisfactory answer and admits that he was sadly mistaken in this matter.[9]

We find the same idea expressed in a number of other discourses in a slightly different form: "If, for instance, the physical body could be considered as self, then this physical body would not be subject to affliction; one should be able to say [with practical results]: 'Let my physical body be like this; let not my physical body be like that.' Because the physical body is nonself, therefore it is subject to affliction."[10]

If anything could be called my own self, then I should have full control over it, so that it behaves in the way I want it to behave. If something is really my own, I should be able to exercise full mastery, full sovereignty over it. Otherwise, how can I call it my own? This is how Buddhism understands the idea of ownership or possession. Since we do not have full control over our possessions, when something adverse happens to them, it is we who come to grief. So it is our possessions that really possess us.

In a commentarial gloss, "absence of control" is defined as "absence of own sway" or "absence of own power" (*a-vasavattitā*).[11] In the case of phenomena that depend on impermanent conditions, none among them can exercise their own sway, their own power.

In fact, it is this meaning of nonself as absence of full control that is most important from the point of view of realizing nibbāna, the final emancipation according to Buddhism. However, this meaning of nonself does not appear to have got due attention in the later schools of Buddhist thought or in modern writings on Buddhism. Perhaps this may indicate a shift of emphasis from Buddhism as a practicing religion to Buddhism as an academic philosophy.

Where the "Self" Notion Originates

The whole world of experience, as Buddhism understands it, is comprised within the five aggregates, namely, materiality (*rūpa*), feelings (*vedanā*), perceptions (*saññā*), volitional constructions (*saṃkhāra*), and consciousness (*viññāṇa*); hence the totality of our experience can be explained with reference to them. Therefore, if there were to be any kind of "self" notion, such a notion should originate only on the basis of these five aggregates, taken selectively or collectively. They are the only ground for the origination of such an assumption. Yet none of the aggregates can be so identified as such. Why? It is because the cause and condition for the arising of materiality and the other four aggregates is nonself; so how can materiality and the other four aggregates, which are brought into being by what is nonself, be the self?[12]

If, for example, someone assumes materiality, the first aggregate, to be the self, such an assumption could manifest in four ways: (1) materiality is the same as the self, (2) the self possesses materiality, (3) materiality is within the self, or (4) the self is in materiality. A further elaboration of this fourfold manifestation of the "self" notion takes the following form:

> *How does he see materiality as self?*
> Just as if a man saw a lighted lamp's flame and color as identical, thus "What the flame is, that the color is; what the color is, that the flame is."
>
> *How does he see self as possessed of materiality?*
> Just as if there were a tree possessed of shade such that a man might say, "This is the tree, this is the shade; the tree is one, the shadow another; but this tree is possessed of this shade in virtue of this shade."
>
> *How does he see materiality in self?*
> Just as if there were a scented flower such that a man might say, "This is the flower, this is the scent; the flower is one, the scent another; but the scent is in this flower."
>
> *How does he see self in materiality?*
> Just as if a gem were placed in a casket such that a man might say,

> "This is the gem, this is the casket; the gem is one, the casket another; but this gem is in the casket."[13]

The same goes for the other four aggregates. Thus, there are in all twenty possible relations between the five aggregates and the hypothetical self. This is how Buddhism explains what is called the origin of "the belief in a self-entity."

The Buddhist teaching on nonself is intended as a remedy for the cessation of this belief in a self-entity. The cessation of this belief is to be achieved through the opposite process, that is, by negating each aggregate as a self-entity so as to eliminate all possibilities for the emergence of the "self" view. The final conclusion of this process of negation is that none of the five aggregates that make up the empiric individuality can be identified as one's own self.

If each aggregate is not the self, then can their combination provide a collective basis for the "self" notion?

In this connection, what we need to remember is that although Buddhism analyzes the living being into several aggregates, it does not say that they just lump together to form the individual, just as a random collection of bricks is not a wall. The individual is the sum total of the five aggregates when they are structurally organized according to the principle of dependent arising (*pañca-upādānakkhandhā paṭiccasamuppannā*).[14] It is dependent arising that ensures causal continuity and interdependent functioning. The individual is, in fact, defined as "the aggregation (*saṅgaha*), collocation (*sannipāta*), and coming together (*samavāya*) of the five aggregates of clinging."[15] What Buddhism denies is not the concept of "the person" (*puggala*) but of a self-subsisting entity within the person. As such, Buddhism has no objection to the concept of "personhood," if "person" is understood not as an entity distinct from the sum total of the properly organized five aggregates, nor as a substance enduring in time, nor as an agent within the five aggregates. The person is the sum total of the five aggregates combined according to the principle of dependent arising, and which are constantly in a state of flux.

What really matters here is not how one tries to understand the nature of the five aggregates in their combination. Rather, what really matters is that even the combination is in a state of constant flux. What is in constant flux is not under one's control and hence is nonself.

Nonself from Another Perspective

Since nonself means absence of intrinsic reality and substantial being, the idea of "nonself" comes into focus from another perspective, that of the Buddhist teaching on nutriment. "All living beings," the Buddha says, "subsist on food" (*sabbe sattā āhāraṭṭhitikā*). By "food" Buddhism means not only what we eat and drink for the sustenance of our physical body, which is called "morsel-made food" (*kabaḷīkāra-āhāra*), but also three other kinds, namely, sensory contact (*phassa*), mental volition (*mano sañcetanā*), and consciousness (*viññāṇa*).[16] As to sensory contact, there are six kinds: eye contact, ear contact, nose contact, tongue contact, body contact, and mind contact. It is through these six sensory contacts that our six sense faculties partake of food. What is visible is food for the eye, what is audible is food for the ear, and so on. If not for this kind of food our sensory apparatus will suffer starvation and thereby not function at all. The third kind of food, which is mental volition, is the conative or motivating aspect. It is the most dynamic, indeed, the will to live. The fourth kind of food, which is consciousness, has to be understood in the context of the saṃsāric process, the cycle of births and deaths. Although consciousness does not migrate from birth to birth, as we saw in the previous chapter, it functions as a condition in the twelve-factored formula of dependent arising. It is mainly this factor that functions as "food/nutriment" for the saṃsāric dimension of individual existence.

Individual existence thus turns out to be a process of nutriment, a process of alimentation: it is kept going by four kinds of food. If there were a static self-entity within the empiric individuality, then it would not be necessary to keep it going by four kinds of food. It is just like a burning fire, a dynamic process with no static entity in it: a fire cannot go on burning without being supplied by fuel.

How the "Self" Notion Emerges

As the Buddha says, the notion of the "self" does not occur to a "young tender infant, lying prone on its back. Such an infant has only a latent tendency to the 'self' view."[17] The emergence of the "self" view can, however, be traced to the cognitive process, the process through which we cognize sense objects. In every cognitive act, an act consisting of a series of cognitive events, the latent tendency for the ego-consciousness awakens and gradually solidifies, eventually becoming fully crystallized at the final stage called conceptual proliferations (*papañca*). Once the ego-consciousness has arisen, it cannot exist in a vacuum: it needs ontological support; it needs concrete form and content. What the unenlightened ordinary person does, in this regard, is identify the ego-consciousness with one or more of the five aggregates into which individual existence is resolved. This process of identification takes the following forms: "this is mine" (*etaṃ mama*), "this I am" (*eso'ham asmi*), "this is my self" (*eso me attā*). Here the first form is due to craving (*taṇhā*), the second, to conceit (*māna*), and the third, to view (*diṭṭhi*). Craving, conceit, and view are thus three different aspects of the ego-consciousness.[18]

In the above process of identification, "this I am" is "the 'I' conceit" (*asmi-māna*) and "this is my self" is to be understood as "the 'self' view" (*attavāda*). The "I" conceit arises at a prereflective level. As to its arising, we need to understand the difference between two cognitive functions, that of perceiving (*saññā*) and that of conceiving (*maññanā*). Whenever an unenlightened person perceives, he or she also automatically conceives, for the act of conceiving involves an "I" tendency to what is perceived. This results in the person's perceptual experience becoming automatically distorted because of the "I" tendency involved in the act of conceiving. It creates an "I" relation, an "I" perspective to what is perceived. This relationship to what is perceived arises in one of four ways: as identical with it, as contained in it, as separate from it, as owning it as "mine."[19]

On the other hand, the "self" view arises at an elementary reflective level, conditioned by the "I" conceit. Nonetheless, both the "I" conceit and the "self" view are conditioned by craving. Both are two of the ten fetters that bind the individual to the saṃsāric process. Only when a person enters the stream of the noble eightfold path (*sotāpatti*) does the "self" view come to an end. On the other hand, the "I" conceit has such a sway over unenlightened living beings that it persists until one attains nibbāna.

Why the "Self" Notion Persists

Although the "self" view has a purely psychological origin, it can be buttressed and perpetuated by many other factors. Among them is our deep-seated craving that provides an emotional attachment to the belief in a permanent self:

> Here someone entertains this view: "This is self, this is the world; after death I shall be permanent, everlasting, eternal, not subject to change, I shall endure as long as eternity." Then he hears a tathāgata or a tathāgata's disciple teaching the True Idea for the elimination of all standpoints for views, all decisions (about "my self"), insistencies, and underlying tendencies, for the stilling of all formations, for the relinquishment of all essentials (of existence, *upadhi*), for the exhaustion of craving, for fading out, cessation, extinction. He thinks thus: "So I shall be annihilated! So I shall be lost! So I shall be no more." Then he sorrows and laments, beating his breast, he weeps and becomes distraught.[20]

Two kinds of anguish (*paritassanā*) are distinguished by the Buddha. One is the anguish due to an absence of something external (*bahiddhā asati*), as, for example, when we do not have the tangible material objects that we want to have. The other form of anguish is very much subtler and hidden. It is the anguish due to an absence of something within (*ajjhattaṃ asati*).[21] It is this latter kind of anguish that a person who believes in a self experiences when he is told that there is no such self, for the notion of an "abiding self" gives a person a sense of identity, security, and certainty. When this same person hears the true teaching that there is no self, he comes to grief and experiences an inner vacuum—a sense of complete loss.

Nonself and Dependent Arising

The idea of "nonself" should not be understood in isolation from dependent arising. If we take the idea of "nonself" separately and overemphasize it, this idea can lead to a form of reductionism. At the time of the Buddha, a Buddhist monk, after listening to the teaching on nonself, thought: "So it seems materiality is nonself, nor are feeling, perception, mental formations, and consciousness. Then what self will the action done by the nonself touch?" He was afterward reprimanded by the Buddha for ignoring the Buddha's teaching on dependent arising owing to his ignorance and craving.[22]

When we combine the ideas of "nonself" and "dependent arising," it becomes clear that what we are now has been conditioned by what we were in the past. The preceding moment conditions the succeeding moment and thus there is causally ordered continuity to the whole process. At the moment of death, the quality of the last consciousness conditions the arising of the rebirth consciousness. Nothing is carried over. Yet the new consciousness arises in dependence on the previous consciousness.

Nonself and Emptiness

Both nonself and dependent arising combine to show how early Buddhism understands the notion of "emptiness." When Ānanda asked the Buddha: "Venerable Sir, it is said, 'Empty is the world, empty is the world.' In what way, Venerable Sir, is it said, 'Empty is the world'?" The Buddha said in reply: "It is because it is empty of self and what belongs to self, Ānanda, that it is said, 'Empty is the world.'"[23]

In the Suttanipāta we find the Buddha bidding Mogharāja to see the world as empty (*suññato lokaṃ avekkhassu*).[24] As noted earlier, for early Buddhism, "world" means the world of experience, the world we experience with our six sense faculties. And it is precisely this world that early Buddhism resolves into the five aggregates, the twelve sense bases, and the eighteen elements of cognition. If the world is empty, then it logically and inevitably follows that the factors into which the world is analyzed are also empty. "Empty" and "nonself" become mutually convertible expressions. What is nonself is empty and, likewise, what is empty is nonself.

As the Buddha's reply shows, "emptiness" is not a separate characteristic. Rather, it is another expression for "nonself."

Therefore, from the early Buddhist perspective, we have the full liberty of restating the well-known statement "all things are nonself" (*sabbe dhammā anattā*) as "all things are empty" (*sabbe dhammā suññā*). "All things" (*sabbe dhammā*) embrace not only the conditioned (*saṅkhata*) phenomena but the unconditioned nibbāna as well.[25] Thus both the world of sensory experience and the unconditioned reality that transcends it are empty. What this means is that the characteristic of "nonself" or "emptiness" is more universal than even impermanence. So thorough is Buddhism's rejection of substantialism.

The Putative Overself

In light of what has been discussed above, we need to examine now the issue of the "overself." Is there a self-entity over and above the five aggregates, a self that transcends the five aggregates, taken selectively or collectively? As far as early Buddhism is concerned, the question has no relevance, for Buddhism explains the totality of phenomenal existence, and emancipation from it, in such a way that it simply rules out the very necessity of raising the question.

That being said, as we have noted at the beginning of this chapter, the above question is raised particularly by modern scholars with a Vedantic orientation, and also by those who profess a perennial philosophy based on the supposed transcendental unity of all religions.

Their basic assumption is that when the Buddha says that the five aggregates are nonself, this does not mean that there is no self. It only means that none of the five aggregates can be identified as our true self because they are subject to impermanence and are a source of suffering. The true self, it is contended, is besides the five aggregates and could be discovered only by transcending the false, empirical self. If the false self that is thus transcended is impermanent, subject to suffering, and marked by nonsubstantiality, the true self so discovered has the opposite three characteristics, namely, permanence (*nicca*), happiness (*sukha*), and the fact of being the true self (*atta*).

If one suffers, so runs their argument, it is because of one's estrangement from one's true self, and therefore, in their view, attainment of nibbāna means "a positive return of the self to itself."

One canonical passage often cited by those who maintain this theory is the passage where the wandering philosopher Vacchagotta asks the Buddha whether the self exists or not. In each case the Buddha remains silent.[26] This silence on the part of the Buddha has been interpreted in two ways. According to some, it was because the Buddha did not want "to shock a weak-minded hearer" by saying that there is no self.[27] According to others, "the logical conclusion from this would be that something is, though it is not the empirical self."[28]

In fact, the correct position can be seen from the same discourse when the Buddha told Ānanda why he decided to remain silent:

> If, Ānanda, when Vacchagotta asked, "Is there a self?" I had said, "There is a self," then I should have been one of those who hold the doctrine of eternalism. But if I had replied, "There is no self," then I would have been one of those who hold the doctrine of annihilation. And if, when Vacchagotta asked, "Is there a self?" I

> had replied, "There is a self," would it have been in accordance with the knowledge that all things are without self?
>
> "No, Lord."
>
> If I had said, "There is no self," the bewildered Vacchagotta would have become still more bewildered, thinking, "Then did my self exist before, and now it does not exist anymore?"[29]

If any conclusion can be drawn from this, it is that Buddhism does not subscribe to the theory of the "self" as recognized both in the eternalist and the annihilationist ideologies, not that the Buddha believed in a self.

What is most intriguing is that some modern scholars who quote this dialogue between the Buddha and Vacchagotta, either by design or by accident, bypass the Buddha's own explanation to Ānanda as to why he remained silent when Vacchagotta raised the question about the existence of the self.

If the theory of the "overself" is valid, it raises the very important question about why the Buddha was silent on this matter. The teaching of the Buddha is not an esoteric doctrine confined to a select few. The Buddha himself says that he does not have the closed fist of the teacher.[30]

The theory of the "overself" also raises the equally important question of why none of the schools of Buddhist thought belonging to the three traditions of Theravāda, Mahāyāna, and Vajrayāna have not arrived at such a conclusion. It leads to the most improbable situation that they all misunderstood the original teaching of the Buddha.

It is also instructive to note that in the history of Buddhist thought there has never been a Buddhist school that has openly acknowledged a theory of the "self." If there was one doctrine that every school was committed to defend, it was the doctrine of "nonself." Furthermore, every Buddhist school was very sensitive to the charge of being criticized as upholding some sort of "self" theory. At the same time, it is of course true that some Buddhist schools may have developed certain theories that amounted to a veiled recognition of the "self" theory. For instance, the Vātsīputrīyas admitted a sort of quasi-permanent self, neither identical with nor different from the mental states. However, what matters here is the fact that the Vātsīputrīyas themselves vehemently denied that their theory was some kind of "self" theory in disguise. Despite their protests and denials, they nonetheless came to be rather sarcastically referred to by other Buddhists as "heretics within our midst" (*antaścara-tīrthaka*), outsiders masquerading as insiders.[31]

The Buddhist teachings on the theory of knowledge and *jhāna* experience are two relevant areas that should be examined here in relation to the issue of the "overself."

It is well known that Buddhism recognizes not only different means of knowledge but also different levels of knowledge. Besides the ordinary sensory knowledge indicated by such cognitive terms as *viññāṇa* (bare awareness) and *saññā* (sensory perception), Buddhism speaks of a higher nonsensuous knowledge, indicated by such cognitive terms as *abhiññā* (higher knowledge), *pariññā* (comprehensive knowledge), *paññā* (wisdom), and *aññā* (gnosis). As to means of knowledge, Buddhism recognizes not only sensory perception and inductive inference but also extrasensory perception, which enables one to cognize things that do not come within the ken of ordinary sensory knowledge. For our present purpose we need not go into the details of the Buddhist understanding of the means and the levels of knowledge. What matters here is that, although Buddhism recognizes different means and levels of knowledge, it is never claimed that a permanent overself (the true self) transcending the empirical self (the false self) becomes an object of such knowledge. If anything becomes the object of higher knowledge, it is the five aggregates (the empiric individuality), and not an elusive self that transcends them. In fact, one theme that runs throughout the Buddhist discourses is that it is the five aggregates that become an object of higher knowledge.[32]

The Buddhist teaching on jhāna recognizes an experience gained through the higher stages of the mind's concentration and unification. The question that arises here is whether one who attains jhāna gets a glimpse of the true self that was hidden to him or her during normal times. Can jhānic experience be interpreted as communion or absorption with a metaphysical reality? As the Venerable Nyanaponika Thera observes:

> A fertile soil for the origin and persistence of beliefs and ideas about a self, soul, god or any other form of an absolute entity is misinterpreted meditative experience occurring in devotional rapture or mystical trance. Such experience is generally interpreted by the mystic or theologian as revelation of, or union with, a godhead; or it is taken for a manifestation of man's true and eternal self.[33]

That Buddhism does not interpret jhānic experience in a mystical or metaphysical sense is shown by a Buddhist discourse where the Venerable Sāriputta analyzes its content. Here the content of each jhāna is fully itemized without leaving any residue for any kind of mystical interpretation. What is significant is the observation made that the mental factors of each jhāna are said to arise in full awareness of the meditator: "He is fully aware of their arising, their persistence, and their passing away. Then he comes to the conclusion that these mental factors, having not been, come to be (*ahutvā sambhonti*), and, having been, they pass away (*hutvā paṭiventi*)." It is further observed that, since the Venerable Sāriputta fully comprehends the constituents of jhānic experience, he does not get attracted by them, nor does he get repelled by them, nor attached to them, nor infatuated by them. Without getting overwhelmed by them he thus comes to the conclusion that there is an emancipation higher than that (*atthi uttariṃ nissaranan'ti pajānāti*).[34]

This account on the nature of jhānic experience establishes three basic facts: One is that its content can be fully analyzed without leaving any residue. The second is that its constituents arise and vanish in full knowledge of the meditator. The third is that it does not in itself constitute final emancipation, for, according to Buddhism, the jhānic experience too is impermanent (*anicca*), unsatisfactory (*dukkha*), and devoid of a self (*anatta*); it is conditioned (*saṅkhata*) and dependently arisen (*paṭiccasamuppanna*). In fact, Buddhism seems to be fully aware of the possibility of misinterpreting jhānic experience on the basis of theological or metaphysical theories. This seems to be the reason why the meditator is advised to review the content of jhānic experience in light of the three marks of phenomenal existence (*tilakkhaṇa*), that is, as impermanent (*anicca*), unsatisfactory (*dukkha*), and devoid of a self-subsisting entity (*anatta*).[35]

Another aspect that we need to consider here is *nibbānic* experience. Does it provide evidence for the belief in an overself? For our present purpose, it is sufficient to refer here to the position of the tathāgata, that is, one who has attained nibbāna, in relation to the five aggregates (*khandhas*). In this connection, it is maintained that the tathāgata cannot be comprehended either with reference to the five aggregates or without reference to them. The first shows that the tathāgata does not identify himself with any of the five aggregates. The second shows that he does not identify himself with anything outside the five aggregates, that is, something that transcends them, as, for example, the overself. Both mean that the tathāgata is free from all forms of self-identification.[36]

Concluding Remarks

From what we have observed so far it should become clear that if there is a doctrine that is unique to Buddhism, it is the doctrine of "nonself." From its very beginning Buddhism was aware that the doctrine of "nonself" was not shared by any other contemporary religious or philosophical system. This is clearly shown by the *Shorter Discourse on the Lion's Roar.* Here it is said that there are four kinds of clinging: clinging to sense pleasures (*kāma-upādāna*), clinging to speculative views on the nature of the self and the world (*diṭṭhi-upādāna*), clinging to rites and observances as a means to salvation (*sīlabbata-upādāna*), and clinging to a doctrine of "self" (*attavāda-upādāna*), that is, to a view of a truly existent self.

The discourse goes on to say that there could be other religious teachers who would recognize only some of the four kinds of clinging, and that at best they might teach the overcoming of the first three forms of clinging.[37]

What they cannot teach because they have not comprehended this for themselves is the overcoming of clinging to a doctrine of "self," for this, the last type of clinging, is the subtlest and most elusive of the group. As clearly articulated here, the doctrine of "nonself" is the unique discovery of the Buddha and the crucial doctrine that separates his own teaching from all other religious and philosophical systems. As the Venerable Bhikkhu Ñāṇamoli says, the title given to this discourse, namely, the *Shorter Discourse on the Lion's Roar,* is clearly intended to show that the Buddha's proclamation of the "nonself" doctrine is "bold and thunderous, as a veritable lion's roar in the spiritual domain."[38]

When it comes to other Buddhist teachings, the teachings on impermanence, suffering, kamma, rebirth, causality, and so forth, we find Buddhism referencing parallel teachings on the part of other religious teachers. However, what is most important to note here is that when it comes to the doctrine of "nonself," we do not find similar references to parallel doctrines. This also shows that the doctrine of "nonself" was not shared, in any form, by other religious teachers during the time of the Buddha.

The status of the doctrine of "nonself" as the most crucial thing that separates Buddhism from all other religions came to be recognized in the subsequent schools of Buddhist thought as well. Ācārya Yaśomitra, a celebrity of the Sautrāntika school, categorically asserts that in the whole world there is no other teacher who proclaims a doctrine of "nonself."[39] Ācariya Buddhaghosa, the Theravādin commentator, says that the characteristics of impermanence (*anicca*) and suffering (*dukkha*) are known whether buddhas arise or not, but that of nonself (*anatta*) is not known unless there is a Buddha, for the knowledge of it is the province of none but a Buddha. The Blessed One in some instances shows no-selfness through impermanence, in some instances through suffering, and in some instances through both. Why is that? Whereas impermanence and suffering are both evident, nonself is not evident and appears impenetrable, hard to illustrate, and hard to describe.[40]

The doctrine of "nonself," with some variations in interpretation, is commonly accepted by all schools of Buddhist thought, and it is on this basis, therefore, that we can speak of the transcendental unity of Buddhism.

If there is a doctrine that is commonly accepted by all schools of Buddhist thought, it is the doctrine of "nonself." If there is a doctrine on the basis of which we can speak of the transcendental unity of Buddhism, it is none other than the doctrine of "nonself." If there is any doctrine that while uniting all Buddhist schools, separates Buddhism from all other religions and philosophies, it is, again, the doctrine of "nonself." Finally, if there is any doctrine on the basis of which Buddhism seeks to explain the psychological genesis of all speculative and theoretical views, it is also the Buddhist doctrine of "nonself."

What is most radical about the Buddhist doctrine of "nonself" is that it is through this doctrine that Buddhism sets itself aloof from the two perennial worldviews of spiritual eternalism and materialist annihilationism. The doctrine of "nonself" has also provided a new dimension to the concept of the "human personality" and has laid the foundation for a psychology without the psyche—if by "psyche" is understood a self-subsisting entity within the recesses of our mind. As Edward Conze observes, the specific contribution of Buddhism to religious thought lies in its insistence on the doctrine of "nonself."[41]

In fact, Buddhism's other contributions to philosophy, psychology, and ethics have all flowed from the doctrine of "nonself." If Buddhist philosophy shows why the idea of a "self-entity" is a wrong assumption, Buddhist psychology shows how it comes to be; if Buddhist ethics shows how it can be got rid of, Buddhism's highest goal, which is nibbāna, shows the final state whereby it is completely eliminated.

5

THE ANALYSIS OF MIND

> The world is led around by mind;
> by mind it's dragged here and there.
> Mind is the one thing that has
> all under its control.[1]

THE VERSE demonstrates how Buddhism brings into focus the primacy and centrality of mind as the fundamental reality of human existence, the ever-changing sequence of thoughts, feelings, and perceptions that comprise our conscious experience. What is emphasized, however, is not only a grasping aright of the nature of the mind in bondage, but more important, the immense potentialities the mind possesses to realize higher cognitive capacities as well as to elevate itself to the highest level of freedom. If bondage means to come under the control of one's own mind, freedom means to have a mind under one's own control. Both bondage and freedom have mind as their common locus. To free the mind from bondage, it is necessary to develop the mind; to develop the mind, it is necessary to know the mind.[2] Here we find the rationale for Buddhism's preoccupation with psychology and for the relevance of psychology to Buddhism as a religion.

The Basic Principles of the Buddhist Analysis of Mind

The Buddhist analysis of mind, as we find it in the Pāli discourses, recognizes three basic principles. First is the dependent arising of consciousness, expressed in the well-known saying: "Apart from conditions, there is no arising of consciousness."[3] Consciousness is not some kind of potentiality residing in the heart and becoming actualized on different occasions. Nor is it a static entity that runs along and wanders without undergoing any change. Consciousness always springs up on a duality.

> What is that duality? It is (in the case of eye-consciousness, for example) the eye, the visual organ, which is impermanent, changing, and becoming-other, and visible objects, which are impermanent, changing, and becoming-other. Such is the transient, fugitive duality (of eye-cum-visible objects), which is impermanent, changing, and becoming-other. Eye-consciousness, too, is impermanent. For how could eye-consciousness, arisen by depending on impermanent conditions, be permanent? The coincidence (*saṅgati*), concurrence (*sannipāta*), and confluence (*samavāya*) of the three factors, namely, the eye, the eye-object, and eye-consciousness, which is called sensory contact, and those other mental phenomena arising in consequence, are also impermanent.[4]

Just as the friction of two sticks produces fire, in the same way, consciousness springs up from the interaction of sense organs with sense objects. Depending on whether it springs up with respect to the eye, or the ear, or any other sense organ, it is named accordingly.[5]

From the Buddhist perspective, therefore, to have a consciousness means to be aware of an object. It is of course true that consciousness needs many factors for it to arise. Nonetheless, it is to the object that most importance is given. As such, in the Theravāda Buddhist exegesis, consciousness came to be defined as "that which grasps its object" (*ārammaṇika*). This definition is intended to refute the notion that consciousness can arise without an object (*nirālambanavāda*).[6]

The second basic principle of the early Buddhist analysis of mind is that consciousness does not exist as an isolated phenomenon. It always exists in conjunction with the other four aggregates into which the living being is analyzed. Hence the Buddha declares:

> Bhikkhus, though someone might say: "Apart from corporeality, apart from feeling, apart from perception, apart from volitional formations, I will make known the coming and going of con-

> sciousness, its passing away and rebirth, its growth, increase, and expansion"—that is impossible.[7]

Although consciousness cannot be separated from the other four aggregates, nevertheless it can be distinguished from them. Indeed, it is this circumstance that makes it possible to define and describe consciousness as well as the other four aggregates.

The third basic principle of the early Buddhist analysis of mind is the reciprocal dependence of consciousness, on the one hand, and mentality-materiality (*nāma-rūpa*), on the other. Here "mentality" denotes five mental factors, namely, feeling (*vedanā*), perception (*saññā*), volition (*cetanā*), sensory contact (*phassa*), and attention (*manasikāra*).[8] These are the five basic, nonrational mental factors that necessarily arise together with every type of consciousness. Such factors come within the aggregates of feeling, perception, and mental formations.

The idea behind this categorization is that as the knowing or awareness of an object, consciousness cannot arise as a solitary condition. It must be simultaneously accompanied at least by five mental factors that exercise more specialized tasks in the act of cognition. "Materiality" in the compound "mentality-materiality" denotes the four great elements of matter (*mahābhūta*), along with the matter that is dependent on them (*upādā-rūpa*).[9] It refers to organic matter, as, for example, the five physical sense faculties, that enters into the composition of a living being.

The three basic principles of early Buddhist psychology, which we have discussed so far, combine to dispense with the notion of a "mental substance." In lieu of these three principles, there is no thing-in-itself beneath or behind the mental phenomena into which the mental continuum is analyzed. Strictly speaking, consciousness is neither that which cognizes (agent) nor that through which cognition takes place (instrument), but is only the process of cognizing an object. Consciousness is not an entity that exists but an event that occurs, an occurrence due to the appropriate conditions. It is an activity, yet an activity without an actor behind it. The point being emphasized is that there is no conscious subject behind consciousness. Consciousness is in no way a self or an extension of a self-substance. Hence the Buddha says:

> It would be better, bhikkhus, for the uninstructed worldling to take as self this body composed of the four great elements rather

> than the mind. For what reason? Because this body composed of the four great elements is seen standing for one year, for two years, for three, four, five, or ten years, for twenty, thirty, forty, or fifty years, for a hundred years, or even longer. But that which is called "mind" and "mentality" and "consciousness" arises as one thing and ceases as another by day and by night. Just as a monkey roaming through a forest grabs hold of one branch, lets that go and grabs another, then lets that go and grabs still another, so too that which is called "mind" and "mentality" and "consciousness" arises as one thing and ceases as another by day and by night.[10]

The Three Pāli Terms for Mind

We find three terms used in the Pāli discourses to mean what we understand by mind. These are *citta*, *mano*, and *viññāṇa*. Very often they are used as near synonyms, as overlapping and complimentary. Thus we have: "This is *citta*, this is *mano*, this is *viññāṇa*,"[11] and also, "what is called *citta*, *mano*, or *viññāṇa*."[12] However, it is only by examining their contextual usage that we can understand their minor differences of nuance.

Of the three terms, *viññāṇa* seems to occur in an elementary sense to mean basic awareness. Thus in the statement "depending on the eye and the visible, visual consciousness arises," the expression "visual consciousness," as we shall see in the sequel, seems to mean "mere seeing." This meaning of *viññāṇa* can also be seen when it occurs as "consciousness element" in a list together with five other items, namely, earth element, water element, fire element, air element, and space element.[13] It seems this list is intended to refer to the most basic factors of the world of experience, an idea confirmed by an exegetical gloss, where it is described as "the basic data of individual existence."[14] The usage of *viññāṇa* in this elementary sense should explain why, unlike *citta* and *mano*, it is never ethically qualified as wholesome or unwholesome. There is also no evidence to suggest that, in contrast to *citta* and *mano*, *viññāṇa* is something to be developed and cultivated. When it comes to explaining rebecoming (rebirth), the term used is *viññāṇa*, not *citta* or *mano*. It is also in this sense that *viññāṇa* functions as one of the four nutriments that maintain the empiric individuality in its saṃsāric wayfaring.[15] However, in the commentarial exegesis, the term used for both death consciousness and rebirth-linking consciousness is *citta* (*cuti-citta*, *paṭisandhi-citta*).

The term *mano* often occurs in a sense to mean mind when it functions as a sense faculty. When used to connate a sense faculty, *mano* is called either mind base (*manāyatana*) or mind element (*mano-dhātu*). When the individual is analyzed into six internal and six external bases (*āyatana*), the sixth internal base is called mind base (*manāyatana*). Moreover, when the individual is analyzed into eighteen elements, the mind element (*mano-dhātu*) represents mind as a sense faculty.

The term *citta* often occurs in a sense to mean consciousness in general. Sometimes it is used to mean consciousness and sometimes to mean consciousness in combination with its concomitant mental factors. It is in this twofold sense that *citta* occurs in the books of the Abhidhamma Piṭaka as well. When it occurs in the first sense, the term is used in the singular. When it occurs in the second sense, the term is used either in the singular or in the plural, for there can be many kinds of consciousness in the second sense, depending on the mental factors with which they come into combination. This should explain why in Pāli discourses as well as in the Abhidhamma, the term *citta* is found in singular as well as plural forms. In contrast, as noted by the PTS *Pali-English Dictionary*, *viññāṇa* and *mano* do not occur in the Pāli discourses in their plural forms. Furthermore, when it comes to mental culture, *citta* is the term often used.[16] It is *citta* that should be cultivated, developed, and elevated to its highest level of perfection.

Mind and the Threefold Analysis of Individual Existence into Khandha, Āyatana, and Dhātu

We can elicit more psychological material by going through the early Buddhist analyses of individual existence. Among them the best known is the analysis of the individual into the five aggregates, that of corporeality, feeling, perception, mental formations, and consciousness. In the Abhidhamma, consciousness is called *citta* to mean bare awareness, while feeling, perception, and mental formations are represented as *cetasika*, or concomitants of consciousness. This division into *citta* and *cetasika* is not an Abhidhammic innovation. In one Buddhist discourse we read that perception and feeling are mental factors (*cetasikā dhammā*) and that they are conjoined with consciousness (*citta-paṭibaddhā*).[17] This shows that consciousness as that which constitutes the knowing or awareness of an object can never arise in its true separate condition. It always arises in immediate conjunction with mental factors, such as feeling, that perform more specialized tasks in the act of cognition.

The aggregate of feeling represents the affective dimension of our psychological experience. It has sensory contact as its immediate condition because sensory contact refers to the immediate descent of consciousness on the object.

There cannot be any cognitive act that is not affected by the object of cognition. This affective tone of feeling could be pleasant, painful, or neutral depending on the response to the object of cognition. The third species of feeling indicates the line that divides the affective quality into pleasant and painful. This affective neutrality is not the same as equanimity or balance of mind (*tatramajjhattatā*). The latter is not a variety of feeling; it is a higher intellectual state included in the aggregate of mental formations.[18]

Feeling is reckoned as a faculty (*indriya*) as well, that is, as a phenomenon exercising control over its associated phenomena. When analyzed as a faculty, the threefold feeling (pleasant, painful, or neutral) becomes fivefold. The pleasant feeling of the threefold division is here arranged into two as pleasure (*sukha*) and joy (*somanassa*). The first is bodily, whereas the second is mental. Similarly, the painful feeling of the threefold division is arranged here into two as pain (*dukkha*) and displeasure (*domanassa*). The former is physical and the latter, mental. Feeling that is neither painful nor pleasant is as a faculty called neutrality (*upekkhā*).

Third is the aggregate of perception. Its connection with feeling is shown by the statement: "What one feels, one perceives."[19] Perception means the recognition of the object appearing at any of the sense-doors or at the mind-door. "What does it recognize? It recognizes what is blue as blue, what is yellow as yellow, and so on."[20] Thus perception means our ability to relate present sense stimuli to past experience and thereby recognize the sense data. A commentarial gloss likens it to a carpenter recognizing a piece of wood by the mark he had made on it, or to our recognizing a man by the sectarial mark on his forehead, which we have noted, and then say he is so and so.[21] In this connection, it may be noted here that the Pāli word *saññā* means not only perception but sign, symbol, or mark as well.

As the Venerable Nyanaponika Thera observes, the function assigned to perception shows the vital role it plays in the arising of memory. Memory is not listed as a mental factor either in the Pāli discourses or in the Abhidhamma. This is perhaps because memory "is a complex process and as such it cannot be assigned to a single mental factor. Remembering is connecting with the past, and it is a function of cognition in general. However, among the many mental factors involved in a cognitive act it is perception (*saññā*) that plays the initial role in this complex process. And, therefore, perception (*saññā*) has to be considered as cognition as well as recognition."[22]

Next come mental formations or volitional constructions (*saṅkhāra*) as the fourth aggregate. In contrast to the previous two aggregates, feeling and perception, volitional constructions stand for something more complex. The term *saṅkhāra* occurs in a variety of contexts, suggesting many connotations, but here we will be limiting ourselves to what it connotes as the fourth aggregate of individual existence. Volitional constructions represent the most dynamic and the constructive component of the human personality. The standard definition takes the following form:

> They construct constructed material form as material form;
> they construct constructed feeling as feeling;
> they construct constructed perception as perception;
> they construct constructed volitional construction as volitional construction;
> they construct constructed consciousness as consciousness;
> they construct the constructed, . . .
> therefore they are called volitional constructions.[23]

Here "to construct the constructed" should be understood in the same way as "to bake the cake." Although the cake is what is already baked, yet we say, "Bake the cake." The above definition should show that although volitional constructions are one of the five aggregates, they construct not only other aggregates but also themselves. What this clearly demonstrates is that, from the Buddhist perspective, what is called individual existence is a process of construction, a construction based on the threefold appropriation: this is mine, this I am, this is my self. This is precisely why, as we shall see in our chapter on nibbāna, nibbāna is defined as "deconstruction" (*visaṅkhāra*), a deconstruction due to the destruction of passion, aversion, and delusion.

Consciousness, the fifth aggregate, means bare awareness, yet bare awareness cannot arise in its true separate condition without being simultaneously accompanied by mental factors. As noted earlier, it must arise in immediate conjunction with at least five mental factors, namely, feeling, perception, volition, sensory contact, and attention. When correlated to the five aggregates, the first two mental factors represent the two aggregates of feeling and perception, while the last three represent the aggregate of mental constructions. Why these five mental factors are listed as necessary concomitants of consciousness needs explanation. We have already discussed the role feeling and perception play in a cognitive act. So we need to explain why the other three, volition, contact, and attention, are necessarily present in any cognitive act.

Volition is the most dynamic mental factor, being the conative or motivating aspect of cognition. Its nature and intensity can vary depending on the feeling or the affective mode in which the object is experienced. If the feeling is one of pleasure due to a pleasant object, then there will be the decision to possess that object. If the feeling is one of displeasure due to an unpleasant object, then there will be the decision to repel from that object. If, owing to the presence of a neutral object, the feeling is neither pleasant nor unpleasant, then there will be some sort of indecision.

Contact means sensorial or mental impression. It is the correlation between the sense faculty, sense object, and sensory awareness. Sometimes it is more elaborately defined as "the coincidence, concurrence, and confluence" of these three factors.[24] Considered in relation to the three factors whose correlation is sensory contact, contact itself divides into six types as eye contact, ear contact, nose contact, tongue contact, body contact, and mind contact. These six types are further distinguished into two as resistant contact (*paṭigha-samphassa*) and designation contact (*adhivacana-samphassa*). The term "resistant" applies to the five physical sense organs because they, so to say, collide with their objects, which are also physical. So resistant contact is so called because it arises with the fivefold physical sensory apparatus as its base. What is called designation contact is another expression for mind contact. Yet why is mind contact called designation contact?

This is a question to which there does not seem to be a clear answer in the Pāli commentarial exegesis. However, if we go by the Sanskrit Buddhist exegesis, we can find a satisfactory explanation for this term. Here it is said that "designation" (*adhivacana*) is another expression for name: "Speech bases itself on names; it illuminates the meaning of names. Therefore, designation means name." Further, "Name is the object par excellence of contact associated with mind consciousness. It is, in fact, said: Through visual consciousness one 'knows blue' (*nīlaṃ vijānāti*), but one does not know 'it is blue.' Through mental consciousness one 'knows blue' (*nīlaṃ vijānāti*) and one [also] 'knows it is blue' (*nīlam iti ca vijānāti*)."[25]

According to another, but similar, explanation, only mental consciousness is activated in relation to its objects, or applies itself to its objects, through expression or speech. Therefore, mental consciousness is called "designation contact."[26]

What both explanations show is the intimate association between language and mental consciousness. If mental consciousness recognizes blue as "this is blue," this activity involves some kind of judgment and the participation of language—verbalization at a very subtle level—in the act of recognizing the object. In other words, the above explanations suggest that language has no role to play in the five kinds of contact based on the physical sense organs.

The last factor of mentality is attention (*manasikāra*). In this instance, "attention" means advertence to the object. Without this mental factor no cognitive act can arise. It is said that three conditions are necessary for any act of cognition to take place. The first is that the sense faculty must be unimpaired, that is, it must have the faculty of sight or hearing, as the case may be. The second is that external objects must come within its range. Finally, there must be an appropriate act of attention (*tajjo samannāhāro*) to the object. Where any one of these conditions fails to operate, there will be no resulting cognition.[27]

A second analysis of individual existence is into the twelve sense bases, six internal and six external. The internal six are the six sense faculties, the eye, ear, nose, tongue, body, and mind. The six external are the corresponding objective bases, the visible, sound, smell, taste, touch, and mental objects. In this division, while mind base (*manāyatana*) represents mind as a sense faculty, all its objective data is subsumed under the base of mind objects (*dhammāyatana*). It should be noted here that the three mental aggregates of feeling, perception, and mental formations also fall under the base of mind objects. Since mind base is internal and the base of mind objects is external, as Fyodor Stcherbatsky observes, the principle of externality of one element in relation to another is recognized in the mental sphere as well.[28] For in this twelvefold division, while the mind base (the mind faculty) becomes the subjective part, such things as feeling, perception, and so on are placed in the objective part (within the base of mind objects). This Buddhist distinction between the internal and the external, it may be noted here, does not correspond to the modern distinction between the subjective and the objective. This situation is perhaps traceable to the Buddhist denial of a self-entity as the agent of experience.

From the Buddhist perspective, the analysis into the twelve bases also shows that what we call individual existence is in fact a process of interaction between the internal sense faculties and the external sense objects.

The third analysis of individual existence into eighteen elements (*dhātus*) is an expansion of the analysis into twelve bases through the addition of the six kinds of consciousness that arise from the contact between the sense faculties and their objects. The six additional items are the visual, auditory, olfactory, gustatory, tactile, and mental consciousness.

It will be noticed that in this analysis, consciousness, as that which constitutes knowing, is represented by one element, called the mind element (*mano-dhātu*). What we need to remember here is that the five consciousnesses, based on the five physical sense organs, refer to this same mind element when it takes one of the five physical sense organs as its physiological base. The sixth consciousness, which is mind-consciousness, is the consciousness having nonsensuous objects.

The relative position of the mind element and the six kinds of consciousness should show that mind in its capacity as a sense faculty performs two functions. One is its function as that which cognizes nonsensuous objects, that is, as the sense faculty sensitive to ideas. Second is its function as that which organizes and integrates the separate experiences of the physical sense faculties. While each separate sense is active in its own sphere, the mind is the resort of them all.[29]

One important idea that we can elicit from the analysis into eighteen elements is that consciousness is neither a soul nor an extension of a soul substance. It is a mental phenomenon that comes into being as a result of certain conditions. There is no independent consciousness that exists in its own right.

The Process of Cognition

Early Buddhist teaching on cognition is based on two fundamental ideas. One is that mind is a process without an enduring substance. The other is that all psychological experience is a continuum of mental phenomena. Accordingly, cognition is not the immediate result of the contact between the sense faculty and the sense object. It is the cumulative result of a continuum of cognitive events. The process begins from sensory contact and proceeds by degrees until it reaches its final stage called "conceptual proliferations" (*papañca*):

> Depending on the eye and visible forms eye-consciousness arises. The correlation (union) of the three is sensory contact (impingement). With sensory contact as condition there is feeling. What one feels, one perceives. What one perceives, one examines. What one examines, one conceptually proliferates. Because one conceptually proliferates, perceptions and notions born of conceptual proliferation beset one with respect to past, future, and present visible forms cognizable through the eye.[30]

It must be clearly noted here that the different cognitive events, enumerated above, do not arise in the mind. Rather, the different cognitive events themselves are the mind.

The above quotation refers to seven different stages that occur in the cognitive process:

1. Eye-consciousness arising in dependence on the eye and the visible.
2. Sensory contact, that is, the correlation between the sense organ, the sense object, and the sense consciousness.
3. Feeling.
4. Perception.
4. Examining.
5. Conceptual proliferation.
6. The overwhelming impact, on the percipient individual, of the conceptual proliferation.

Eye-consciousness, which is the initial stage in the above process of cognition, means not full cognition but an elementary level of seeing. It is some kind of "bare sensation" or some sort of "anoetic sentience." This meaning of the term as it occurs in this particular context is recognized in the Pāli Buddhist exegesis as well. In a commentarial gloss, it is described as "mere seeing" (*dassana-matta*). "Mere seeing," as described by the Venerable Bhikkhu Bodhi, is the consciousness "by which the sense datum is experienced in its bare immediacy and simplicity prior to all identificatory cognitive operations."[31] Accordingly, consciousness in this particular context is not ethically qualified as morally wholesome or unwholesome.

Sensory contact is the second stage in the process of cognition. It is the correlation that is set up between the sense organ, the sense object, and the sensory awareness. Sometimes it is more elaborately defined as "the coincidence, concurrence, and confluence of the three factors."[32]

With sensory contact as its condition, the third stage in the cognitive process is feeling. It is the affective tone brought about by the object. This affective tone could be pleasant, unpleasant, or neutral. At this stage, the latent tendency for the ego-consciousness awakens. As the Venerable Ñāṇananda observes, the earlier stages are impersonal in the sense that they occur as a process of dependent arising. For this stage the words used are not "feeling arises," but "feels," suggesting the intrusion of the ego-consciousness as an agent in addition to the feeling.[33] However, it is important to remember that, strictly speaking, even here it is a case of dependent arising. The ego-consciousness is only a superimposition on a purely impersonal process. What the "feeler feels" could be pleasant, unpleasant, or neutral depending on how the feeler responds to the stimuli.

As the fourth stage, we find perception. As explained in chapter 3 on dependent arising, when an unenlightened person perceives (*sañjānāti*), at that very same time, he or she conceives (*maññati*). The original percept is now converted into a concept.

Next comes initial examination. The Pāli word is *vitakka*. This is a technical term for which it is difficult to give a proper English word. *Vitakka* is often translated as "initial application of the mind on the object." It often occurs together with *vicāra*, which means "sustained application of the mind on the object." Both initial and sustained application have a causal connection with meaningful vocal expression. Hence they are defined as verbal constructions (*vacī-saṅkhāra*), that is, subvocal operations of the mind preceding vocal utterance. Hence we read: "Having first had initial thought (*vitakka*) and discursive thought (*vicāra*), one breaks out into speech."[34] Therefore the reference to initial application (*vitakka*) in the cognitive process shows the participation, at least in a very subtle form, of language, the tendency to give a label to the object.

After initial examination comes conceptual proliferations. At this stage, the latent ego-consciousness that awakened earlier becomes fully solidified and crystalized. This stage also involves a more marked verbalization, a process of labeling the object, all resulting in a profuse proliferation of conceptual constructs. If the object is interpreted as something pleasurable because of greed, the percipient individual will be assailed by greed-driven thoughts; if it is interpreted as something repulsive because of aversion, the individual will be assailed by aversion-driven thoughts; if the object is interpreted as something neither pleasurable nor repulsive, he or she will be assailed by delusion-driven thoughts.

Furthermore, the object of cognition reminds the individual of similar experiences that were in the past and similar experiences to be in the future. In fact, it is the past and the future that, more than the present, engages the attention of the individual. What is of critical importance is that the individual is now engulfed, overwhelmed, and rendered powerless to control his or her own conceptual proliferations. In other words, at this stage individuals come under the control of their own minds rather than having their minds under their own control.

The sixth and the seventh stages, referred to above, can be understood as the saṃsāric dimension of individual existence. In a way, saṃsāra means conceptual proliferation and its impact on the individual. This should explain why nibbāna is sometimes defined as the absence of conceptual proliferation (*nippapañca*).[35]

It will be noticed that according to the cognitive process sketched above, the original raw stimulus that has impinged on the eye is not cognized as it is. In the cognitive process that it triggers, the raw stimulus comes to be gradually edited and interpreted until it becomes a fully fledged concept, dressed with a label. The external world is there, yet it is not cognized as it is. Our familiar world of substantial objects turns out to be a mass of conceptual constructs superimposed on the raw sense data. From an epistemological perspective, what this means is that Buddhism sets itself equally aloof from both naïve realism and idealism. What we cognize is not mind made but mind interpreted.

The Mind-Body Relationship

How early Buddhism understands the nature of the mind-body relationship can be seen from the following statement on the inseparable nexus between consciousness (*viññāṇa*) on the one hand and mentality-materiality (*nāma-rūpa*) on the other:

> Mentality-materiality has consciousness as its condition (*viññāṇa-paccayā nāmarūpaṃ*); consciousness [in turn] has mentality-materiality as its condition (*nāmarūpa-paccayā viññāṇaṃ*).

This statement, as we have already noted, occurs in the twelve-factored formula of dependent arising. Mentality-materiality and consciousness are the only two factors, among the twelve, where the relationship is not one-sided but reciprocal. Here "consciousness" (*viññāṇa*) is that which constitutes the knowing or awareness of an object. "Mentality" in "mentality-materiality" (*nāma-rūpa*) denotes the five mental factors of feeling, perception, volition, contact, and attention. These are the five mental factors that necessarily arise together with every type of consciousness.[36]

"Materiality" in "mentality-materiality" denotes the four great material elements, earth (solidity and extension), water (viscidity and liquidity), fire (temperature of cold and heat), and air (distension and mobility), along with the matter that is dependent on the four great material elements. In this particular context, they all refer not to matter in general but to the (organic) matter that enters into the composition of a living being.

Considered in relation to the five aggregates, materiality is the same as the aggregate of matter (*rūpakkhandha*), whereas mentality represents the three aggregates of feeling (*vedanā*), perception (*saññā*), and volitional constructions (*saṅkhāra*).

The reciprocal dependence of consciousness and mentality-materiality is compared to two sheaves of reeds leaning against each other. "Just as if, friend, two bundles of reeds were to stand, one supporting the other, even so consciousness is dependent on mentality-materiality and mentality-materiality is dependent on consciousness . . . If one of the two bundles of reeds is drawn out, the other one would fall down."[37]

As to the reciprocal dependence of consciousness and mentality-materiality, we find the following words of the Buddha:

> Then, bhikkhus, it occurred to me: "When what exists does consciousness come to be? By what is consciousness conditioned?" Then, bhikkhus, through careful attention, there took place in me a breakthrough by wisdom: "When there is mentality-materiality, consciousness comes to be; consciousness has mentality-materiality as its condition." Then, bhikkhus, it occurred to me: "This consciousness turns back; it does not go further than mentality-materiality. It is to this extent that one may be born and age and die, pass away and reborn, that is, when there is consciousness with mentality-materiality as its condition."[38]

It is thus on the essential interdependence of consciousness and mentality-materiality that the whole saṃsāric process of births and deaths revolves. In this sense, their reciprocal dependence constitutes the irreducible ground of saṃsāric existence. This situation remains the same all throughout life, whether the dependently arising series is traced back to the remote past or traced forward to the distant future.

It is to this extent, namely, the reciprocal dependence of consciousness and mentality-materiality, that all designations, descriptions, and linguistic expressions can go—and no further.[39] For, as noted above, consciousness and mentality-materiality represent the five aggregates into which individual existence is analyzed. The entire gamut of the world of experience is comprised within the five aggregates. No description can go beyond them. All interpretations, all fabrications, all views and ideologies coming under both spiritual eternalism and annihilationist materialism are all based on them. The same situation is true of right views as well. Even right views cannot go beyond the five aggregates. The wrong view says: this pentad of aggregates is mine, this I am, this is my self. The right view says: this is not mine, I am not this, this is not my self.

The idea that consciousness does not go beyond mentality-materiality, but turns back from mentality-materiality, is of great philosophical significance. It is mostly consciousness that is identified as the unchanging subject, as the agent of experience, as the quality of a permanent soul, if not as the soul itself. Yet despite this, when the Buddha says that consciousness invariably depends on mentality-materiality, he aims to show that individual existence cannot be reduced to mind (idealism). This amounts to a complete rejection of spiritual eternalism, which advocates the metaphysical version of the self. Again, the fact that materiality cannot be separated from mentality and that both mentality and materiality are necessarily dependent on consciousness shows that individual existence cannot be finally reduced to matter (materialism) either. This amounts to a clear rejection of annihilationist materialism, which advocates the physical version of the self. Here again what comes into focus is how Buddhism remains as a middle position in relation to the two perennial ideologies that polarize our thinking on the nature of individual existence.

If the organic physical body and the mental factors necessarily depend on consciousness, this means that it is only when consciousness is present that a compound of material phenomena functions as a sentient body, and only when consciousness is present do the mental factors participate in cognition. The reciprocal dependence of consciousness and mentality-materiality shows how Buddhism understands the nature of the mind-body relationship: Buddhism avoids the dualistic theory, which says that mind and matter are strictly separate entities. Buddhism also avoids the monistic theory, which says that mind and matter are finally reducible to one, either to mind (idealism) or to matter (materialism). Keeping itself equally aloof from both theories, Buddhism explains the mind-body relationship as one of reciprocal dependence.

The mind-body relationship, as explained thus, does not mean that consciousness is located in the physical body, as assumed by some.[40] Consciousness is not a discrete entity to be located in one particular place of the body or in the whole body. The correct position is that consciousness is dependent on the physical body. This situation becomes all the clearer from the *Paṭṭhāna* of the Abhidhamma Piṭaka, where we find specific reference to the physiological bases of the six kinds of consciousness.

The *Paṭṭhāna* begins by saying that the eye, ear, nose, tongue, and body are conditions by way of support (*nissaya-paccaya*) to the five kinds of consciousness named after them. Then it says that whatever materiality on which mind and mind-consciousness occur, that materiality is a condition by way of base to mind and mind-consciousness and what is associated therewith.[41] What we find here is the language of conditionality, the dependence of the six kinds of consciousness on their respective physiological bases.

One question that now arises is that if the mind depends on a physiological base, is not the mind completely determined by matter? In answering this question, we need to take the following data into consideration. There are six sense organs: the eye, ear, nose, tongue, body, and mind. These are also called doors (*dvāra*) because it is through them that consciousness and its concomitant mental factors gain access to the object. The six sense organs are also called faculties (*indriya*). A faculty is so called because it exercises lordship or control over its associated phenomena. Since they exercise a controlling power over the five kinds of consciousness named after them, as eye-consciousness and so on, the five physical sense organs are recognized as faculties. For example, whereas good eyes produce good vision, weak eyes produce poor vision. For our present purpose, what is most important to remember here is that mind is also recognized as a faculty. It is called the mind faculty (*manindriya*). Therefore, although the mind is dependent on the physical body, it is the mind in its capacity as a faculty that exercises lordship and control over the physical body. With the recognition of mind as a faculty, the preeminence of mind is maintained, although it is said to depend on the organic physical body. Hence the question of mind being completely determined by matter does not arise.

In a commentarial exegesis, we find a classic example to illustrate this situation. In the case of a boat and a boatman, it is the boat that the boatman has as his physical support. However, it is the boatman that controls the boat. It is he who decides where to go. The mind is like the boatman and the physical base on which the mind depends is like the boat. Another example is the case of a man born blind and a cripple who wanted to go on a journey. The blind man had the cripple climb up on his shoulders and made the journey following the instructions given by the cripple. The cripple who can see is like the mind, and the blind man who can walk is like the physical base of the mind.[42]

Yet the reciprocal dependence of consciousness and mentality-materiality should be understood as the reciprocal interaction between mind and body. One good example of how the mind influences the physical body is shown in the higher levels of the mind's concentration (unification), called *jhāna*. When a person is, for instance, in the first jhāna, he "drenches, saturates, permeates, suffuses, this very body with joy and happiness."[43] Similarly does physical health ensure mental health. Physical well-being and a good digestion are among the many factors that enable a person to make speedy progress toward final emancipation.[44]

We can also argue that if Buddhism keeps equally aloof from the two practices of self-mortification and sensual indulgence, it is in order to maintain a healthy mind in a healthy body, for both self-inflicted austerities and inordinate sensual indulgence are equally injurious to mental and physical health.

For Buddhism, the physical body is not a source of bondage to the mind's freedom but a necessary instrument for the mind's development. All gains, as the *Dhammapada* says, have health as the highest attainment.[45] Buddhist discourses often describe physical health in terms of pliability (*lahu*) and wieldiness (*kammañña*) of the physical body.[46] Overeating renders the body heavy and unserviceable; the feeling is like a load of soaked beans. Such a body is not conducive to putting forth energy in the right direction.[47] In the *Theragāthā* we read of the Elder Khitaka exulting in the thought that his physical body is light and wieldy, that "it floats" like a piece of cotton in the air.[48]

The importance of physical health is expressly recognized in the Theravāda Abhidhamma as well. Among the many basic factors of materiality recognized by the Ābhidhammikas, three are called corporeal lightness (*rūpassa lahutā*), corporeal malleability (*rūpassa mudutā*), and corporeal wieldiness (*rūpassa kammaññatā*). These three represent the physical body when it is healthy and amenable to work. Agreeable food, suitable weather, and a wholesome mind are the prerequisites for physical health.[49] These three corporeal factors have their mental counterparts as well.[50] Thus what is emphasized in Buddhism is the necessity and desirability not only of mental health but of physical health as well.

6

DIAGNOSIS OF THE HUMAN CONDITION

IT IS ON the pivotal notion of *dukkha*, a term often rendered into English as "suffering," that the Buddha's diagnosis of the human condition is based. This rendering of the term, it must be noted, does not bring out its full implications. Dukkha has a far wider significance that reflects a comprehensive philosophical vision. Accordingly, what Buddhism means by dukkha is any kind of conditioned experience, an experience dependent on impermanent conditions. Conditioned experience could be extremely pleasant or extremely unpleasant. Nevertheless, it is subsumed under dukkha. Even the nonsensuous jhānic experience that represents higher levels of mind's unification, and therefore higher levels of happiness, is also brought under dukkha, for in the final analysis, even jhānic experience is impermanent and therefore conditioned.[1] What all this amounts to is that any experience other than the unconditioned experience that is nibbāna is reckoned as dukkha.[2]

Addressing Anurādha, the Buddha says: "Both formerly and now also, Anurādha, it is just suffering and the cessation of suffering that I proclaim."[3] This should show what the teachings of the Buddha are and what they are not. The teachings are concerned totally with our existentialist predicament, which according to the Buddha is the problem of suffering and how suffering can be brought to a complete end. If Buddhism is to be understood in this context, it follows that all Buddhist teachings are ultimately related to the problem of suffering and its final solution. It is on this theme that all early Buddhist teachings converge and it is in relation to this that they assume their significance. Dependent arising, which the Buddha himself wants us to consider as the heart of the Dhamma,[4] does in fact amount to a statement of the origin of suffering when the causal formula is understood in its progressive order, and to a statement of the cessation of suffering when it is understood in its regressive order.

That the teachings of the Buddha converge on the problem of suffering and its solution is also shown by the reference in the Pāli discourses to two kinds of teaching. The first is called the "graduated talk" (*ānupubbī kathā*). Talks on charity, on morality, on heaven as a reward for virtuous living, on the disadvantages, the folly, and the defiling nature of sense pleasures and the advantages of renunciation—this is what constitutes the graduated talk.[5] It is the emphasis on these subjects that Buddhism seems to have shared with many other religions of the day in a variety of moral teachings (*kammavāda*). The second kind of teaching is called the "all-exalting discourse" (*sāmukkaṃsika-desanā*).[6] It consists of the four noble truths, that is, the Buddha's diagnosis of the human condition and its solution. "Graduated talk" could be understood in two ways: It is a type of teaching that gradually prepares the background necessary for the deliverance of the "all-exalting discourse." It also gradually prepares the mind of the listener as a proper receptacle (*kallacitta*, a proper mind, *muducitta*, a pliable mind, and so on) for a correct understanding of the second kind of teaching. If the Buddha begins with the "graduated talk," it is not for its own sake, but for the sole purpose of preparing the ground for the deliverance of the characteristically Buddhist doctrine of the four noble truths.

It is through four propositions that the Buddha presents his teaching on suffering and deliverance from suffering: there is suffering, there is a cause for this suffering, there is cessation of suffering through the removal of the cause of suffering, there is a way that leads to the removal of the cause of suffering that results in the cessation of suffering. When the Buddha proclaims the presence of suffering, he proclaims something factual; he does not express his personal feelings or emotions.

Suffering is not due to our being ignorant of some kind of metaphysical reality and of our relation to it. Nor is it due to our being estranged from our true self, or to our identifying our true self with what is not the true self, since for Buddhism there is neither a true self nor a false self. There is only the false notion of the "self." The cause of suffering, according to the Buddha, is self-centered craving. Obviously it is a cause that is within us and not out there in the external world. Therefore we ourselves can liberate ourselves from all suffering.

When suffering arises, it arises within us; when it ceases, it also ceases within us. Thus both saṃsāra and nibbāna are within us. "Within this very body," declares the Buddha, "mortal as it is and only a fathom high, but conscious and endowed with mind, is the world and the waxing thereof and the waning thereof and the way that leads to the passing away thereof."[7]

The four noble truths do not exhibit a hierarchical order. What they bring into focus is the progressive sequence between four facts. It is of course true that cessation of suffering is "higher" (better) than suffering. Yet the truth of the cessation of suffering is certainly not higher than the truth of suffering. As four propositions, the four truths are all coordinate. Hence they are all introduced as noble truths: they are equally true and therefore equally noble.

Because of the progressive sequence between the four noble truths, the significance of one cannot be understood in a context from where the other three are excluded. Each assumes its significance in relation to the other three. If the truth of suffering is sought to be understood in isolation from the other three truths, such an understanding will necessarily lead to the conclusion that Buddhism advocates a pessimistic view of life. Any such misconception could be easily removed if it is understood in its proper context, that is, in relation to the other three truths. Even nibbāna, which is the final goal of Buddhism and which corresponds to the third noble truth, assumes its significance in the context of the other three noble truths. Their mutual relation and interconnection are such that it would not be incorrect to say that they are not four different propositions, but four aspects of one and the same proposition.

In fact, it is maintained in the Pāli discourses themselves that "when the first noble truth is comprehended, the second suggests itself; when the second is comprehended, the third suggests itself; when the third is comprehended, the fourth suggests itself."[8]

The progressive sequence the four noble truths exhibit is also taken into consideration when they become the basis for actual practice of the religious life. Hence it is said that the fact of suffering is to be *understood* (*pariññeyya*), the cause of suffering is to be *removed* (*pahātabba*), the cessation of suffering is to be *realized* (*sacchikātabba*), and the path that leads to the cessation of suffering is to be *developed* (*bhāvetabba*).[9] If the second (the need to remove) and the fourth (the need to develop) are taken as two aspects relating to practice, then here we have the three main dimensions of Buddhism as a religion, namely, understanding, practice, and realization. It is under these three aspects that all Buddhist teachings are presented.

Like many other Buddhist teachings, the Buddha's teaching on suffering is presented against the background of similar theories current at the time. Mention is made in the Pāli discourses of four theories as to why human beings suffer. According to the first, suffering is self-caused. This theory is based on the view that there is an identically persisting self-entity that acts and suffers its consequences. According to the second, suffering is other-caused: someone acts and someone else suffers. This second theory is based on the view that there is complete otherness between the one who acts and the one who suffers. The first, as the Buddha says, leads to eternalism, the second, to annihilationism. According to the third theory, suffering is both self-caused and other-caused. This theory is an attempt to combine the first two theories, which are equally false. The combination of two false theories makes it doubly false. The fourth rejects the first three theories and seeks to explain human suffering as befallen by chance, that is, due to fortuitous circumstances.[10]

By explaining the fact of suffering as a case of dependent arising, the Buddha goes beyond these four theories. This is the significance of the twelve-linked causal formula, where each succeeding link is said to result from what immediately precedes it. What the twelve-linked causal formula clearly demonstrates is that the causes of suffering are not outside individual existence, that they are identifiable and therefore removable.

As to the Buddhist view of suffering, one pertinent question that has been raised is this: Does it mean there is suffering in life or that life itself is suffering? The answer to this question will become clear if we examine how the fact of suffering is defined in Buddhism.

The Buddhist definition of suffering has three levels: The first level identifies four concrete occasions of suffering, namely, "the trauma of birth" (*jāti*), "the morbidity of decrepitude" (*jarā*), "the pathology of sickness" (*vyādhi*), and "the phobia of death" (*maraṇa*). At this level suffering appears as physical pain and oppression. To this may be added such experiences as hunger, thirst, privation, and accident. The second level is more comprehensive, and it defines suffering in three ways: "to be dissociated from what is pleasant" (*piyehi vippayoga*), "to be associated with what is unpleasant" (*appiyehe sampayoga*), and "to not get what one expects"—unfulfilled expectations or impeded will (*yam p'icchaṃ na labhati*). At this level, what is focused on is suffering as psychological experience. The third level of definition is a comprehensive summing up of what suffering is: "In brief, the five aggregates of grasping are suffering."[11]

All seven occasions of suffering listed before the third level of definition could be accepted by almost all as veritable sources of suffering. However, it is the conclusive summing up of what suffering is that is most significant, the one that could be the most controversial. It says that, in brief, the five aggregates of grasping, namely, corporeality, feeling, perception, mental constructions, and consciousness, are "suffering." What this clearly demonstrates is not that the five aggregates of grasping are a source of suffering but that the five aggregates of grasping themselves are the suffering. Both "suffering" and "the five aggregates of grasping" become mutually convertible expressions.

Now the five aggregates of grasping themselves constitute individual existence in its saṃsāric dimension. The very fact that they are described as suffering should show that from the Buddhist perspective, it is not correct to say that there is suffering in life. The correct saying should be that life itself is suffering.

If life itself is suffering, is this not contradicted by empirical evidence? Are there not pleasures in sensual gratification, in the titillation of the senses? Buddhism would not quarrel with such an assertion. If there were no satisfaction in the world—so runs the Buddhist argument—living beings would not be attached to the world. Mention is made of many kinds of pleasure and happiness, which could be obtained through righteous or nonrighteous means. The very fact that Buddhism rejects sensual gratification as a means to emancipation shows that what it questions is not the impossibility of sensual pleasure but rather its validity as a means to true happiness. Sensual gratification is not even described as suffering, as is its opposite, self-mortification. Again, the very fact that nibbāna is defined not as happiness but as the highest happiness shows that there are many other levels of happiness that are lower than nibbāna.

What all this suggests is that Buddhism recognizes different levels of happiness that culminate in nibbāna. Hence happiness itself came to be defined as that which has nibbāna as its consummation (*nibbāna-paramaṃ sukhaṃ*).[12]

Is there then a contradiction between the assertion that life itself is suffering and the recognition of the actuality and the possibility of pleasures in life? As we have pointed out, the answer to this question is that what Buddhism means by "suffering" is any kind of conditioned experience, an experience dependent on impermanent conditions.

Why are the five aggregates of grasping suffering? What we need to remember is that it is not the five aggregates (*pañca-khandha*), but the five aggregates of grasping (*pañca-upādānakkhandha*), that are described as suffering. This distinction should show that although the five aggregates in themselves are not a source of suffering, they constitute suffering when they become objects of grasping (*upādāna*). Strictly speaking, therefore, what Buddhism calls the individual in its saṃsāric dimension is not the five aggregates, but the five aggregates when they are grasped, appropriated, and clung to. That which is called "individual existence" can thus be reduced to a causally conditioned process of grasping. It is this process of grasping that Buddhism describes as suffering.

Another question that arises here is, by whom are the five aggregates grasped? The answer is that besides the process of grasping, there is no agent who performs the act of grasping. This answer may appear rather enigmatic; nevertheless, it is understandable in the context of the Buddhist doctrine of nonself and the Buddhist doctrine of dependent arising. What both doctrines seek to show is that the individual is a conditioning and conditioned process, without an agent either inside or outside the process. The grasping process manifests in three ways: this is mine (*etaṃ mama*), this I am (*eso'ham asmi*), and this is my self (*eso me attā*). The first is due to craving (*taṇhā*), the second to conceit (*māna*), and the third to the mistaken belief in a self-entity (*diṭṭhi*). It is through this process of threefold self-appropriation that the idea of "mine," "I am," and "my self" arises. If there is a phenomenon called "individuality" in its saṃsāric dimension, it is entirely due to the superimposition of these three ideas on the five aggregates.[13]

At this juncture, another question arises: Why and how does the process of grasping lead to suffering? In answering this question, it is important to note that the five aggregates that become the object of self-appropriation and grasping are in a state of constant change, in a state of continuous flux with no persisting substance. Their nature is such that they do not remain in the way we want them to remain. As such, the aggregates are not under our full control. Thus by identifying ourselves with what is impermanent (*anicca*), with what does not come under our full control (*anatta*), we come to suffering. This should explain why Buddhism traces the fact of suffering to the fact of impermanence (*yad aniccaṃ taṃ dukkhaṃ*). When the process of self-appropriation and self-identification is terminated, suffering too comes to an end. As long as this process persists, there is suffering. The moment it stops, the saṃsāric process also ceases to be, and together with it all suffering comes to an end.

Sometimes the totality of suffering is presented under three aspects. First there is suffering-suffering (*dukkha-dukkhatā*). This reduplicated form of the term refers to suffering as generally understood, that is, physical pain as well as its deeper psychological experience as sorrow and anxiety. This aspect therefore corresponds to the first two levels of our classification of definitions mentioned above. Second there is "suffering through change" (*vipariṇāma-dukkhatā*). This aspect refers to situations when, even though we are happy, suffering stares at us in the background. Moments of happiness do not obtain in uninterrupted continuity but have a tendency to become interrupted through change of circumstances. Third there is "suffering as construction" (*saṅkhāra-dukkhatā*). This aspect corresponds exactly to the suffering involved in grasping the five aggregates.[14]

Buddhism's great concern with the problem of suffering may, on a superficial appraisal, appear as an inordinate obsession with an unwarranted problem, particularly when it is considered in the context of the joys and pleasures of life. What should not be overlooked here is that if Buddhism is concerned with the problem of suffering, it is only in order to get rid of it completely. If Buddhism identifies all sources and occasions of suffering, it is in order to provide not a mere palliative, but a complete cure for the disease, which, in turn, ensures that happiness is based on a sure and solid foundation. Therefore, the Buddhist teaching on suffering is the Buddhist teaching on the pursuit of happiness.

Experience of suffering is sometimes described as "real and objective" (*tatha, avitatha, anaññatatha*).[15] The reason seems to be that although suffering is a subjective experience, it is presented as an objective fact in order to emphasize its universality.

If Buddhism emphasizes the universality of suffering, this could be understood from another point of view, from the point of view of the cause of suffering. The cause of suffering is self-centered craving, which manifests itself in many forms. Hence the universality of suffering also means the universality of the cause of suffering. As such, to say that a human being suffers is the same as saying that a human being is motivated by self-centered craving. The two statements are mutually convertible, although the first is by way of the effect, whereas the second is by way of the cause. If we have the liberty of reversing the progressive sequence of the first two noble truths, thereby presenting the second truth as the first, then we can say: "A human being is motivated by self-centered craving." And if we present the first truth as the second, then we can further claim: "Therefore he or she suffers." Understood in this way, the whole purpose of the four noble truths is to bring imperfect human beings to perfection.

The Buddhist attitude to suffering is very accurately analyzed by Alexandra David-Neel.[16] She refers to four possible attitudes to suffering. The first is the denial of suffering in the face of all evidence. This may be interpreted as irrational, naïve optimism. The second is one of "passive resignation, the acceptance of a state of things which one considers inevitable." This attitude may be interpreted as out-and-out pessimism. The third is "camouflage of suffering by the help of pompous sophistry or by gratuitously attaching to it such virtues and transcendent aims as one thinks may ennoble it or diminish its bitterness." Such an attitude may be interpreted as rationalization of suffering. The fourth is "the war against suffering, accompanied by the faith in the possibility of overcoming it." This can be described as the most rational and the most acceptable attitude to suffering. Indeed, it is this fourth attitude to suffering that Buddhism adopts. Such a position should explain why Buddhism does not make any attempt to "interpret" suffering, for any interpretation of suffering implies an attempt to rationalize it. Rationalization of suffering, in turn, implies an attempt to "hide its bitterness" on spiritual or other grounds. It amounts to some kind of escapism in the face of suffering, which, in other words, means a postponement of a solution to it.

Accordingly, Buddhism emphasizes the urgency of the need for a solution to the problem of suffering. The human being's existentialist predicament is therefore compared to a person who has been pierced with a poisoned arrow (*salla-viddha*).[17] This comparison draws attention not only to our present predicament but also to the urgency of solving it. It also draws attention to two other things: what one should do and what one should not do in such a situation. In the first place, one must not waste one's time by asking such silly questions as who shot the arrow or what his name, caste, and so on, are. Nor should one insist that one would not get the poisoned arrow removed until one knows the answers to these questions. To raise such questions is to create more questions, questions that have no relevance to the problem; what is more, the patient would die before he or she could receive satisfactory answers to such impertinent questions.

It is in light of this illustration that the Buddha's attitude to the problem of suffering and to the solution of metaphysical questions should be understood. When Māluṅkyaputta, a Buddhist monk, asked the Buddha whether the world is eternal or noneternal, or whether the world is finite or infinite, the Buddha refused to answer. Māluṅkyaputta then decided to leave the order. Addressing him after this decision, the Buddha said: "The religious life, O Māluṅkyaputta, does not depend on the dogma that the world is eternal or not, nor does it depend on the dogma that the world is finite or not. Whether the world is eternal or not, whether the world is finite or not, there is birth, there is death, there are grief, sorrow, pain, lamentation, and despair, and it is for their extinction in this very life itself that I preach the doctrine." It was in illustrating this point that the Buddha used the simile of the poisoned arrow. If the Buddha refused to answer such metaphysical questions, it was because their solution, whether they are solvable or not, is another question, has no relevance to the understanding of our present predicament or to solving it altogether. These questions, as the Buddha insists, are not concerned with the practice of the higher life: "They do not conduce to dispassion, to cessation [of suffering], to calming, to higher knowledge, to awakening, or to nibbāna." What is most significant is that immediately after saying so, the Buddha goes on to explain the four noble truths, which is the Buddha's formulation of the problem of suffering and its solution. It is in this context that the quotation that we cited at the beginning of this chapter becomes significant: "Both formerly and now also, Anurādha, it is just suffering and the cessation of suffering that I proclaim."[18]

7

THE THEORY OF MORAL LIFE

Right View and the Theory of Moral Life

As is well known, the Buddhist moral life begins with right view (*sammā diṭṭhi*). The elevation of right view to this fundamental level serves the purpose of drawing our attention to the importance of the way we look at the nature of reality in pursuing the moral life, for our perspectives on the nature of reality play a crucial role in how we conduct ourselves in our individual and social life, how we respond to the social environment. The Buddha asserts that he sees no single factor so responsible for the suffering of living beings as wrong view (*micchā diṭṭhi*), and no factor so potent in promoting the good of living beings as right view.[1] This is the rationale for Buddhism's emphasis on the importance and relevance of right view for the practice of moral life. A system of morality, if it is to be oriented toward the right direction, should be based on a correct view of reality, on a proper understanding of our world of experience.

Although the Buddha draws our attention to the importance of right view, he does not endorse dogmatic adherence to views, even if they are right. "To be infatuated with 'the rightness' of our own views and ideologies" (*sandiṭṭhi-rāga*) and to have a "dogmatic attachment to speculative views" (*diṭṭhi-parāmāsa*) are at the root of the belief that "this alone is true, all else is false" (*idaṃ eva saccaṃ, moghaṃ aññaṃ*).[2] It is this kind of warped mindset that provides a fertile ground for bigotry and dogmatism (*idaṃ-saccābhinivesa*).[3] The external manifestations of such a mindset, as we all know, are interpersonal conflicts, acts of fanaticism and militant piety, indoctrination and unethical conversion, fundamentalism and persecution, as well as acts of terrorism, often leading to internecine warfare. From the Buddhist point of view, dogmatic attachment to ideologies is exponentially more detrimental and fraught with more danger than our inordinate attachment to material things. Interreligious and intra-religious wars, wrongly referred to as holy wars, are a case in point. If Buddhism does not encourage dogmatic attachment to views, it is because, from the Buddhist way of looking at it, a view is only a guide to action. In his well-known discourse on the Parable of the Raft (*kullūpamā*), the Buddha tells us that his teaching should be understood not as a goal in itself, but as a means to the realization of the goal.

Hence the teaching of the Buddha, as the Buddha himself says, has only relative value, relative to the realization of the goal. It is a vehicle to be used, not an icon to be ritually adulated. What this attitude clearly implies is that even the right view, like all other views, is a conceptual model, serving as a guide to action. If it is called the right view, it is because it leads us properly to the right goal. The right goal, according to Buddhism, is a right vision (*sammā dassana*) into the true nature of the world both within and outside us (*yathābhūta-ñāṇa*).[4]

The Three Foundational Principles of the Buddhist Theory of Moral Life

There are three cardinal principles that according to Buddhism are axiomatic to a truly rational theory of morality. Among them, the first is called *kammavāda*.[5] This principle is the advocacy of moral life and the recognition of moral consequences, the recognition that there is a causal correlation between what we do and what we reap. It is best understood as the exact opposite of moral nihilism, which denies the validity of moral distinctions and questions the possibility of moral consequences. From the Buddhist point of view, all religions in concert espouse the supremacy of moral life. Hence the Buddha called his contemporaneous religious teachers "those who advocate the moral life" (*kammavādino*). The second principle is called *kiriyavāda*.[6] It is the recognition of the need to do morally wholesome acts and to refrain from morally unwholesome acts. This principle is the opposite of moral acausalism (*ahetukavāda*), according to which "there is no cause or condition for the defilement or purification of beings. Beings are defiled and purified without cause or condition."[7] Lastly there is the principle called *viriyavāda*.[8] It is the recognition and provision for the role of human effort in the pursuit of moral life.

These three principles—*kammavāda*, *kiriyavāda*, and *viriyavāda*—bring into focus the three important dimensions of the Buddhist teaching on the theory of moral life. What they seek to show is that the advocacy of moral life in itself is not adequate. To be meaningful, the advocacy of moral life must be supplemented, first with a rational explanation as to the efficacy of moral actions, and second, with a justification for the necessity and desirability of the role of human effort in the practice of moral life.

This will become clear if we examine the Buddha's observations on three "sectarian views," namely, theistic determinism, karmic determinism, and strict indeterminism. The first view maintains that everything is due to the fiat of a creator god. The second view contends that everything is due to past kamma. The third view rejects both versions of determinism and argues that everything happens owing to fortuitous circumstances, as if befallen by chance.[9]

Criticism of the first two theories by the Buddha takes the following form: If everything is due to a creator god or to past kamma, then man is not morally responsible for any of his actions. He is reduced to the level of a hapless object in the presence of an external power over which he has no control. Although the two theories espouse moral life (*kammavāda*), they fail to establish moral responsibility, that is, a rational correlation between our actions and their consequences. In other words, both fail to establish *kiriyavāda*. Consequently, these two views also fail to justify the necessity and desirability of human effort in practicing the moral life. The third, the theory of strict indeterminism, fares no better. If, as it claims, events happen fortuitously, then no rational correlation can be established between what we do and what we experience. In this situation, it makes no sense to speak of moral responsibility or the role of human effort. The theory of strict indeterminism undermines the very foundation of moral life; thus it becomes another expression for moral nihilism.[10]

It is through the principle of dependent arising that Buddhism avoids both strict determinism and strict indeterminism. The principle of dependent arising establishes a causal correlation between moral actions and their consequences. According to the Buddha, human effort (*attakāra*) is not strictly determined. It can in fact serve as a factor in the myriad causal processes of life. The very evident fact that we feel free to act and exercise our initiative-effort (*ārambha-dhātu*) in many situations is cited as an example for the possibility of human effort. Hence the Buddha asks: "*How can one, while walking up and down with one's own effort, say that there is no personal effort?*"[11]

In the Buddhist practice of moral life, the need for human effort plays a vital role. Human effort is described as "the mental inception of energy, the striving and the onward effort, the exertion and endeavour, the zeal and ardour, the vigour and fortitude, the state of unfaltering effort, the state of sustained desire, the state of unflinching endurance, the solid grip of the burden."[12] It is one of the five spiritual faculties (*indriya*) and spiritual powers (*bala*). Human effort appears as right effort (*sammā vāyāma*), or as the four modes of supreme effort (*sammappadhāna*) in the noble eightfold path. It is elevated to the sublime position of a factor leading to awakening (*bojjhaṅga*). What is more, as one Pāli commentary observes, "right energy should be regarded as the root of all attainments."[13]

Kamma and the Criteria of Moral Evaluation

The term *kamma* literally means action. Yet despite this, the Buddha gives it a psychological meaning when he defines it as volition, or willed action (*cetanā*): "I declare, O monks, that volition is moral action. Having willed one acts by body, speech, and mind."[14] It is not action but the intentionality of the action that is recognized as moral action per se. If I simply raise my arm, that is not kamma, though if I raise it with the intention of assaulting someone, then that intention translates that action into kamma. For any action to be morally responsible, it has to be carried out with a purposeful intention. Only willed action produces an effect that is eventually experienced by the actor, while the nature of the effect will be determined by the intention with which the action is performed.

As shown in the Buddha's definition, kamma can manifest in three different ways: physically, vocally, and mentally. Despite its threefold manifestation, kamma is but one, that is, volition or intention. Kamma, which is volition, should be clearly distinguished from its result, which is called *vipāka*. Accordingly, the Buddhist term *kamma* by no means connotes the result of kamma. Kamma, be it repeated, is nothing but volition.

Both kamma and its result are part of our psychological experience. The result of kamma could be experienced either in this life (*diṭṭhe'va dhamme*), or in the next life (*upapajje*), or in future lives (*apare vā pariyāye*).[15]

Even kamma is condition-originated. In this connection, we can distinguish between three causative factors: the first is external stimulation, the second is conscious motivation, and the third is the impact of unconscious motives.

External stimulation refers to sensory contact through the five physical sense faculties: the eye, ear, nose, tongue, and the body. Our contact with the external world triggers diverse thoughts within us, thoughts of attraction to what is interpreted as attractive, or thoughts of repugnance to what is interpreted as repugnant. Objects or events in themselves are neither attractive nor repugnant. It is our discrimination by way of interpretation that makes the difference.

Conscious motivation is the second causative factor. Among the factors that drive unenlightened people in their behavior are craving for sense pleasures (*kāma-taṇhā*), craving for being (*bhava-taṇhā*), and craving for nonbeing (*vibhava-taṇhā*). Another set of causal factors are greed (*lobha*), hatred (*dosa*), and delusion (*moha*), along with their opposites. The unwholesome factors lead to unwholesome acts, and the wholesome factors to wholesome acts. In a further analysis of conscious motivation, we have what is called the four "wrong courses," namely, partiality (*chanda*), aversion (*dosa*), delusion (*moha*), and cowardice (*bhaya*).[16] When overcome by them, we lose our sense of impartiality and all our judgments become distorted.

Among the clearly nonconscious factors determining human behavior are seven proclivities, or inclinations, that are deep-seated and innate: (1) the desire for sensual gratification (*kāma-rāga*), (2) the desire for self-perpetuation (*bhava*), (3) grudges, aggression, the predisposition to acts of violence (*paṭigha*), (4) egocentric beliefs and various perspectives (*diṭṭhi*), (5) obsessive doubting, diffidence, skeptical doubt (*vicikicchā*), (6) conceit that manifests as feelings of equality, superiority, and inferiority (*māna*), and (7) ignorance, ignorance of the nature of actuality (*avijjā*).[17] These mental proclivities or hidden psychological dispositions are so called since they remain in a state of latency. When there are suitable conditions they manifest as mental turbulence, as excited feelings. What is deposited in the inner recesses of our mind as latencies are our conscious activities that have merged into the unconscious. Many of them are gathered through our array of lives in the saṃsāric process. As such, their presence cannot be explained with reference to the present life alone.

Our minds' proclivities and propensities have a role to play in determining the quality of our kammic activities. The Buddha says: "Whatever a person habitually reflects on and ponders over, in accordance with that will be his mental bent."[18] Each mental bent lays down an imprint. When this imprint is repeated, we develop habits and patterns of behavior. Habitual patterns help shape our character and our character in turn determines our destiny. This determination is true in either way, whether for our own betterment or for our downfall.

Whether the stimulus for kammic activities comes from external stimulation, from conscious motivation, or from unconscious motives, the ethical value of kamma depends on its being motivated by what are known as the six radical roots of moral evil and moral good. They are called "roots" since all manifestations of moral evil and moral good can ultimately be traced to them.

Greed (*lobha*), aversion (*dosa*), and delusion (*moha*) are the three roots of all moral evil. In this context, greed covers all degrees of egocentric desire, longing, attachment, and grasping. Aversion includes all forms of ill will, anger, animosity, irritation and annoyance, along with so-called righteous anger and moral indignation. Aversion can range from mild irritability to uncontrollable rage. Delusion is another expression for ignorance (*avijjā*). It is the absence of clear comprehension and objectivity, or as a Pāli commentary describes, it is "the mind's blindness."[19] These are the three psychological mainsprings of all defilements, all pollutants, all unwholesome mental dispositions that manifest themselves either mentally, vocally, or physically.

Absence of greed (*alobha*), absence of aversion (*adosa*), and absence of delusion (*amoha*) are the three roots of moral good. The first two should be understood in a positive sense as well. The first root refers not only to the absence of greed but also to its positive manifestation as charity, liberality, and renunciation. In the same way, the second root refers not only to the absence of aversion but also to the positive qualities of amity, goodwill, gentleness, benevolence, and loving kindness. Loving kindness (*mettā*), for instance, is not a separate mental factor, but the highest manifestation of the absence of hatred. On the other hand, as the Venerable Bhikkhu Nyanaponika observes, the negative term "absence of delusion" has always a positive significance, for here the reference is to knowledge and understanding: "If the other two roots provide the volitional impetus and the emotional tone required for wholesome consciousness, this particular root represents its rational or intellectual aspect."[20] It is, in fact, the mental factor called "absence of delusion" that elevates itself to the level of liberating wisdom.

It is with reference to these six roots, the unwholesome and the wholesome, that Buddhism makes its moral evaluation as morally unwholesome (*akusala*) and morally wholesome (*kusala*). Any volitional action that is conditioned by the three unwholesome roots is evaluated as unwholesome. Conversely, any volitional action that is motivated by the three wholesome roots is evaluated as wholesome. *Kusala* literally means "skillful"; it is precisely this literal meaning that comes into focus in its technical sense as well.

The Buddhist evaluation of kammic activities according to the six roots of moral evil and moral good shows that a mind that is obsessed with greed, malice, and delusion is a mind that is "defiled" (*kiliṭṭha-citta*), "diseased" (*ātura-citta*), and "in bondage" (*avimutta-citta*). Such a mind cannot see things in their proper perspective. A defiled and diseased mind is in a state of disharmony with actuality. It is therefore called "unskillful" (*akusala*).

On the other hand, when the mind has the opposite skillful qualities, namely, generosity, compassionate love, and wisdom, it experiences the positive qualities of mental purity, mental health, and mental freedom. It is a mind that is in harmony with actuality. Such a mind is therefore described as "skillful" (*kusala*).[21]

As the commentarial exegesis observes, when we have "skillful" qualities, we experience mental health (*ārogya*), mental purity (*anavajjatā*), as well as dexterity (*cheka*), all of which result in mental felicity (*sukha-vipāka*).[22] If negative mental dispositions, such as animosity and jealousy, are called "unskillful," it is because they impair our mental (as well as physical) health and reduce the mind's skillfulness.

Thus the Buddhist moral evaluation, in terms of "skillful" and "unskillful," is based on psychology, on a distinction made between positive mental dispositions that enhance our mental health, on the one hand, and negative mental dispositions that impair our mental health, on the other.

Kamma-based Buddhist ethics is thus an ethics of intention, an ethics of volition. As such, it is an ethics with universal application. Greed, aversion, and delusion, which are the three radical roots of moral evil, along with their opposites, are, needless to say, commonly experienced by all unenlightened human beings. They are not confined to one geographical region, nor are they confined to one historical period. As a result, the Buddhist evaluation of what is morally good and bad is not relative, in the sense that it does not change in relation to shifting social conventions, cultural norms, government-enforced laws, or political ideologies.

The moral order is not an imposition from above by a supreme deity, nor is it an invention on the part of the Buddha. For Buddhism, the basic moral law is inherent in life: it is a special case of the principle of cause and effect. The Buddha only discovers it. In this regard, the Buddha explains his own position in the following words: "You yourselves ought to do what ought to be done. The tathāgatas [only] show the way."[23] The Buddha does not claim to be a savior who can redeem humankind. He is the Awakened One who shows the way to the awakening of others, an awakening from the slumber of ignorance. He is the Enlightened One who shows the way to the enlightenment of others. The Buddha is therefore called the torch-bearer to human beings (*ukkādhāro manussānaṃ*).[24]

For those who follow the Buddha, the Buddha is a moral authority—not in the sense that he has authoritative power to impose his "moral will," but in the sense that he has authoritative knowledge on the subject of morality. Accordingly, we need to understand the moral teachings in Buddhism not as injunctions and commandments but as guidelines for moral action. They are not coercive, but persuasive; more descriptive than prescriptive. This also means that according to Buddhism, morally good and morally bad actions are neither rewarded nor punished. Rather, they have their own consequences according to the principles of moral causation.

Although kamma is universally applicable, it is not the only factor that matters in human experience. In fact, as indicated above, the Buddha rejects the view that all human experience is due to past kamma. If past kamma were the sole determinant factor, then my present kamma, which is purposeful intention, would also be determined by my past kamma. This state of affairs would imply two situations. The first is that I had no free choice in deciding between two or more possible alternatives, for my decision was forced on me by my past kamma. The second is that such a situation would lead to a process of interminable kammic determinism, with no possibility of escape from the inexorable sway of the previous kamma.

When it was reported to the Buddha that some recluses and brahmins maintained that "whatever a person experiences, all that is caused by past kamma," the Buddha says that this view can easily be falsified by the empirically observable fact that people experience diverse feelings due to diverse factors. Some feelings, for instance, arise from bile disorders, from phlegm disorders, from wind disorders; some are due to an imbalance of the three humors, to climatic change, to careless behavior; while some are due to self-inflicted pain or to past kamma. As enumerated here, past kamma is one among eight factors responsible for the experience of diverse feelings.[25]

On another occasion the Buddha makes the humorous point that if all human experience is due to past kamma, as maintained in Jainism, "then the tathāgata surely must have done good deeds in the past, since he now feels such taintless pleasant feelings."[26]

That kamma is not the only factor that activates in our experience is further recognized by the Abhidhamma when it mentions some twenty-four conditional relations, among which kamma is only one. Then in the postcanonical commentarial exegesis we find reference to five orders, among which kamma corresponds to one alone. These are:

1. Physical inorganic order (*utu-niyāma*), e.g., the unerring order of seasons, the causes of winds and rains.
2. Physical organic order (*bīja-niyāma*), e.g., the order of germs and seeds, the peculiar characteristics of certain fruits.
3. Moral order (*kamma-niyāma*), e.g., the causal order of kammic acts and their results (*vipāka*).
4. Psychological order (*citta-niyāma*), e.g., the arising of cognitive acts as a patterned continuum wherein the immediately succeeding one is conditioned by the immediately preceding one.
5. Spiritual order (*dhamma-niyāma*), e.g., specific phenomena arising at the advent of a bodhisatta in his last birth.[27]

As to the operation of kamma, there is this important question: Should a person reap the consequences of his kamma in the same way as he performed the kamma? In this connection, the Buddha says:

> Were one to declare thus: "Just as this man does a deed, so does he experience," this being so, the living of a religious life would be

> rendered meaningless. For there would be no opportunity for the complete destruction of suffering. Yet if one were to say, "Just as this man performs a deed of which the consequence is to be experienced, so does he experience its consequence," this makes the religious life meaningful and there will be an opportunity for the complete destruction of suffering.[28]

The above explanation by the Buddha clearly demonstrates that there is no mechanical one-to-one correspondence between kamma and its consequence. If, for instance, a person kills someone, it is not the case that he too will be killed as a consequence of his kamma. From the Buddhist perspective, the consequence of kamma is certainly not tit for tat, an eye for an eye. The Buddhist teaching on kamma has nothing to do with revengeful justice. What we find in Buddhism is not kammic determinism but kammic conditionality.

There is another question that concerns the operation of kamma: Should one experience retribution for all previously committed bad kamma? As recorded in one Buddhist discourse, the opinion of Nigaṇṭha Nātaputta on this matter is as follows: anyone at all who, for instance, destroys life or takes what is not given is bound for a state of misery, bound for hell. The Buddha's position on this matter is quite different. If, for instance, a person committed such evil deeds as killing and taking what is not given, he could reflect like this: "In many ways, the Buddha criticizes and censures such evil acts as destruction of life and taking what is not given. However, now I have destroyed life to such and such extent. That was not proper; that was not good. Yet my feeling of regret and guilt cannot undo the evil I have done." Having reflected thus, he abandons the destruction of life and he abstains from the destruction of life in the future. He abandons all other vocal and bodily evil acts. Having abandoned wrong view, now he is one of right view.

Then that noble disciple—who is thus devoid of covetousness, devoid of ill will, unconfused, clearly comprehending, ever mindful—dwells one quarter with a mind imbued with loving kindness, likewise the second quarter, the third quarter, and the fourth quarter. Thus above, below, across, and everywhere, and to all as to himself, he dwells, pervading the entire world with a mind imbued with loving kindness, vast, exalted, measureless, without hostility, without ill will." He does so in respect of the other three immeasurables, namely, kindness, altruistic joy, and equanimity. Then as a result of the *immeasurable* (*appamāṇa*) compassionate love, *immeasurable* kindness, *immeasurable* altruistic joy, and *immeasurable* equanimity, the *measurable* kamma (*pamāṇa-kata-kamma*) that was committed earlier does not remain anymore, does not persist anymore.[29]

According to the Buddhist teaching on kamma, one does not have to accept the resultant effects of kamma with a sense of resignation and submission. As we have noted in the course of this chapter, the Buddha espouses not only "moral life" (*kammavāda*) but "the efficacy of human effort" (*viriyavāda*) as well. From the Buddhist perspective nobody is incorrigible, everybody is capable of reform and is rehabitable. The best evidence for conscious moral evolution comes from the story of Aṅgulimāla, who had been a serial killer. Despite his horrific deeds, in this life itself he was able to become an arahant.

There are two facts that need emphasis: The first is that Buddhism rejects kammic determinism, the theory that our present behavior is completely determined by past kamma. The second is that we do not have to experience retribution for all previously committed kamma. Our present kamma, if sufficiently powerful, can nullify the possible results of past deeds. "The past gives us certain tendencies and latencies. It is for us to fashion them how we will."[30]

> The Buddhist doctrine of *kamma* has nothing to do with predestination. That which we have done in the past has made us what we are now; that which we are in the process of doing now, this day, this minute, is making what we shall be in the future. The future will be a process of becoming largely what we make it. It is always being shaped, but never finished. There is no evidence of its being predetermined independently of us, but we do know that we largely determine it by our own acts. There is no fixed future, even as regards tomorrow, but only possible futures, which depend largely on our present thoughts and actions. Just as we have been making ourselves in all our previous lives, so now it lies with us to determine our future; there is no god that can stop our doing so.[31]

The Issue of One's Own Good and the Good of Others

One problem closely connected with the subject of moral evaluation in Buddhism is how this evaluation addresses the problem concerning the relative position of one's own good and the good of others. Buddhism approaches this issue from many perspectives, though the basic idea underlying them all can be seen from the following two statements of the Buddha:

> Herein a certain person is one who abstains from taking life, from stealing and so forth. This one is called *the worthy man.* Herein a certain person not only himself abstains from taking life and so forth, but also encourages another to abstain from so doing. This one is called *the still more worthy man.*

> Herein a certain person is a believer, modest, conscientious, of wide learning, of ardent energy, of good memory, and strong in wisdom. This one is called *the worthy man.* Herein a certain person is possessed of faith and encourages another to possess faith, is himself modest and encourages another to be modest, is himself conscientious and encourages another to be so, is himself widely learned . . . of ardent energy . . . of settled mindfulness . . . strong in wisdom and encourages another to be the same. This one is called *the still more worthy man.*[32]

What the above two statements amount to is this: one who pursues his own moral good is morally good, but one who pursues his own moral good as well as the moral good of others is morally better.

There is, however, another important aspect that has to be noted here. It comes into focus from a Buddhist classification of individuals into four groups, as follows:

1. The individual who pursues neither his own well-being nor the well-being of others.
2. The individual who pursues the well-being of others but not his own well-being.
3. The individual who pursues his own well-being but not others' well-being.
4. The individual who pursues his own well-being as well as the well-being of others.[33]

The four individuals are mentioned here according to an ascending order of excellence, such that the first individual is the worst and the fourth is the best. It is palpably clear why this is so. What is intriguing, however, is why the third individual who pursues his own well-being without pursuing the well-being of others is better than the second individual who pursues the well-being of others without pursuing his own well-being.

If we are to understand this situation correctly in its proper context, it is of the utmost importance that we clarify first what the term "well-being" (*hita*) means in the fourfold classificatory scheme. At first glance, the term seems to mean well-being based on such extraneous factors as material or economic conditions. Any such understanding could easily lead to a conclusion that is just the opposite of what is intended, for it must be clearly noted here that in the early Buddhist discourses, the two terms, "one's own well-being" (*atta-hita*) and "the well-being of others" (*para-hita*), are always used in an ethical context to mean "one's own moral well-being" and "the moral well-being of others," respectively.

Then the question that arises next is why the pursuit of one's own moral well-being is considered more important than the pursuit of the moral well-being of others. The answer is found in the following words of the Buddha, addressed to Cunda, as an illustration of this situation:

> It is not possible, Cunda, for one who is stuck in the mud to pull out another who is [also] stuck in the mud. But, Cunda, it is possible for one who is not stuck in the mud to pull out another who is stuck in the mud. [Similarly] it is not possible, Cunda, for one who is himself not tamed, not disciplined, having defilements not extinguished, to tame and discipline another and help extinguish his defilements.[34]

This illustration draws our attention to two equally important points: The first is that one who is stuck in the mud of moral depravity cannot save another who is in the same predicament. The second is that one who has pursued his own moral well-being is in a sure position to help others pursue their own moral well-being. We find this situation exemplified in the life of the Buddha himself. It is after realizing his own moral perfection that the Buddha began his mission for the moral uplift of others.

> Being himself enlightened, the Buddha teaches the Dhamma for the enlightenment of others; being himself tamed, he teaches the

> Dhamma for others to be tamed; being himself at peace, he teaches the Dhamma for others to be at peace; having himself crossed over, he teaches the Dhamma for others to cross over, having himself attained nibbāna, he teaches the Dhamma for others to attain nibbāna.[35]

This situation is also exemplified in the lives of the Buddha's early disciples, as we find them recorded in the early Buddhist texts. It is best illustrated in the Buddha's admonition to the first sixty arahants to go forth and preach the Dhamma "for the benefit, well-being, and happiness of the many." The conclusion to be drawn is that one who has realized his own highest moral well-being, rather than remaining indifferent to others, addresses himself to the task of promoting the moral well-being of others.

From these observations, we can come to an important conclusion as to why the individual who pursues only his own moral well-being is held in higher esteem than the individual who pursues only the moral well-being of others. The reason is not that the moral well-being of others is less important than our own, or that our moral well-being is more important than the moral well-being of others. Indeed, the hierarchy of persons only means that we should give priority to our own moral well-being so that we will be in a position to help others. If we pursue our own moral well-being first, this could be considered not as a case of helping ourselves first, but as a case of preparing ourselves to help others. What is taken into consideration here is not whose moral well-being is more important but whose moral well-being should get priority.

On the other hand, an individual who pursues the moral well-being of others without pursuing his own moral well-being is like one who seeks to reform the world without reforming himself. He is only assuming the role of a savior. Such a person can easily succumb to fantasies of moral superiority and to delusions of moral grandiosity. He will certainly have many admirers, but not true followers.

In this connection, it is also important to remember that the benefits of moral cultivation are reciprocal. When we eliminate from our own minds such unwholesome mental dispositions as greed and hatred, we thereby eliminate the possibility of their external manifestation in relation to others. In the same way, when we develop within ourselves such wholesome moral qualities as generosity and compassionate love, we in turn ensure the possibility of their external manifestation in relation to others. Thus, moral cultivation has an individual as well as a social dimension. In actuality, when it comes to the practice of moral life, the very distinction between our own good and the good of others tends to be obliterated. We find this situation beautifully expressed by Buddha:

> Monks, one who takes care of oneself takes care of others. One who takes care of others takes care of oneself. How, monks, is it that one who takes care of oneself takes care of others? It is by moral training, moral culture, and moral development. And how, monks, is it that one who takes care of others takes care of oneself? It is by forbearance, by harmlessness, by goodwill, and compassion.[36]

Illustrating this situation, the Buddha recounts:

> Once in the past an acrobat set up his bamboo pole and said to his apprentice: "Climb the bamboo pole and stand on my shoulders." When the apprentice did so, the acrobat said. "You protect me, and I'll protect you. Thus guarded by each other, we'll display our skills, collect our fee, and get down safely from the bamboo pole." Then the apprentice said: "That's not the way to do it, teacher. You protect yourself, teacher, and I'll protect myself. Thus, each self-guarded and self-protected, we'll display our skills, collect our fee, and get down safely from the bamboo pole."[37]

As for the criticism made by some that the early Buddhist ideal of *arhatship* is individualistic and self-centered, all that needs to be said here is that it is by uprooting all traces of individualism and self-centricity that one becomes an arahant. How then can it be said that the ideal of arhantship is individualistic and self-centered? The very criticism amounts to a self-contradiction.

The Role of Knowledge and Awareness in the Practice of Moral Life

Another important aspect that concerns the Buddhist teaching on moral life is the role of knowledge and awareness in moral conduct. All moral cultivation, in Buddhism's view, should be based on knowledge and should be constantly accompanied by awareness. "Just as one washes hand with hand or foot with foot," runs the illustration, "both knowledge and conduct should help each other."[38] A person who is cultivating moral qualities should be fully aware of what he is doing and the different levels of moral purification he has attained to. A person who is morally perfect, if he is not aware of his moral perfection, is not morally perfect. Such a situation may sound rather paradoxical, though that is the case from the Buddhist perspective.

We find this situation very well illustrated in the Buddha's response to the idea of moral perfection as taught by Uggahamana, a religious teacher during the time of the Buddha. In his view, "a person is perfected in what is wholesome when he does not do an evil act with his body, speaks no evil speech, intends no evil intention, leads no evil livelihood."[39] Apparently this is how the Buddha himself teaches moral perfection. All the same, the Buddha found it necessary to make the following observation:

> If that were so, then a young tender infant lying prone is accomplished in what is wholesome. For a young tender infant lying prone does not even have the notion "body," so how should he do an evil bodily action beyond mere wriggling? He does not even have the notion "speech," so how should he utter evil speech beyond mere whining? He does not even have the notion "intention," so how does he have evil intention beyond mere suckling? He does not even have the notion "livelihood," so how should he make his living by evil livelihood beyond being suckled at his mother's breast?[40]

The naïve innocence of a baby boy cannot be equated with moral perfection. It is based on sheer ignorance and is not accompanied by awareness. Nor is it consciously and deliberately cultivated. To give an example: As we all know, elephants and some other animals in the wild are vegetarians. Yet surely it is not after pondering the virtues of vegetarianism that they have become so. Their physical constitution is such that they have to be vegetarians.

Of an entirely different kind is the moral cultivation and moral perfection that Buddhism speaks of. It has to be grounded on knowledge, accompanied by knowledge, and culminate together with knowledge. "Just as a man whose hands and feet are cut off, knows that his hands and feet are cut off, even so, one who is morally perfect, whether he is walking or standing still or asleep or awake, in him there is constant and perpetual presence of knowledge to the effect that all mental defilements are destroyed by him."[41]

We find this same idea expressed in a classification of individuals into four groups: The first individual has a blemish, but he does not know: "I have a blemish in myself." The second person also has a blemish, but he knows: "I have a blemish in myself." Between them the second is better than the first. The third individual has no blemish, but he does not know: "I have no blemish in myself." The fourth individual has no blemish and he knows: "I have no blemish in myself." Here the fourth individual is better than the third.[42]

It is not assumed by the Buddhist theory of moral life that either the sense organs or the sense objects are in themselves an obstacle to mental culture. If two oxen, one white and the other black—so runs the illustration—are tied by a yoke, it is not correct to say that the black ox is a bond for the white ox, or that the white ox is a bond for the black ox. It is the yoke that constitutes the bond, that which unites them both. In the same way, what constitutes an obstacle to mental culture is neither a sense organ nor a sense object, but craving or attachment. This situation is true of the relation between the whole cognitive apparatus on the one hand, and the external sense objects on the other. If it were otherwise, then one would have to rule out the very possibility of practicing the moral life.[43]

More or less the same idea is reflected in an early Buddhist discourse where the Buddha questions a disciple of a contemporary religious teacher as to how his master teaches mental culture. In reply, the latter says that the senses are to be trained to the extent that they fail to fulfill their respective functions: the eye does not see forms, the ear does not hear sounds, and so on. The Buddha rejoins that this kind of mental culture will lead to the conclusion that the blind and the deaf have their senses best cultivated.[44] The clear implication is that mental culture is not to be associated with the suppression of the senses. The senses should be cultivated to see things as they truly are (*yathābhūta*).

8

THE PRACTICE OF MORAL LIFE

The Noble Eightfold Path

PRESENTED by the Buddha as the fourth noble truth, the noble eightfold path lays the foundation for the practice of the Buddhist moral life. Altogether, the noble eightfold path consists of right view (*sammā diṭṭhi*), right motivation (*sammā saṅkappa*), right speech (*sammā vācā*), right action (*sammā kammanta*), right livelihood (*sammā ājīva*), right effort (*sammā vāyāma*), right mindfulness (*sammā sati*), and right concentration (*sammā samādhi*). This path is called "the middle way," as it steers clear of the two extremes of self-mortification and sensual indulgence.

One misunderstanding about the path is that it is meant only for those who have renounced the lay life, not for the laity. The best evidence that counters this misunderstanding comes from the Buddha's reference to two paths. One is the wrong path (*micchā paṭipadā*) and the other the right path (*sammā paṭipadā*). After defining the wrong path as the direct opposite of the noble eightfold path, the Buddha declares: "Monks, I do not uphold the wrong path either for laymen or for monks."[1] Thus the noble eightfold path is intended not only for monks (*bhikkhu*) and nuns (*bhikkhunī*) but also for laymen (*upāsaka*) and laywomen (*upāsikā*).

That the noble eightfold path is meant for the laity as well is also shown by the definition given by the Buddha to right livelihood (*sammā ājīva*), which is the fifth factor of the path. It is defined as abstaining from such means of livelihood as trafficking in weapons, in human beings (the slave trade, for example), in living beings (butchery and meat production), in poison, and in intoxicating drinks.[2] Obviously, though not necessarily, it is the members of the lay society who follow these five trades as a means of livelihood. As such, when right livelihood is defined as abstaining from these morally reprehensible trades, its definition is made by taking the laity into consideration.

From the fact that it is said to be conducive to three things, namely, happiness in this life (*diṭṭhadhamma-sukha*), well-being in the life after (*samparāya-hita*), and the realization of nibbāna (*nibbāna-gāminī paṭipadā*), the all-embracing applicability of the noble eightfold path is clear.[3]

What this means is that the path can be followed at different levels or in varying degrees of intensity. If one cannot follow it fully, one can follow it as far as possible. If the best situation is to realize the ideal, the next best situation is to be nearer the ideal. We often see a gap between precept and practice. This situation is not peculiar to religion alone, but is true of all other ideals of individual and social life. Yet just because there are varying degrees of difference between the ideal and the practice we do not propose to give up the ideal. The ideal is the source of inspiration to do right and to resist from doing wrong.

The Path Factors

As noted above, the noble eightfold path begins with right view. Right view, as defined by the Buddha, is to know wrong view as wrong view and right view as right view.[4] It is the forerunner of the path (*pubbaṅgama*), since it ensures proper direction to the other seven path factors. In a general sense, right view, as the opposite of wrong view, means the recognition of religious and moral values as a proper basis for right living. In a more specific sense, it means an initial knowledge of the four noble truths, for, as a goal-oriented path, the noble eightfold path's ultimate purpose is the emancipation from all suffering.

If right view provides the proper direction, the second path factor, that of right intention, is the mind's commitment to follow the path. It is the mind's intentional function, the purposive or volitional aspect of mental activity. Right intention is of three kinds: (1) intentions of renunciation, that is, intentions free from self-centered desires and egocentric impulses, (2) intentions free from aversion, and (3) intentions free from harmfulness, that is, those of benevolence and compassionate love.[5] Such wholesome intentions constitute the psychological foundation for benevolent moral actions. All actions that are socially harmful, all forms of social conflict, violence, and oppression, can ultimately be traced to our ill intentions. Actions are the external manifestations of our thoughts motivated by passion, aversion, and delusion or their opposites. Hence our mind's intentional function has a profound impact on our social environment in its widest sense.

Our speech, physical actions, and livelihood constitute the focus of the next three path factors. Together they represent the vocal and physical manifestations of our right or wrong intentions, which in turn are conditioned by our right or wrong views. It is at the level of vocal and physical action that our private thoughts and intentions begin to have a concrete impact on our social environment, for better or worse. In the context of social ethics, it is these three path factors that assume the greatest significance.

Four aspects are taken into consideration by the Buddha's instruction on right speech. The first aspect is that right speech should be dissociated from all forms of falsehood (*musāvāda*). Positively framed, this means devotion to truth that makes one reliable and worthy of confidence. The second aspect is abstention from calumny or slanderous speech (*pisuṇā vācā*) that is intended to create enmity and division among people. Its opposite is the speech that heals divisions and promotes amity, harmony, and friendship (*samagga-karaṇī*). The third aspect is abstention from harsh speech (*pharusā vācā*). All forms of abuse, insult, and even sarcastic remarks constitute the myriad variations of harsh speech. Its opposite is the speech that is "blameless, pleasant to the ear, lovely, reaching to the heart, urbane, pleasing, and appealing to the people." Fourth, right speech means abstaining from frivolous and vain talk (*samphappalāpa*), which is defined as "idle chatter and pointless talk, all lacking in purpose and depth." Its opposite is "meaningful, purposeful, useful, and timely speech."[6] Right speech requires us to refrain from uttering even what is true if it leads to harmful consequences (*anattha-saṃhita*). In uttering what is true, one should take into consideration not only its potential effect but also the proper time for its utterance (*kālavādī*).[7] The effects of speech are as pervasive as the effects of physical action, while their potential and consequences for good or bad are limitless. Hence the Buddhist instruction on right speech enjoins us to exercise our capacity for verbal expression with great caution and circumspection, always being watchful of our words (*vācānurakkhī*).[8]

If right speech is related to vocal acts, the next path factor, that of right action, is concerned with bodily acts. Right action requires us to refrain from injury to life and from all forms of violence. Negatively understood, it is "the laying aside of all cudgels and weapons," and taken positively, the cultivation of love and compassion for all creatures that have life. Second, the teaching on right action directs one to abstain from "taking what is not given by others." All kinds of thievery, robbery, fraudulence through false claims, and deceiving customers by using false weights and measures are some of its many variations.[9] In a constructive sense, right action means cultivation of honesty and purity of heart at all levels of interpersonal relations. Third, right action requires us to abstain from wrongful gratification of sensual desires through illicit sexual relations.

Following a morally acceptable means of livelihood is a necessity related to the fifth path factor. The Buddha mentions five specific modes of livelihood that are to be avoided, namely, trading in weapons, in human beings (the slave trade, for example), in living beings (butchery and meat production), in poison, and in intoxicating drinks. Among other wrongful means of livelihood mentioned in the Buddhist texts are deceit, treachery, soothsaying, trickery, and usury.[10] In short, any occupation that involves harmful consequences to others is to be considered morally reprehensible, although it could be materially rewarding.

As the last three factors of the noble eightfold path, right effort, right mindfulness, and right concentration form a closely interrelated group involving direct mental training. They have as their basis the purification of vocal and physical conduct brought about by the three immediately preceding factors. Right effort requires putting forth energy to eliminate unwholesome dispositions and to prevent them from arising anew, along with the energy needed to cultivate and stabilize wholesome dispositions. This particular path factor brings into focus the indispensability of right effort and diligence, of exertion and unflagging perseverance for the successful practice of mental culture. The seventh factor, that of right mindfulness, is presence of mind, attentiveness, alertness, or awareness. It plays the role of an inward mentor watching over and guiding all mental activity. For purposes of surveilling all mental activity, it is necessary that the mind remain in the present, without judging, evaluating, editing, and interpreting thoughts that arise. The ultimate aim of right mindfulness is to give proper moral direction to all volitional acts, as well as to their mental, vocal, and physical manifestations. The last path factor, right concentration, is to be realized by unifying the usually differentiated mind. Right concentration is the calm, clear, unconfounded state of mind, "the centering of all mental activity rightly and evenly." Right concentration is the indispensable prerequisite for wisdom, an insight into the nature of actuality, for it is only a properly concentrated mind that can see things as they actually are.[11]

This is a general survey of the (eight) factors of the noble eightfold path. It must be noted that the eight factors are not like the steps of a ladder that we normally follow in sequence or that we sometimes bypass for purposes of expediency. On the other hand, the path factors should be followed more or less together. And at the beginning some sequence is necessary until the factors begin to support one another. We should also understand the metaphor of the "path" in its proper context. Any other path we can leave behind once we have reached the destination. Not so the noble eightfold path. For the eight path factors are in fact eight moral qualities that are to be cultivated, developed, absorbed, and internalized. Once the eight factors are fully developed and brought to perfection, they help to gain two other factors, right knowledge (*sammā ñāṇa*) and right emancipation (*sammā vimutti*). These are "the ten skillful qualities" (*kusala-dhamma*) that one who is enlightened and morally perfect (*arahant*) is said to be endowed with.[12] Accordingly, the highest level of moral perfection coincides to a great extent with the very path that leads toward it.

The Psychological Foundation of the Practice of Morality

The Buddhist scheme of moral practice can also be understood with reference to the three aspects of moral discipline (*sīla*), concentration (*samādhi*), and wisdom (*paññā*). These three aspects are mutually dependent and gradually progress toward a higher ideal. There is a clearly presented psychological theory behind this threefold scheme of moral culture. According to this theory, all our moral evil exists and activates at three distinct levels. The first level is called "latency" (*anusaya*). It is the level at which moral evil remains dormant and latent in the form of inner dispositions and proclivities. We are not aware of these deep-seated psychological proclivities in us until they manifest themselves as excited feelings and emotions. The second level is called "arising all around" (*pariyuṭṭhāna*). It is the level where what remained earlier as latent proclivities are now fully awake. This awakening is what we experience as the mind's turbulence, excited feelings, or negative emotions. The third level is called "going beyond" (*vītikkama*). It is the stage when our emotions and excited feelings externalize in the form of vocal and physical actions.[13]

Clearly it is at the third level, called "going beyond," that our moral evil begins to have a direct and concrete impact on others. All kinds of evil committed vocally and physically—lying, slandering, thievery, sexual misconduct, violence, interpersonal conflicts, acts of terrorism and internecine warfare, to name but a few—are all instances of moral evil manifesting at the third level. On the other hand, whatever detrimental impact the other two levels may have is private to ourselves. Therefore, of the three levels in which moral evil activates, the third level is the most dangerous. Nonetheless, of the three levels, the third is also the easiest to bring under control. At first this may not appear to be so. Yet a little reflection should convince us that this is really the case. We all know by experience that it is easier to refrain from acts of violence but much more difficult to prevent thoughts of violence from welling up within us. The same situation is true of many other kinds of moral evil such as sexual misconduct, fraud, and falsehood. Temptation is much more difficult to control than its external expression. It is of course true that external factors, such as public opinion, social conventions, and laws of the country, serve as restraining factors. Nevertheless, the fact remains that acts of transgression due to temptation are more easily avoided than thoughts of temptation themselves.

So although the third level is the most dangerous, it is the easiest to control. The Buddhist scheme of moral cultivation thus begins at the third level when moral evil is externalized. The function of controlling this level is assigned to moral discipline (*sīla*), which is listed as the first step in the threefold moral training. Since all moral evil at the third level expresses itself either vocally or physically, moral discipline is defined as moral discipline in speech and body. Once this is fully accomplished, the next step is to control moral evil at the second level, when it is "arising all around." This task is assigned to concentration (*samādhi*), which is listed as the second step in the threefold scheme of moral training. Concentration is one-pointedness of mind or mental composure. It is the unification of the mind that usually remains differentiated. A unified mind is exceedingly more powerful than a differentiated mind. However, the function of concentration is only to still the mind and bring it under our conscious control. It cannot remove the roots of moral evil that remain as latent tendencies embedded in the deepest recesses of our minds. The responsibility of uprooting moral evil at this level is assigned to wisdom (*paññā*), which is the third step in the threefold moral training.

Wisdom is insight. It is the mind's ability to see phenomena and events as they actually are (*yathābhūta-ñāṇa*). It is by wisdom that moral evil is discarded at its very roots. With the help of a cognitive faculty refined by wisdom, one can observe and identify the roots of all moral evil lying dormant in the deep recesses of one's own mind. This observation takes place as bare awareness, without allowing our mind to edit or interpret what comes to be observed, for it is only then that bare awareness is able to uproot all roots of moral evil without leaving any remainder.

For Buddhism, the practice of moral life is a graduated discipline (*anupubba-sikkhā*), a graduated course of conduct (*anupubba-cariyā*), and a graduated mode of progress (*anupubba-paṭipadā*).[14] The practice involves self-transformation from a lower to a higher level. It has a beginning, an intermediate stage, and a consummation. The threefold scheme of moral training shows that the way to moral perfection is gradual, leading systematically from one step to the next. If moral discipline paves the way to concentration, concentration in turn paves the way to wisdom. The premise behind this progressive system is that it is only by first disciplining one's vocal and physical acts that one can develop right concentration, while it is only by developing right concentration that one can realize wisdom, that is, the mind's ability to see reality as it is.

Why Buddhist morality begins with the observance of the five precepts (*pañca sīla*) becomes clear when one further examines the threefold scheme of moral training. The five precepts refer to abstaining from depriving a living being of its life, refraining from taking what is not given by others (thievery, robbery, and so on), and renouncing sexual misconduct or illicit sexual relations, false speech, and taking intoxicating beverages that impair our diligence and vigilance. These are five moral transgressions at the "going beyond" level that have the most detrimental impact on the social environment. It is obvious that the five transgressions do not represent all moral violations at the third level, though as they constitute five of the most dangerous, abstaining from them is considered as the very beginning of the moral life.

Moral Guidelines

In order to prevent moral evil surfacing at the level of transgression, that is, as vocal and physical acts, Buddhism provides us with a set of moral guidelines. Their purpose is to help us make the right moral decision and to refrain from moral transgressions. One such moral guideline is called self-comparison (*attūpamā*). Self-comparison invites us to put ourselves in another person's position and to refrain from inflicting on others what we do not wish inflicted on ourselves. This moral guideline finds expression in the *Dhammapada*, the Buddhist anthology of ethical verses, in the following form: "All tremble at punishment; all fear death. Comparing oneself to the other, let one refrain from killing others, let one refrain from tormenting others."[15]

The same idea is more poignantly expressed in the following quotation from an early Buddhist discourse.

> Here a noble disciple reflects thus: "I like to live. I do not like to die. I desire happiness and dislike unhappiness. Suppose someone should kill me. Since I like to live and do not like to die, it would not be pleasing and delightful to me. Suppose I too should kill another who likes to live and does not like to die, who desires happiness and does not desire unhappiness. It would not be pleasing and delightful to the other person either. How could I inflict on another that which is not pleasant and delightful to me?" Having reflected in this manner, he, on his own, refrains from killing and speaks in praise of refraining from killing.[16]

The quotation demonstrates that the moral guideline of self-comparison also bids that while refraining from killing and from other moral evil, one must also dissuade others from committing the same evils. The quotation further implies that the Buddhist precept relating to abstaining from violence toward any living being is based on the Buddha's observation that all living beings seek happiness and recoil from suffering.[17]

Another guideline for moral reasoning is the one based on what is called the "threefold authority" (*ādhipateyya*).[18] Reasoning based on the threefold authority requires us to examine the possible consequences of what we intend to do from three different points of view. The first point of view is called "self-authority" (*attādhipateyya*). It enjoins us to examine whether what we intend to do would result in self-blame or repentance, that is, whether our own self would censure us for what we have done (*attā' pi attānaṃ upavadati*).[19] Thus what is called self-authority is a case of allowing ourselves to be controlled by ourselves.

Public authority (*lokādhipateyya*) is the second point of view. It requires us to examine whether what we are going to do would be censored particularly by the intelligent people in the society. What is called public authority is thus a case of allowing ourselves to be controlled by public opinion. The Buddhist idea of "public opinion" does not exactly correspond to how we understand it today, that is, as the opinion of the majority. For Buddhism, what matters is neither the opinion of the majority nor the opinion of the minority, but the opinion of those who really know, the wise people in the society, the people who are knowledgeable (*viññū purisā*). This is the yardstick that Buddhism would like us to consider when we are confronted with what others say. What is morally approvable is therefore referred to as "praised by the wise" (*viññuppasattha*), and what is morally reprehensible as "censored by the wise" (*viññū-garahita*).[20]

The third guideline for correct moral reasoning is called "dhamma-authority" (*dhammādhipateyya*). It requires us to examine whether what we are going to do is in accord with the moral norm (Dhamma) and to avoid all actions that deviate from it. It is an appeal to man's higher moral sense. It is man's higher moral sense that separates him from other living beings that are on a lower level of evolution. The necessary concomitants of dhamma-authority are moral shame (*hiri*) and moral dread (*ottappa*). Where these two are lacking, there is no civilization. Hence the Buddha aptly calls them "guardians of the world" (*loka-pālā dhammā*).[21]

What the three moral guidelines combine to illustrate is the idea that before one performs an action one should be thoughtful of its consequences for oneself as well as for others. We find this idea beautifully brought into focus in the Buddha's advice to his son Rāhula:

> "What do you think, Rāhula? What is the purpose of a mirror?"
>
> "For the purpose of reflection, venerable sir."
>
> "So too, Rāhula, an action with the body should be done after repeated reflection; an action by speech should be done after repeated reflection; an action by mind should be done after repeated reflection."[22]

A fitting conclusion to this chapter on the practice of Buddhist moral life would be the Buddha's advice on morality to some brahmin householders who had no faith in any religious teacher. To these householders, the Buddha recommended the following "incontrovertible (infallible) teaching" (*apaṇṇaka*). In a situation where there is no certainty of conviction, the most rational approach for a rational-minded person (*viññū puriso*) is to reflect thus:

> Even if there is no life after death, a person who leads a morally bad life in this life will be censored by the wise for his moral misbehavior. If, on the other hand, there is life after death, he will suffer in the life after as well. Thus he is bound to lose both worlds. If a person leads a morally good life, even if there is no life after death, he will be praised by the wise in this very life for his good behavior. And, if there is going to be life after death, he will be happy in the next life as well. Thus he is bound to gain both worlds.[23]

The main thrust of this "incontrovertible teaching" is that whether one believes in a particular religion or not, whether one believes in survival or not, everyone should practice the moral life.

9

THE PURSUIT OF HAPPINESS

ALL LIVING BEINGS, says the Buddha, desire happiness and recoil from suffering.[1] Indeed, the pursuit of happiness is what is common to Buddhism and the other two worldviews from which it keeps equally aloof. If spiritual eternalism advocates self-mortification, it is precisely in order to obtain eternal happiness in the distant future; if annihilationist materialism advocates sensual indulgence, it is precisely in order to experience happiness in the immediate now.

Yet what Buddhism means by "true happiness" differs from how others conceive of it. "What the noble ones call happiness others call suffering. What others call suffering the noble ones have found it to be happiness."[2] In this context the Buddha says: "There are some divines (*brāhmaṇas*) and philosophers (*samaṇas*) who call the day the night and night the day. I say that this is a delusion on their part."[3]

What, then, is happiness? How can we define happiness?

Happiness means many things to many people. It is not possible, therefore, to define happiness with mathematical precision. There are some who argue that what constitutes happiness is entirely relative: it depends on people's emotions and attitudes. They also maintain that sources of happiness cannot be properly identified. On this issue, Buddhism takes a different position.

The Buddhist position is that there is a necessary causal correlation between morality and happiness. That which is morally good leads to happiness, whereas that which is morally bad leads to unhappiness. The Buddhist term for what is morally good is "skillful" (*kusala*), and the Buddhist term for what is morally bad is "unskillful" (*akusala*). Accordingly, a mind that is poisoned with the three poisons of greed, hatred, and delusion is a mind that is "unskillful" (morally bad), a mind that is defiled, a mind that is ill, a mind that is in bondage—in other words, a mind that suffers. In contrast, a mind that is free from the three poisons is a mind that is "skillful" (morally good), a mind that is pure, a mind that is well, a mind that is in freedom—in other words, a mind that is happy. Here the Buddhist argument is that when we have skillful qualities we experience mental health (*ārogya)*, mental purity (*anavajjatā*), mental ability (*cheka*)—all resulting in happiness (*sukha-vipāka*).[4]

If we want to be happy there are, in fact, two options before us. One option is to change the nature of the world to conform to our desires. The other option is to change ourselves to be in harmony with the nature of the world. It is the second option, though difficult, that Buddhism adopts, because the first option is simply not possible.

How can we be truly happy? How can we experience sustainable happiness? According to the Buddha, it is only when we have a mind under our own control that we can be truly happy, not when we come under the control of our own mind. We find this idea clearly articulated in the early Buddhist theory of the cognitive process, which we discussed in our chapter on the analysis of mind. In the cognitive process, which begins with sensory contact and proceeds by degrees until it reaches the final stage called "conceptual proliferations," we can identify three stages:

1. At the first stage, the eye-consciousness arises according to the principle of dependent arising.
2. At the second stage, from "feeling" up to "conceptual proliferations," the individual assumes the role of an agent and directs the cognitive process.
3. At the third stage, the individual loses his role as the agent and becomes an object of his own uncontrollable conceptual proliferations.

If the individual becomes an object of his own uncontrollable conceptual proliferations, what this really means is that he does not have a mind under his own control; he is being controlled by his own mind.

If one wants to have a mind under one's own control, one should develop mindfulness (*sati*) and clear comprehension (*sampajañña*): "When one is going forward or coming back, when one is looking ahead or looking aside, when one is drawing in or extending out the limbs, when wearing one's clothes, when eating, drinking, chewing, and tasting, when defecating and urinating, when walking, standing, sitting, falling asleep, waking up, speaking, and keeping silent," in all these occasions and activities one should have mindfulness and clear comprehension.[5]

To be mindful is not the same as to be self-conscious. When we are self-conscious we are obsessed with ourselves; we tend to react to situations thoughtlessly instead of responding to them after careful reflection. When we are mindful, our mental and physical efficiency strengthens. Rather than reacting to situations recklessly, we respond to them after proper reflection. It is by letting go of the self that one becomes truly active and creative.

What prevents us from experiencing true happiness are greed, hatred, and delusion. They are the three poisons that corrode our mental and physical health and destroy our happiness. Of these three, it is hatred, not greed and delusion, that is most poisonous and corrosive. It is the Buddhist position that a mind primarily motivated by greed gives rise to some kind of pleasure (*somanassa*) or indifference (*upekkhā*), but it never gives rise to displeasure (*domanassa)*. Greed is due to some kind of attraction to someone or something judged as pleasant and appealing. In such a situation, the object of cognition gives rise to a feeling of pleasure. A mind primarily motivated by delusion always gives rise to some kind of indifference (*upekkhā)*. The reason for this is that a deluded mind is not in a position to judge something as pleasant or unpleasant. Therefore, such a mind does not experience either pleasure or displeasure. On the other hand, a mind primarily motivated by hatred always gives rise to displeasure (*domanassa*). Hatred arises when someone or something is judged as unpleasant or repulsive. Obviously in such a situation the object of cognition triggers some kind of displeasure (*domanassa*). Greed means the desire to possess an object; the moment that desire is frustrated it will be immediately followed by a moment of hatred. It is not at the moment of greed, but at the immediately succeeding moment of hatred, that one experiences displeasure. What corresponds to greed and hatred are attraction and distraction. Since attraction and distraction are mutually exclusive, they cannot activate in one and the same mind-moment.[6]

Hatred can range from mild irritability to uncontrollable rage. So-called righteous anger or moral indignation is, in fact, another form of hatred, though very subtle. So is a sarcastic remark with ironic intent.

> When anger does possess a man,
> he looks ugly and lies in pain.
>
> No being but seeks his own self's good,
> none dearer to him than himself,
> yet men in anger kill themselves,
> distraught for reasons manifold:
> For crazed they stab themselves with daggers,
> in desperation swallow poison,
> perish hanged by ropes,
> or fling themselves over a precipice.
>
> Yet how their life-destroying acts
> bring death unto themselves as well,
> that they cannot discern, and that
> is the ruin anger breeds.[7]

The most effective antidote for the poison of hatred is loving kindness (*mettā*). This is how, says the Buddha, one should develop loving kindness:

> Just as a mother would protect her only child at the risk of her own life, even so, let one cultivate a boundless heart of compassion toward all beings. Let one's thoughts of boundless compassion pervade the whole world: above, below, and across without any obstruction, without any hatred, without any enmity. Whether one stands, walks, sits, or lies down, as long as one is awake, one should develop this mindfulness. This is the noblest living here.[8]

There are eleven blessings, says the Buddha, that one can have by developing loving kindness: One sleeps in comfort, one wakes up in comfort, one dreams no evil dreams, one is dear to human beings, one is dear to nonhuman beings, the gods protect one, no fire or poison or weapon harms one, one's mind can be quickly concentrated, the complexion of one's face becomes serene, one will face death with no mental confusion, and even if one fails to realize the highest goal in this life, one will pass on to the world of High Divinity (*Brahmaloka*).[9]

The Buddha spoke of happiness through the four sublime states or divine abodes (*Brahma-Vihāra*):

1. Loving kindness (*mettā*): Love without the desire to possess. Love without selecting and excluding. Love embracing all living beings. Loving kindness is not the same as selfish affection.
2. Compassion (*karuṇā*): Compassion to all suffering living beings. Compassion is not the same as sentimentality, which is a state of mind accompanied by sorrow.
3. Altruistic joy (*muditā*): The ability to feel happy and joyful at the success of another. Sharing the happiness of others as if it were our own. Altruistic joy is the best antidote for the poison of jealousy. Jealousy is the resentment and bitterness one experiences when another succeeds.
4. Equanimity (*upekkhā*): Perfect, unshakable balance of mind. It is not negative indifference, but a positive social virtue. Equanimity is our ability to remain calm and unruffled when we face "the eight vicissitudes" or the "eight ups and downs" of life. These are gain and loss, blame and honor, insult and praise, delight and despair.[10]

When a person faces these vicissitudes of life, it is instructive for him or her to remember what the *Dhammapada* says in this connection:

O Atula!
Indeed, this is an ancient practice,
not one only of today.
They blame those who remain silent.
They blame those who speak much.
They blame those who speak in moderation.

There is none in this world,
who is not blamed.

There never was,
there never will be,
nor is there now,
a person who is wholly blamed,
or a person wholly praised.[11]

Equanimity also means an attitude of impartiality. As such, equanimity enables us to transcend all divisive thoughts and feelings based on class, caste, race, religion, nationality, ethnicity, and all forms of parochialism as well as gender distinctions.

Mundane Happiness

Buddhism speaks of two levels of happiness: mundane and supramundane. Mundane happiness is the happiness that one can experience until one realizes nibbāna, the supramundane happiness. The idea of mundane happiness does not contradict the Buddhist definition of "suffering." As we have noted, dukkha has a philosophical connotation that means any kind of conditioned experience, an experience depending on impermanent conditions. Conditioned experience can be extremely pleasant or extremely unpleasant. Within conditioned experience, therefore, there can be many levels of pleasure and happiness.

One of the most important prerequisites to leading a happy life is adequate wealth. As a religious teacher, the Buddha never praised poverty. The Buddha singled out hunger to be "the worst disease"[12] and poverty to be the most socially destabilizing factor. As the Buddha says, the division of the world into the haves and the have-nots paves the way for the collapse of the moral foundation of the society:

> When there is no proper distribution of wealth, poverty grows rife; from poverty growing rife, stealing increases; from the spread of stealing, violence and use of weapons increases; from violence and use of weapons, destruction of life becomes common; when destruction of life becomes common, people's lifespan decreases, their beauty decreases.[13]

One Buddhist discourse says:

> If the king of the kingdom were to think, "I will get rid of this plague of robbers by executions and imprisonments, by confiscation, threats, and banishment," by such means the plague would not be ended. Those who survived would later harm the kingdom.

There is another plan, the discourse goes on to say:

> To those in the kingdom who are engaged in cultivating crops and raising cattle, let Your Majesty distribute grain and fodder; to those in trade, give capital; to those in government service, assign proper living wages. Then those people, being intent on their own occupations, will not harm the kingdom. Your Majesty's revenues will be great, the land will be tranquil and not beset by thieves, and the people, with joy in their hearts, will play with their children and will dwell in open houses.[14]

What the two quotations show is that the duty of kings is not merely to preserve law and order but also to develop the economy. In this connection, one Buddhist discourse observes: "The king provided for the righteous protection and security of his subjects (*dhammikañ ca rakkhāvaraṇaguttiṃ saṃvidahi*), but failed to give property to the needy (*na ca kho adhanānaṃ dhanaṃ anuppadesi*), and as a result poverty became rife."[15]

Poverty, it may be noted, has not only objective indicators but also a psychological dimension. Even if a person is very rich, in the presence of another who is richer, he will feel poor by comparison. So poverty can be a state of mind as well. It is in this context that we need to understand the well-known saying of the Buddha: "Contentment is the highest wealth."[16]

Advice to Householders on How to Be Happy

One day a person called Dīghajāṇu came to the Buddha and said:

> Lord, we householders are immersed in the round of pleasures; we are cumbered with bedmate and sons, we delight in the muslins from Benares and in sandalwood, we deck ourselves with

> flowers, with garlands and cosmetics, we enjoy the use of both silver and gold. Lord, to such as us, let the Exalted One also teach the Dhamma, teach the things that will be conducive to our advantage and happiness here on earth and to our advantage and happiness in the world to come.[17]

In response to this request, the Buddha refers to four requirements that are conducive to happiness in this life:

1. Accomplishment in effort (*uṭṭhāna-sampadā*): The honest effort needed to earn one's living. "One should be energetic, tireless, of an inquiring turn of mind and capable of organizing and carrying out one's work systematically and efficiently."
2. Accomplishment in protection (*ārakkha-sampadā*): "One should see that the wealth one has earned is properly guarded and protected."
3. Good companionship/friendship (*kalyāṇa-mittatā*): "One should associate and cultivate friendship with people who are virtuous, faithful, charitable, and wise."
4. A balanced life (*samajīvikatā*): "One should neither be unduly extravagant nor unduly miserly in one's living. One should know that one's income will stand in excess of one's expenditure, but not expenses in excess of income. Just as the goldsmith knows on holding up a balance that by so much it has dipped down, by so much it has tilted up, even so, a householder, knowing his income and expenses, leads a balanced life, neither extravagant nor miserly."[18]

> He should divide his wealth in four
> (this will bring the most advantage).
> One part he may enjoy at will,
> two parts he should put to work,
> the fourth part he should set aside
> as reserve in times of need.[19]

The wealth earned by a householder can have four sources of loss: looseness with women, addiction to intoxicating drinks, gambling, and associating with evil-minded people. "There are six evil consequences in indulging in intoxicants: Loss of wealth, increase of quarrels, susceptibility to illness, loss of one's good name and reputation, shameless and indecent exposure of one's body, and weakening of one's intellect. There are six evil consequences when one indulges in gambling: The winner makes enemies, the loser bewails his loss, the loss of wealth, the gambler's word is not relied on in a court of law, he is despised by his friends and associates, and he is not in demand for marriage, for people would say he is a gambler, how can he look after a wife. There are six evil consequences in being addicted to idleness: The idler does no work, saying that it is extremely cold, that it is extremely hot, that it is too early in the morning, that it is too late in the evening, that he is extremely hungry, that he is too full."[20]

Happiness through Family Life

Filial piety or devotion to parents plays an important role in the teachings of the Buddha. One's parents, the Buddha says, are the "first teachers" (*pubbācariyā*), the "first deities" (*pubbadevatā*), and "worthy of offerings" (*āhuṇeyyā*). The mother and father are elevated to the level of high divinity (*Brahmāti mātāpitaro*).[21] "One's mother is the friend in one's own home" (*mātā mittaṃ sake ghare*).[22] "In five ways should a child minister to his mother and father: Having been supported by them, I will support them, I shall perform their duties for them, I shall keep up the family tradition, I shall be worthy of my heritage, after my parents' death I shall offer alms in honour of my departed parents. There are five ways in which the parents so ministered to by their children will show compassion to their children: They restrain them from evil, they encourage them to do good, they train them for a profession, they arrange a suitable marriage, and at the proper time they hand over their inheritance to them."[23]

"A man's wife," the Buddha says, "is his greatest friend" (*bhariyā'va paramā sakhā*).[24] Marriage between man and woman thus becomes the greatest friendship. "There are five ways in which a husband should minister to his wife: By being courteous to her, by not despising her, by being faithful to her, by handing over authority to her, and by providing her with adornments. The wife thus ministered to by her husband shows her compassion to her husband in five ways: She performs her duties well, she is hospitable and courteous to relations and attendants, she is faithful to her husband, she protects what he brings, and she is skilled and industrious in discharging her duties. In five ways should a householder minister to his servants and employees: By assigning to them work according to their ability, by supplying them with food and with wages, by tending them when they are sick, by sharing special delicacies with them, and by granting them leave from time to time."[25]

The Four Winning Ways:

Generosity, sweet speech,
helpfulness to others,
impartiality to all,
as the case demands.

These four winning ways make the world go 'round,
as the linchpin in a moving car.
If these in the world exist not,
neither mother nor father will receive
respect and honor from their children.

Since these four winning ways
the wise appraise in every way,
to eminence they attain,
and praise they rightly gain.[26]

Levels of Happiness

The Buddha draws our attention to many levels of happiness, ranging from the lowest to the highest, from the grossest to the most refined. There is a gradual refinement and sublimation of happiness until it reaches the highest level of happiness. The process begins with sensual pleasure (*kāma-sukha*), the pleasure that we experience by gratifying our fivefold sensuality through the five physical sense organs. What is unsatisfactory with this kind of pleasure is that it alternates with feelings of displeasure and nourishes more and more desire for sensory gratification. This situation is compared to a leper with sores and blisters on his limbs cauterizing his body over a burning charcoal pit. He will certainly enjoy some momentary pleasure by cauterizing his body, though this act will increase the problem rather than cure it.[27] Then come in gradual sequence higher levels of nonsensuous happiness, as, for example, the happiness one experiences when one unifies and concentrates one's mind in higher levels of jhāna-experience.

Since there are many levels of happiness, the Buddha has asked his disciples to make a "proper evaluation of happiness" (*sukha-vinicchaya*). The purpose of this evaluation is to forgo lower levels of happiness in order to pursue higher levels of happiness.[28] Engrossed in sensual pleasure, the ordinary people think that there is no happiness higher than sensual pleasure. So they are scared of any happiness that goes beyond sensual pleasure. It is this psychological resistance that prevents them from pursuing higher levels of nonsensuous happiness. Such happiness, the Buddha says, should not be feared (*na bhāyitabbaṃ*).[29] An important motivation for pursuing abiding, sustainable happiness is the reflection that it is better to give up a lower level of happiness if, by doing so, one can experience a higher level of happiness.[30] The psychological principle is that "one who pursues happiness will certainly obtain happiness" (*sukhaṃ sukhattho labhate*).[31]

The Path to the Highest Level of Happiness

It was the belief among some ascetics who lived during the time of the Buddha that happiness could be realized only through suffering. Even the Buddha-to-be, before his enlightenment, accepted this widespread belief and underwent ascetic practices, only to realize that they were "fraught with suffering, ignoble, and not leading to the goal." Immediately after this realization, another occurred to the Buddha-to-be: Why am I afraid of that happiness that has nothing to do with sensual pleasure and unwholesome states?[32] This realization by the Buddha-to-be is the most momentous occasion in his search for true happiness. It signifies his complete break away from self-mortification, the practice associated with spiritual eternalism (*sassatavāda*).

The path discovered by the Buddha for the realization of nibbāna, the highest happiness, is the noble eightfold path. It sets itself aloof not only from sensual indulgence but also from self-mortification, which is "painful and ignoble." Therefore, the Buddhist path to the highest happiness is certainly not through suffering: it "does not involve suffering, vexation, despair, and anguish."[33] Accordingly, the Buddha describes the noble eightfold path as the path "to be trodden with joy (*pīti-gamanīyo*).[34]

The Buddha reminds us that "it is only when one does not give up happiness that accords with the Dhamma that the effort will be fruitful."[35] This shows the indispensability of happiness in order to pursue higher levels of happiness. As a matter of fact, monks and nuns during the time of the Buddha delightfully pursued their religious life. King Pasenadi of Kosala once told the Buddha that he "sees Buddhist monks and nuns smiling and cheerful, sincerely joyful, plainly delighting, their faculties fresh, living at ease, unruffled." This was in contrast to non-Buddhist recluses and brahmins, "who are lean, wretched, unsightly, jaundiced, with veins standing out of their limbs as if they were leading the holy life in discontent."[36]

It is certainly not through suffering but through happiness that the Buddha penetrated the truth of suffering. In this connection, the Buddha says:

> I do not say that the breakthrough to the four noble truths is accompanied by suffering or displeasure. Rather, the breakthrough to the four noble truths is accompanied only by happiness and joy.[37]

Through happiness to the highest happiness is also the theme of the spontaneous poetic utterances of some arahants, as recorded in the *Theragāthā*. They claim: "Happiness has been attained through happiness."[38]

In the quest for the highest happiness, the decisive turning point is not fear but a real encounter with suffering. From then onward the sequence is not one of suffering, but degrees of happiness leading to the highest happiness. We find this idea clearly explained in what is called the "transcendental dependent arising, a dependent arising that leads to the transcendence of the world":

> Thus, monks, ignorance is the supporting condition for kamma formations, kamma formations are the supporting condition for consciousness, consciousness is the supporting condition for mentality-materiality, mentality-materiality is the supporting condition for the sixfold sense base, the sixfold sense base is the supporting condition for contact, contact is the supporting condition for feeling, feeling is the supporting condition for craving,

> craving is the supporting condition for clinging, clinging is the supporting condition for existence, existence is the supporting condition for birth, birth is the supporting condition for suffering, suffering is the supporting condition for faith, faith is the supporting condition for joy, joy is the supporting condition for rapture, rapture is the supporting condition for tranquility, tranquility is the supporting condition for happiness, happiness is the supporting condition for concentration, concentration is the supporting condition for the knowledge and vision of things as they really are, the knowledge and vision of things as they really are is the supporting condition for disenchantment, disenchantment is the supporting condition for dispassion, dispassion is the supporting condition for emancipation, while emancipation is the supporting condition for the knowledge of the destruction of the cankers.[39]

This sequence of conducing factors is compared to the rain descending on a mountaintop that gradually fills gullies and creeks, pools and ponds, streams and rivers, and finally flows down to the great ocean.

The arising of higher levels of happiness is a natural, not a supernatural, occurrence:

> It is in the nature of things (*dhammatā*) that the absence of remorse is present in a virtuous person. A person who has no (feelings) of remorse need not determine in his mind that joy should arise in him. It is of the nature of things that joy arises in a person who has no remorse. A person who is joyful need not determine in his mind that delight should arise in him. It is of the nature of things that delight arises in a joyful person.[40]

In concluding this chapter on the pursuit of happiness we would like to clarify the position of happiness in relation to the ultimate goal of Buddhism. What exactly is the ultimate goal of Buddhism? If we go by the four noble truths, the quintessence of Buddhism, then we know that the ultimate goal is cessation of suffering. We come to the same conclusion even if we go by the Buddha's summary statement on the be-all and the end-all of what he has taught as a religious teacher. "Both formerly and now also I proclaim two things: suffering and the cessation of suffering."

The "cessation of suffering" is another expression for "happiness." If it is contended that the "cessation of suffering" is a negative expression, then let us remind ourselves that so is "immortality," which many religions, including Buddhism (see next chapter), claim to be the highest goal of religious life.

Happiness is not a means to wisdom, whereas wisdom is a means to happiness. Happiness is not a means to mental purity, whereas mental purity is a means to happiness. Happiness is not a means to compassionate love, whereas compassionate love is a means to happiness. While wisdom and mental purity and compassionate love function as the means, happiness becomes the goal. This is certainly not to downgrade, but to upgrade, the importance and indispensability of wisdom, mental purity, and compassionate love, for true, sustainable happiness is certainly not possible unless it is grounded on a proper understanding of the nature of actuality (wisdom), on the cultivation, to its highest level, of mental purity, and on the development, to its highest degree, of compassionate love.

It is not the case that wisdom, mental purity, and compassionate love arise first, and then comes happiness. We need to understand this arising not in a chronological but in a logical sense. It is only in a logical sense that wisdom, mental purity, and compassionate love come first. In actuality, wisdom, mental purity, compassionate love, and happiness all arise together, exist together. We find a similar situation in the enumeration of the three universal properties of that which is sentient, namely, impermanence, suffering, and nonselfness. Although they are enumerated in sequence, that does not mean that they arise in chronological sequence. What is impermanent is, at one and the same time, suffering and nonselfness. It is only logically that impermanence is prior to the other two. And it is in fact impermanence that provides the rational basis for all Buddhist teachings on the nature of actuality.

Happiness is the only thing we pursue for its own sake.

10

NIBBĀNA: THE FINAL GOAL

THE EARLY BUDDHIST teaching on nibbāna has given rise to a wide variety of interpretations. Most of these interpretations relate to the postmortem status of the arahant, the one who has realized nibbāna. There seem to be two questions raised over this issue: Is the postmortem status of the arahant one of complete annihilation in a physical sense? Or is it one of continual existence in a metaphysical sense? On our view, both questions do not arise. If they arise, it is due to a failure to take into consideration the early Buddhist response to the binary opposition between spiritual eternalism and materialist annihilationism.

Nibbāna as the Third Noble Truth

The best way to understand what nibbāna is and what it is not is to understand nibbāna in its proper context of the four noble truths. These truths are presented in such a way as to show that nibbāna, which is the third noble truth, follows in logical sequence from the first two. If there is suffering and if there is a cause of suffering, then it logically follows that the elimination of the cause of suffering leads to the cessation of suffering, which is nibbāna.

What is important to remember is that nibbāna is defined as the cessation of suffering. It is not the cessation of life (*jīvita-nirodha*), nor is it the annihilation of an independently existing self-entity, for Buddhism does not recognize such an entity to be annihilated in a physical sense or to be perpetuated in a metaphysical sense. When nibbāna is attained, what comes to an end is not a self-entity but the false belief in such an entity.

It is in this context that we should understand the significance of the following statement of the Buddha:

> Some ascetics and brahmins accuse me wrongly, baselessly, falsely, and groundlessly, saying that the recluse Gotama is a nihilist and preaches the annihilation, destruction, and non-existence of an existent being. That is what I am not and do not affirm. Both previously and now I preach suffering and the cessation of suffering.[1]

As this quotation shows, the charge of nihilism was not new; it prevailed even during the time of the Buddha.

Nibbāna as Cessation of Passion, Aversion, and Delusion

In the Pāli discourses, nibbāna is defined more in terms of its experiential characteristics than in terms of metaphysics. An exploration of the etymological meaning of the term *nibbāna* does in fact shed much light on the nature of nibbānic experience. The basic idea conveyed by this term is that of extinguishing a fire. Everything, insists the Buddha, is burning. Burning with what? Everything is burning with the three fires of passion (*rāga*), aversion (*dosa*), and delusion (*moha*).[2] These fires are the three basic factors of moral evil to which all unwholesome mental dispositions and defilements can be traced. When they are eliminated, all other defilements come to an end with no possibility of further growth. Hence the final deliverance that is nibbāna came to be defined as the extinction of passion, aversion, and delusion.[3] One who has extinguished these three fires came to be aptly defined metaphorically as "cool" (*sītibhūta*) or "pacified" (*nibbuta*).[4] Absence of the three unwholesome factors should be understood in a positive sense as well. Absence of passion means the presence of such wholesome qualities as charity, liberality, and renunciation.

Absence of aversion means the presence of amity, goodwill, benevolence, and loving kindness (*mettā*). Lastly, absence of delusion means the presence of higher knowledge (*abhiññā*) and wisdom (*paññā*).

Passion and aversion are the defiling emotive factors, whereas delusion is the defiling cognitive factor. Elimination of the two unwholesome emotive factors gives rise to compassion, while the elimination of the unwholesome cognitive factor gives rise to wisdom: compassion and wisdom are the two main components of the nibbānic experience. Cessation of passion, aversion, and delusion can be considered the standard definition of nibbāna. All other dimensions of nibbāna—nibbāna as the highest emancipation, nibbāna as the highest happiness, and so on—are but different perspectives of understanding nibbāna as the cessation of the three unwholesome factors.

One important dimension of the nibbānic experience comes into focus by the description of passion, aversion, and delusion as "limiting factors" (*pamāṇa-karaṇa*).[5] When one is infatuated with passion (*ratta*), overcome by aversion (*duṭṭha*), and blinded by delusion (*mūḷha*), one does not see things as they actually are. Since nibbāna is free from these "limiting factors," it is described as "limitless" or "immeasurable" (*appamāṇa*). This is the context in which we need to understand why nibbāna is described as limitless or immeasurable, and not in a context-free, abstract sense. The three limiting factors are also described as "boundaries" (*sīmā*), as they set bounds to, and thus circumscribe, our freedom. One who has attained nibbāna is therefore described as "one who has gone beyond the boundaries" (*sīmātiga*),[6] the boundaries of passion, aversion, and delusion. The three limiting factors are also called "barriers" (*mariyādā*). As such, the one who has attained nibbāna is described as one who "lives with a mind in which all barriers have been broken asunder."[7]

Nibbāna as Cessation of Kamma

Kamma, as noted in a previous chapter, is volitional activity, and what is important to remember at this juncture is that not only unwholesome but even wholesome kamma is motivated by self-interest and self-expectation. That is precisely why all kamma has either good or bad results (*vipāka*). It follows, therefore, that all kamma must wane away in the nibbānic experience. What leads to the waning away of all kamma is explained by the Buddha when he speaks of four kinds of kamma:

1. Dark kamma with dark results, that is, bad kamma with bad results.
2. Bright kamma with bright results, that is, good kamma with good results.
3. Kamma that is both dark and bright with dark and bright results.
4. Kamma that is neither dark nor bright with results that are neither dark nor bright.

It is the fourth kind of kamma that leads to the cessation of kamma. The Buddha elucidates it thus:

> And of what sort, monks, is the kamma that is neither dark nor bright, with a result that is similar, which itself being a kamma conduces to the waning of kamma? In this case, monks, the intention to abandon this dark kamma with its dark result, the intention to abandon this bright kamma with its bright result, the intention to abandon this kamma that is both dark and bright with its dark and bright result, this intention is called the kamma that is neither dark nor bright with a result that is neither dark nor bright, that conduces to the waning away of kamma.[8]

At this stage in the discussion, it is important to note that the absence of wholesome kamma in the nibbānic experience does not mean that nibbāna transcends what is wholesome. In order to understand this, it is necessary to refer here to two different contexts in which the term "wholesome" (*kusala*) is used in the Pāli discourses.

First, the term is used in the context of kamma to mean "wholesome volitional acts" (*kusala-kamma*). Second, the term is used to mean "wholesome spiritual qualities" (*kusala-dhamma*). Among the wholesome spiritual qualities are the four bases of mindfulness (*cattāro satipaṭṭhānā*), the four modes of right endeavor (*cattāro sammappadhānā*), the four bases of psychic power (*cattāro iddhipādā*), the five spiritual faculties (*pañca indriyāni*), the five spiritual powers (*pañca balā*), the seven factors of enlightenment (*satta bojjhaṅgāni*), and the noble eightfold path (*ariyo aṭṭhaṅgiko maggo*).[9] It is by cultivating these wholesome spiritual qualities that one realizes nibbāna.

When one has attained nibbāna by practicing the wholesome spiritual qualities, one comes to experience the highest level of wholesomeness: Such a one "is accomplished in what is wholesome (*sampanna-kusala*) and perfected in what is wholesome (*parama-kusala*)."[10] Thus through "wholesome spiritual qualities" one comes to "the highest wholesome" (*parama-kusala*), which is none other than nibbāna.

At this point, it is necessary to understand that nibbāna transcends only kamma-wholesomeness. If it does so, it is precisely in order to reach the highest level of wholesomeness, a wholesomeness that goes beyond kamma-wholesomeness. In the nibbānic experience, one does not face a moral dilemma or a moral struggle: there is no inclination to do what is unwholesome, nor is there any resistance to do what is wholesome. In the nibbānic experience, all actions are spontaneously wholesome.

Nibbāna as the Highest Level of Knowledge

Absence of delusion, as mentioned before, means the presence of higher knowledge or wisdom. In fact, the realization of nibbāna is itself defined as the attainment of knowledge.[11] The knowledge in nibbānic experience is described by a number of terms: "wisdom" (*paññā*), "accurate or exact knowledge" (*pariññā*), "gnosis" (*aññā*), "higher knowledge" (*abhiññā*), and "insight" (*vipassanā*).[12] If nibbāna is knowledge, what exactly is the object or content of this knowledge?

The answer to this question is found in the definition of "higher knowledge" as "knowledge of things as they actually are" (*yathābhūta-ñāṇa*).[13] Now according to Buddhism, the phenomenal world is represented by the five aggregates of grasping (*upādānakkhadhas*). It follows that when Buddhism defines "knowledge" as "knowledge of phenomena as they actually are," the words "phenomena as they actually are" refer to the five aggregates of grasping. To the question raised by the Buddha, "Monks, what are the things that should be thoroughly comprehended through higher knowledge?" the Buddha himself provides the answer: "It is the five aggregates of grasping—so should it be answered."[14] Thus nibbānic knowledge is not the knowledge of a metaphysical reality. Rather, it is the final awakening to the true nature of the world of sensory experience by "fully comprehending the five aggregates of grasping."

What takes place when nibbāna is attained is not a change in the nature of reality but a change in our perspective of the nature of reality. The fact of impermanence is not a problem in itself. This fact becomes a problem when it is wrongly considered as permanence. This is what is called "perception of permanence in impermanence." In the same way, the absence of a self-entity is not a problem in itself. Its absence becomes a problem only when one considers what is nonself as a self-entity. This is what is called "perception of self in what is not the self."[15] Accordingly, what prevents the attainment of nibbāna is not the nature of reality, but the unwarranted assumptions that do not conform to the nature of reality. What comes to an end when nibbāna is attained is not the world, but a wrong interpretation of the world.

Thus, for Buddhism, what matters is not the nature of the world per se but the world as interpreted and constructed through the lens of our egocentric perspectives: our views and beliefs, our speculative theories and dogmatic assertions. This is why the Buddha sometimes explains theoretical views (*diṭṭhi*) using the same framework reserved for explaining suffering: views (*diṭṭhi*), origin of views (*diṭṭhi-samudaya*), cessation of views (*diṭṭhi-nirodha*), and the path that leads to the cessation of views (*diṭṭhi-nirodha-gāminī-paṭipadā*).[16] "Cessation of views" is the "cessation of suffering." When Vacchagotta, the wandering philosopher, asked the Buddha, "But has Venerable Gotama a view of his own?" the Buddha replied, "The Tathāgata, O Vaccha, has given up all *views* (*diṭṭhi*). However, the Tathāgata has *viewed* (*diṭṭha*) thus: This is materiality, this is its arising, this its cessation, this is feeling, . . . this is perception, . . . these are mental formations, . . . this is consciousness, and so on."[17]

Accordingly, in the Pāli Buddhist exegesis we find "freedom from views" (*diṭṭhi-nissaraṇa*) as another expression for nibbāna.[18]

Nibbāna as World Transcendence

In which sense should we understand nibbāna as transcending the world? What is significant here is that in the Pāli discourses the Buddhist notion of "world transcendence" is expressed by the phrase "the cessation of the world" (*loka-nirodha*). "In this fathom-long body, endowed with consciousness and perception," says the Buddha, "I declare the world, the origination of the world, the cessation of the world (*nibbāna*), and the path that leads to the cessation of the world."[19] "Cessation of the world" is sometimes called "the end of the world" (*lokanta*).[20] How are we to understand the cessation or end of the world as transcendence of the world?

The answer to this question comes from the Buddhist definition of the world as "the world of experience," in other words, as the five aggregates of grasping.[21] Hence the Buddha says: "I do not say that the world's end could be known, seen, or reached by traveling. Nor do I say that without reaching the end of the world, an end of suffering can be made."[22]

All suffering, from the Buddhist perspective, is due to self-appropriation, a process that manifests itself in three ways: this is mine (*etaṃ mama*), this I am (*eso'ham asmi*), this is my self (*eso me attā*). It is in relation to the five aggregates that the ordinary unenlightened person imposes this process of self-appropriation. It follows that in order to transcend the five aggregates of grasping (= the world), this threefold self-appropriation should come to an end. The cessation of the threefold appropriation has to be accomplished by the opposite process of self-negation: "this is not mine (*n'etaṃ mama*), this I am not (*n'eso'ham asmi*), this is not my self (*n'eso me attā*)."[23]

The attainment of nibbāna thus means the ending of the threefold process of self-appropriation. The tathāgata does not identify himself with any of the five aggregates, selectively or collectively. Hence it is said:

> The five aggregates on the basis of which one would designate (identify) the tathāgata, in the case of the tathāgata—they are given up, their root broken, uprooted like a palm tree, and are beyond all possibility of their ever again arising in the future. The tathāgata is deep, immeasurable, unfathomable, just as the deep ocean.[24]

If the tathāgata is not comprehensible as such, it is because he does not identify himself with any of the five aggregates. For instance, if I do not identify myself with anything in the world, then from my point of view, I become unidentifiable by others.

In the above excerpt, the idea of giving up the five aggregates should not be understood in a literal sense. In the Pāli suttas "the arising" (*samudaya*) and the "cessation" (*atthaṅgama*) of the five aggregates means not their actual arising and cessation but the arising and the cessation of attachment or clinging to them. "In this way arises material form" means "in this way arises attachment to material form." "In this way ceases material form" means "in this way ceases attachment to material form."[25] This interpretation is true of the other four aggregates as well. Accordingly, when the Buddha says that the five aggregates should be abandoned (*pahātabba*),[26] he means that one should abandon attachment to them. Understood thus, the abandonment of the five aggregates by the tathāgata means the abandonment of the attachment and clinging to them. It is extremely important to remember this psychological meaning of the arising and ceasing of the five aggregates. To overlook this connotation amounts to a gross misinterpretation of the Buddhist teaching on the nature of nibbānic experience. As noted before, it is the five aggregates that constitute the world of experience. So the fact that the tathāgata does not identify himself with any of the aggregates means that he has transcended the world.

Does this attainment then mean that the tathāgata is distinct and separate from the five aggregates? The answer is unequivocally no, since it is also maintained that although the tathāgata is not within the five aggregates, neither is he distinct from them.[27] Given this observation, the relation between the tathāgata and the five aggregates can be subsumed under two headings: The tathāgata is neither identical with nor distinct from the five aggregates. The tathāgata is not the five aggregates nor is he without the five aggregates.

This situation, which appears rather paradoxical, could be explained as follows: The fact that the tathāgata is not identical with any of the five aggregates, or comprehensible with reference to them, means that he has transcended the world. The fact that the tathāgata is not distinct or apart from the five aggregates means that he does not identify himself with anything that transcends the five aggregates (= the world) either, that is, a metaphysical reality that goes beyond the aggregates themselves. This idea is very well expressed in the following statement:

> Monks, when a monk's mind is freed, *devas* headed by Indra, Brahmā, and Pajāpati do not succeed in their search for something to which the mind of the arahant is attached. What is the reason for this? I say that the arahant is not knowable (*ananuvejja*) in this very life itself.[28]

It could of course be argued that the position of the tathāgata in relation to the five aggregates is not different from that of an ordinary unenlightened person. For in the context of the Buddhist doctrine of "nonself," neither the tathāgata nor the unenlightened person has a self-entity of their own. Nonetheless, there is this difference: Although an unenlightened person does not have a self-entity of his own, he in fact imposes the "self" notion on the five aggregates. This is what makes him different from an enlightened person. What all this adds up to is that the tathāgata is not without the five aggregates, but he makes use of them without imposing on them the ego illusion.

We find articulated here the Buddhist idea of "world transcendence," an idea beautifully illustrated by the simile of the lotus flower:

> Just as, O monks, the lotus, born in water, grown in water, rises above the water and stands unsullied by the water, even so the tathāgata grows up in the world, rises above the world, and stays unsullied by the world.[29]

Nibbāna as the One and Only Unconditioned Experience

> Monks, there is not-born, not-become, not-made, and not-constructed. Monks, if not-born, not-become, not-made, not-constructed were not, no deliverance from the born, become, made, and constructed would be known. But, monks, since there is not-born, not-become, not-made, and not-constructed, therefore deliverance from the born, become, made, and constructed is known.[30]

What this excerpt refers to is the difference between saṃsāra, which is born, become, made, and constructed, on the one hand, and nibbāna, which is not-born, not-become, not-made, and not-constructed on the other. The excerpt seems to give the impression that nibbāna is some kind of metaphysical reality into which the tathāgata enters. In fact, some modern scholars interpret the four words, not-born, not-become, not-made, and not-constructed, as conveying four different meanings in support of such a metaphysical interpretation of nibbāna. Quite in contrast to this modern interpretation is the Theravāda commentarial exegesis. This exegesis says that these four words connate the same thing because they are used here in a synonymous sense (*sabbāni'pi padāni aññamañña-vevacanāni*) to show that nibbāna is not brought about by causes and conditions.[31] Indeed, in Pāli suttas we find "become" (*bhūta*), "constructed" (*saṅkhata*), and "dependently arisen" (*paṭicca-samuppanna*) used in a synonymous sense.[32] What these synonyms all entail is that whatever is dependently arisen is born, become, constructed, and made. As such, nibbāna should be understood in the opposite sense, as not subject to the principle of dependent arising.

In the above excerpt, nibbāna as psychological experience is presented in an objective sense, as if nibbāna were some kind of external reality. The kind of language used here is meant to emphasize that nibbāna represents the one and only unconditioned experience, an experience free from the three basic factors of moral evil. Hence the Buddha says: "The cessation of passion, aversion, and delusion is the unconditioned."[33] As noted above, the cessation of passion, aversion, and delusion, in positive terms, implies the presence of generosity, compassion, and wisdom. Could these latter factors function as conditioning factors? The answer is, certainly not. It is passion, aversion, and delusion that function as limiting (*pamāṇa-karaṇa*), and therefore as circumscribing and conditioning factors. In contrast, compassion and wisdom are not conditioning factors. Rather, they are unconditioning factors, factors that free the mind from all that is evil and unwholesome. That is precisely why the nibbānic experience is presented as the one and only unconditioned experience. This presentation, in other words, conveys that all saṃsāric experience is conditioned, and in this sense, is suffering.

Nibbāna as Deconstruction (Visaṃkhāra)

Another way to understand the nature of nibbānic experience is to understand it in light of the term "deconstruction" (*visaṃkhāra*). From the Buddhist perspective, what is called "individual existence" in its saṃsāric dimension is a process of construction. This idea can be clearly seen in the definition given to volitional constructions (*saṃkhāra*):

> And why, monks, do you call them volitional constructions? They construct the constructed, monks, therefore they are called volitional constructions. And what is the constructed that they construct? They construct constructed material form as material form, they construct constructed feeling as feeling, they construct constructed perception as perception, they construct constructed volitional constructions as volitional constructions, they construct constructed consciousness as consciousness.

> They construct the constructed, monks, therefore they are called volitional constructions.[34]

This definition should show that although volitional constructions (*saṃkhāras*) are one of the five aggregates, they construct not only other aggregates but themselves as well. From the Buddhist perspective, individual life is a process of construction through the imposition of the threefold grasping: this is mine, this I am, this is my self.

In contrast, nibbāna represents complete deconstruction (*visaṃkhāra*). Hence it is that immediately after realizing nibbāna, the Buddha declares: "My mind has come to deconstruction (*visaṃkhāra-gataṃ cittaṃ*); I have attained the destruction of cravings (*taṇhānaṃ khayam ajjhagā*)."[35] Thus with the destruction of all cravings that give rise to all volitional constructions, the mind comes not to destruction but to deconstruction.

When the mind has reached deconstruction, the five aggregates remain. Yet they are no more constructed, in the sense that the tathāgata does not impose on them the three kinds of clinging.

> That which is selfless, hard it is to see;
> not easy is it to perceive the truth.
> But who has ended craving utterly
> has naught to cling to, he alone can see.[36]

> For one who is clinging, there is agitation; for one who has no clinging, there is no agitation. When there is no agitation, there is calm; when there is calm, there is no attachment; when there is no attachment, there is no coming and going; when there is no coming and going, there is no disappearance and reappearance; when there is no disappearance and reappearance, there is neither here nor there nor in-between. This is indeed the end of suffering.[37]

Nibbāna as Conceptual Nonproliferation

The difference between saṃsāra and nibbāna can also be understood in light of the difference between conceptual proliferation (*papañca*) and conceptual nonproliferation (*nippapañca*). We discussed earlier how the cognitive process of an unenlightened person gives rise to what is called "conceptual proliferation," a proliferation based not only on present objects but also on objects in the past and in the future.[38] At this stage, the individual is overwhelmed and overpowered by his own thoughts. Rather than having a mind under his own control, he comes under the irrepressible dominance of his own mind. This is another way of referring to saṃsāric experience.

If a person, says the Buddha, does not delight, welcome, and hold fast to such conceptual proliferation, then "this is the end of the underlying tendency to lust, of the underlying tendency to aversion, of the underlying tendency to views, of the underlying tendency to doubt, of the underlying tendency to conceit, of the underlying tendency to desire for being, of the underlying tendency to ignorance; this is the end of resorting to rods and weapons, of quarrels, brawls, disputes, recrimination, malicious words, and false speech; here these evil unwholesome states cease without remainder."[39]

Commentarial exegesis identifies the roots of this conceptual proliferation as craving, conceit, and views, "on account of which the mind 'embellishes' experience by interpreting it in terms of 'mine,' 'I,' and 'my self.'"[40] It is this threefold appropriation of the five aggregates by way of craving, conceit, and views that constitutes saṃsāric experience. It follows that when the three roots of conceptual proliferation are uprooted, there is nibbānic experience. Hence another expression for the nibbānic experience is conceptual nonproliferation (*appapañca*, *nippapañca*).

Since there are six sense faculties, faculties that are called the six internal contact spheres (*phassāyatanāni*), there can be only six kinds of cognitive processes that culminate in conceptual proliferation. Accordingly, it is said: "To whatever extent is the course of the six internal contact spheres, to that extent is the course of the conceptual proliferation. To whatever extent is the course of the conceptual proliferation, to that extent is the course of the six internal contact spheres."[41] Therefore, either "the complete cessation of the six internal contact spheres" or "the complete absence of all conceptual proliferation" entails the same thing: both refer to nibbānic experience from two different angles.

When the six internal contact spheres come to complete cessation, it is not proper to say that something remains, or that something does not remain, or that something both remains and does not remain, or that something neither remains nor nonremains. Why? It is because such a predication amounts to "conceptually proliferating what is not conceptually proliferable" (*appapañcaṃ papañceti*).[42]

The phrase "complete cessation of the six internal contact spheres," as used above, should not be understood in a literal sense to mean the complete cessation of the internal contact spheres themselves. What this phrase means is that when one attains nibbāna one does not cling to the internal contact spheres by way of craving, by way of conceit, and by way of views.

Nibbānic Experience as Freedom from the "I" Conceit (Asmi-Māna)

"I" conceit can manifest in three ways: "I am superior," "I am inferior," or "I am equal" to someone else. Since the arahant is free from the "I" conceit, he does not make such I-based comparisons. Nor does he project the "I" conceit in relation to nibbāna: "Having directly known nibbāna as nibbāna, he does not conceive [himself as] nibbāna, he does not conceive [himself] in nibbāna, he does not conceive [himself apart] from nibbāna, he does not conceive nibbāna to be 'mine,' he does not delight in nibbāna."[43]

It is not that the arahant is not aware of nibbāna. As a matter of fact, awareness is fundamental to the nibbānic experience. If not for awareness, the nibbānic experience would be some kind of mystical experience. What is stressed in the above quotation is that the arahant does not consider nibbāna as an object to be grasped. He is aware of nibbāna, but is not conscious of nibbāna. To be conscious of something is not the same as to be aware of something.

Nibbāna and the Attainment of Cessation

What is known as "attainment of cessation" (*nirodha-samāpatti*) is "the cessation of perception and feeling" (*saññā-vedayita-nirodha*). In one who has reached this state, the state of *saññā-vedayita-nirodha*, the bodily, verbal, and mental functions have been suspended and come to a standstill. Yet life is not exhausted, the vital heat is not extinguished, and the faculties are not destroyed. It is the suspension of all consciousness and mental activity, and not their cessation, that is called the cessation of perception and feeling.[44]

Nibbāna and the attainment of cessation are certainly not identical. Nibbāna means the cessation of passion, aversion, and delusion, whereas "attainment of cessation" is the cessation of perception and feeling. There is, however, a close connection between them. This close connection concerns the Buddhist definition of the highest level of happiness. In a sequence of ascending levels of happiness, it is claimed that happiness culminates in the attainment of cessation. To the question, "If there is no feeling in this attainment, how could there be happiness in it?" the Buddha's answer is that it is the very absence of feeling that qualifies it to be called happiness. The Buddha declares: "Wherever happiness is found and in whatever way, the tathāgata describes that as included in happiness."[45]

As recorded in another discourse, when Sāriputta claimed that nibbāna is happiness, a monk called Udāyin exclaimed: "How could there be happiness, if there is no feeling in nibbāna!" Nibbānic experience is not without feelings. As such, it is obvious that here the reference is to an arahant's experience when he is in "the attainment of cessation." Sāriputta's reply is reminiscent of the Buddha's declaration referred to above. Sāriputta too declares that it is the very absence of feeling that is called happiness.[46]

The conclusion that we could draw from the juxtaposition of the attainment of cessation and nibbāna is this: When an arahant, the one who has realized nibbāna, abides in the attainment of cessation, he experiences the highest happiness.

What we need to remember is that an arahant is one who has extirpated passion, aversion, and delusion. This is precisely what qualifies him to be called an arahant. However, the arahant can experience many levels of happiness while being completely free from passion, aversion, and delusion. For instance, when he is in different levels of jhāna, he experiences different levels of happiness, and when he is in the attainment of cessation, he experiences the highest level of happiness.

Nibbāna as the Immortal

The term "immortal" (*amata*) occurs often in the discourses of the Buddha. In fact, when Brahmā Sahampati invited the Buddha to preach the newly discovered Dhamma, the words he used were: "Let the Enlightened One open the door to the immortal."[47] Again, when the Buddha was on his way to set in motion the wheel of the Dhamma, he told Upaka, the wandering ascetic, that he was going to Benares to beat the drum of immortality (*amata-dundubhi*).[48] These and many other references show that in common with many other religions, Buddhism too has as its final goal the realization of immortality.

Since Buddhism does not recognize an immortal soul or an eternal heaven as its final goal, in what sense are we to understand the nibbānic experience as the experience of immortality?

What we need to remember is this: It is true that the arahant has the five aggregates and that they are subject to impermanence and death. However, since he does not identify himself with any of the five aggregates, taken selectively or collectively, the arahant does not experience death as such. Of course, death as a physical event cannot be overcome. Yet since he does not identify himself with the five aggregates, aggregates that are subject to death, in that sense the arahant has won a psychological victory over the inevitable phenomenon of death. The experience of death is present only when one identifies oneself with what is subject to death. Therefore, the liberated saint does not die per se. If he did he would be born again, for in the Buddhist context death is always followed by rebirth. The truth of the matter is that saints never die. This is precisely why in the Buddhist discourses, the nominal and verbal derivatives from the root *mṛ* (to die) are not applied with respect to the liberated saint. Consequently, the modern practice of using such expressions as "the death of the Buddha," "the dead arahant," and so on, does really amount to a gross misrepresentation of the Buddhist ideal of emancipation.

Although Buddhism also has as its final goal the gaining of immortality, in the context of the Buddhist doctrine of nonself, the concept of "immortality" too assumes a new dimension. Immortality cannot be the perpetuation of a self-entity into eternity. From the Buddhist perspective, immortality is what results from the elimination of the ego-illusion. What is unique about this Buddhist concept of "immortality" is that it can be achieved, here and now, while the mortal frame remains. This is another reason why those who are wont to represent Buddhism as pessimistic should do well to revise their opinion, for what is more optimistic than to be told that death, the greatest hazard one has to face in this world, can be conquered in this very life.

Liberation through Wisdom and Liberation of Mind

What is common to all arahants, those who have attained nibbāna, is complete emancipation from suffering—the absence of passion, aversion, and delusion. Despite this commonality, there can be differences among them as to attainment. In this respect, there are two kinds of arahants: The first kind is called "one who is liberated through wisdom" (*paññā-vimutta*). Such an arahant has fully destroyed all defilements (*āsavakkhaya*). The other kind of arahant is called "one who is liberated in two ways" (*ubhato-bhāga-vimutta*). Such an arahant has also what is called "liberation of mind" (*ceto-vimutti*). "Liberation of mind" is an expression for the ability to unify and concentrate the mind through the four jhānas and the four attainments.[49] What is important to remember is that the "liberation of mind" does not ensure complete emancipation from suffering unless it is supplemented with "liberation through wisdom." Wisdom is the deciding factor: "The extinction of defilements is to be realized by means of wisdom."[50] This is precisely why "liberation through wisdom" is common to both kinds of arahants. Accordingly, liberation through wisdom is rightly defined as the "imperturbable mental freedom" (*akuppā ceto-vimutti*).[51]

In this distinction between two kinds of arahants, what comes into focus is the distinction between concentration (*samatha*) and insight (*vipassanā*). It will be seen that when it comes to emancipation, the deciding factor is not higher levels of concentration but an insight into the nature of actuality. In pre-Buddhist meditational practices, what was sought after was the mind's concentration (*samatha*) as an end in itself, not wisdom (*vipassanā*). This is precisely why, as recorded in the Buddhist discourses, the Buddha-to-be was not satisfied with the meditational practices taught to him by Ālāra, the Kālāma, and Uddaka, the disciple of Rāma. In the Buddha's teaching on emancipation, it is to wisdom that preeminence is given.

Jhāna, or the higher levels of mind's unification, is only a means to an end, the end being the realization of wisdom. Exclusive emphasis only on the higher levels of mind's unification as an end in itself can have many pitfalls. As the Venerable Bhikṣu Saṃgharaksita says: "To get stuck in a super-conscious state—the fate that befalls so many mystics—without understanding the necessity of developing insight is not a blessing but an unmitigated disaster."[52]

The Two Nibbāna Elements

Designated as *sa-upādisesa* and *anupādisesa*, there are two nibbāna elements. We prefer to translate the first as "nibbāna element with base" and the second as "nibbāna element without base." That which is common to an arahant when he is in either of these two nibbāna elements is described thus: "His influxes are extinct, he has lived the higher life to the full, he has done what has to be done, he has laid down the burden, reached the goal, fully destroyed the bonds of existence, and is released with full understanding." Despite this commonality, there is this difference to be noted in the two nibbāna elements.

When an arahant is in the nibbāna element with base, his five physical sense faculties still remain and function. Therefore he experiences likes and dislikes, pleasures and pains. Yet when he experiences such feelings, he knows that they are impermanent and therefore they do not bind him. They are not experienced with passion and aversion or with emotional reaction. However, since the arahant has extirpated passion, aversion, and delusion, this nibbānic experience is called "nibbāna with base." On the other hand, when an arahant experiences nibbāna with no base, "here itself, all that is felt, being not delighted in, will become cool."[53]

In the context of the two nibbāna elements, what exactly is meant by "base" (*upādi*)? Does it refer to the five physical sense faculties, because of which the arahant experiences likes and dislikes, pleasures and pains? Or does it refer to the five aggregates? It is very likely that the reference is to the five aggregates, for the presence of the five aggregates implies the presence of the physical sense organs.

Accordingly, "nibbāna element with no base" should mean when the five aggregates are discarded for good, and hence when "all that is felt, being not delighted in, will become cool." Nibbāna element with no base comes at the last moment of the arahant's life when the five aggregates break up. To state this happening more specifically, it is the final passing away of the arahant. The most convincing evidence for this conclusion comes from two Buddhist discourses that say: "The tathāgata fully passes away through the nibbāna element with no base (*Tathāgato anupādisesāya nibbānadhātuyā parinibbāyati*)."[54]

We could even refer to the nibbāna with no base as the "final nibbāna" if it is understood as taking place not after death, but in this very life. Nibbāna with no base is not some kind of metaphysical reality into which the arahant enters after the final passing away; it is not a place of eternal rest for the arahant.

The Buddhist doctrine of nonself precludes any such metaphysical conclusion. It must be categorically stated that nowhere in the Pāli discourses is there any reference to nibbāna after the final passing away of the arahant. The whole of the nibbānic experience is to be realized in this very life. There is only one unconditioned experience; it is none other than the nibbānic experience—which is to be realized in this very life. Since Buddhism dissociates itself from spiritual eternalism (*sassatavāda*), there is absolutely no possibility within early Buddhism to speak of a postmortem nibbāna, in whichever way it is sought to be interpreted.

It is of course true that the nibbāna element with base is said to occur "in this very life" (*diṭṭhadhammikā*) and the nibbāna element without base is said to occur subsequently (*samparāyikā*).[55] "Subsequent" does not necessarily mean "after death." Rather, in this particular context, it means "subsequently in this very life." That is precisely why the words "here itself" (*idh'eva*) are used in referring to the occurrence of the nibbāna element with no base. According to the very definitions given to the two nibbāna elements, nibbāna element with base comes first and nibbāna element without base comes subsequently. Let it be repeated, both nibbānic experiences occur in this very life, not in a hereafter.

In all other religions, their final goals can be realized only after death. According to Buddhism, however, its final goal, which is nibbāna, not only can be realized but also has to be realized in this very life.

The Postmortem Condition of One Who Has Realized Nibbāna

What, then, is the postmortem position of the tathāgata? Is it complete annihilation in a physical sense (materialist annihilationism)? Or is it eternal continuation in a metaphysical sense (spiritual eternalism)? The state of an enlightened person after death was, in fact, the subject of a dialogue between the Buddha and Vacchagotta, a wandering philosopher who was very much prone to metaphysical speculations.

In this dialogue, Vacchagotta asks the Buddha whether a liberated monk, after the dissolution of the body, reappears or does not reappear, or both reappears and does not reappear, or neither reappears nor does not reappear. When the Buddha told Vacchagotta that none of these four alternatives "fit the case" (*na upeti*), the latter got so bewildered as to tell the Buddha that he had lost whatever faith he derived from the earlier part of his dialogue with the Buddha. The Buddha then goes on to illustrate with a simile why none of the four alternatives fit the case:

> "What do you think, Vaccha? Suppose a fire were burning before you. Would you know: 'This fire is burning before me'"?
>
> "I would, Master Gotama."
>
> "If someone were to ask you, Vaccha: 'What does this fire burning before you burn in dependence on?'—being asked thus, what would you answer?"
>
> "Being asked thus, Master Gotama, I would answer: 'This fire burns in dependence on fuel of grass and sticks.'"
>
> "If that fire before you were to be extinguished, would you know: 'This fire before me has been extinguished'"?
>
> "I would, Master Gotama."
>
> "If someone were to ask you, Vaccha: 'When that fire before you was extinguished, to which direction did it go: to the east, the west, the north, or the south?'—being asked thus, what would you answer?"
>
> "That does not apply, Master Gotama. The fire burned in dependence on its fuel of grass and sticks. When that is used up, if it does not get any more fuel, being without fuel, it is reckoned as extinguished."
>
> "So too, Vaccha, the tathāgata has abandoned that material form by which one describing the tathāgata might describe him, he has cut it off at the root, made it like a palm stump, done away with it so that it is no longer subject to future arising. The tathāgata is liberated from reckoning in terms of material form, Vaccha, he is profound, immeasurable, hard to fathom like the ocean. 'He reappears' does not apply; 'he does not reappear' does not apply; 'he both reappears and does not reappear' does not apply; 'he neither reappears nor does not reappear' does not apply. (The same is true of the other four aggregates: feeling, perception, volitional constructions, and consciousness.)"[56]

The above statement, that none of the four alternatives "fits the case," has given rise to a widespread belief that the postmortem status of the tathāgata is some kind of mystical absorption with an absolute that transcends the four alternative possibilities proposed by Vaccha. In other words, that the liberated saint enters, after death, into a transcendental realm that goes beyond all descriptions in terms of existence, nonexistence, both existence and nonexistence, and neither existence nor nonexistence. It has also been suggested by some that if the four questions were considered meaningless, this meaninglessness is partly due to the inadequacy of the concepts contained in them to refer to this state of transcendence.[57]

In our view, if the four questions are set aside, it is not because the concepts contained in them are inadequate to refer to this so-called state of transcendence. The correct position is that the questions do not arise at all. If the questions do not arise, it is certainly not due to the inadequacy of the concepts contained in the four questions. Rather, it is entirely due to their illegitimacy. They are as meaningless as the four questions regarding where the fire went. Here too what is focused on is not the inadequacy of the four questions but their illegitimacy in explaining a fire that gets extinguished with the exhaustion of its fuel.

A fire can burn only so long as there is fuel. Once the fuel is gone, the fire is extinguished. Being extinguished does not mean that the fire gets released from its fuel and goes out to one of the four quarters. In the same manner, it is not the case that at "death" an entity called tathāgata is released from the five aggregates and finds its way to some kind of transcendent existence. To try to locate a tathāgata in a postmortem position is like trying to locate an extinguished fire. In both cases the questions are equally meaningless and equally unwarranted.

There is in fact direct textual evidence that goes against the metaphysical interpretation of the posthumous status of the tathāgata. Anurādha, a disciple of the Buddha, once held the view that the after-death condition of the tathāgata is such that it cannot be explained with reference to any of the four possibilities mentioned above. His conclusion was that the after-death condition of the tathāgata could be explained with reference to a position outside the four predications, in other words, a position that transcends the four possibilities.

When this matter was reported to the Buddha, the Buddha told Anurādha: "Since even in this very life a tathāgata is not comprehensible in truth and reality (*saccato thetato anupalabbhiyamāne*), it is not proper to say that the after-death condition of the tathāgata could be proclaimed as a position other than these four possibilities." Anurādha confesses that his conclusion is wrong. Finally, the Buddha sums up the correct position: "Anurādha, both formerly and now, it is just suffering and the cessation of suffering that I proclaim."[58] This clearly shows that the after-death condition of the tathāgata cannot be explained either in terms of the fourfold predication or in terms of a position that transcends it.

In fact, when it is said that the four questions on the postmortem status of the tathāgata do not arise (*na upeti*), this explains the present position of the tathāgata, not his postmortem status. The present position of the tathāgata is such that it does not admit any of the four questions relating to his after-death condition, for although the five aggregates are there, the tathāgata does not identify himself with any of them. It is this fact that makes the tathāgata, the liberated saint, incomprehensible in this life itself.

One reason for interpreting nibbāna in a metaphysical sense could be the fact that religion in general believes in a reality that is either transcendental or both transcendental and immanent. Hence some scholars have been inclined to believe that this metaphysical conception, which is common to many religions, should have its counterpart in early Buddhism as well. From the Buddhist point of view, all such attempts at interpreting nibbāna in this manner amount to spiritual eternalism (*sassatavāda*), which upholds the theory of the metaphysical self. Buddhism began by rejecting spiritual eternalism. There is therefore no reason why its final goal should involve a theory that it rejected at its very beginning.

Is the after-death condition of the tathāgata, then, one of complete annihilation? This is the other conclusion to which some modern scholars arrived, particularly during the early stages of the academic study of Buddhism: It is claimed that since Buddhism denies a self-entity, this denial naturally and logically leads to the conclusion that nibbāna is annihilation.

The annihilationist view of nibbāna is not confined to modern scholarship. An identical view was held by a disciple of the Buddha known as Yamaka: "On the dissolution of the body, the monk who is delivered from all defilements is annihilated, perishes, and does not exist after death." This conclusion is equally as wrong as the metaphysical interpretation, as shown by Sāriputta's response to it. The latter tells Yamaka that since the tathāgata cannot be identified either with or without reference to the five aggregates, it is not proper to conclude that at death the tathāgata comes to annihilation.[59] To interpret the after-death condition of the tathāgata as annihilation is to understand it in light of materialist annihilationism (*ucchedavāda*). Buddhism began by rejecting materialist annihilationism. Therefore, there is no reason why the final goal of Buddhism should involve a theory that it rejected at its very beginning.

If the postmortem status of the tathāgata cannot be explained in light of either spiritual eternalism or materialist annihilationism, it is because in this very life itself, there is no identifiable entity called "tathāgata," either to be perpetuated in a metaphysical sense or to be annihilated in a physical sense. Strictly speaking, it is not correct to say that the Buddha was silent on the question of the after-death condition of the tathāgata, for the Buddha's answer to the question is that the question does not arise (*na upeti*). Attainment of nibbāna means the elimination of the very possibility of raising the question.

11

THE UNANSWERED QUESTIONS:

Why Are They Unanswered?

ONE ISSUE that has intrigued modern scholars is why the Buddha left some questions unanswered. Although the Buddha gave his own reasons for leaving the questions unanswered, modern scholars want to know what other reasons lay behind the Buddha's silence. So we find attempts being made to understand the silence in light of such ideological stances as skepticism, agnosticism, pragmatism, logical positivism, and so on. In this chapter, we propose to explain why the Buddha left some questions unanswered, and to examine, in light of this explanation, why some modern interpretations relating to this issue are not tenable.

The Four Kinds of Questions

Four kinds of questions are distinguished by the Buddha, and the category of "unanswered questions" comes under the fourth:

1. A question that ought to be answered unilaterally (*ekaṃsa-vyākaraṇīya*).
2. A question that ought to be answered analytically (*vibhajja-vyākaraṇīya*).

3. A question that ought to be answered by raising a counterquestion (*paṭipucchā-vyākaraṇīya*).
4. A question that ought to be set aside (*ṭhapanīya*).[1]

The four kinds of questions entail four kinds of answers, if we consider "setting aside the question" to be an answer to the fourth question. Among the questions and answers, one kind of question or answer is not considered superior or inferior to any other. The sequence of their enumeration does not imply in any way a hierarchical evaluation. Each kind of answer, when apposite, is equally valid and therefore equally commendable. What determines the validity of the answer is whether it belongs to the same class to which the question belongs. Hence the Buddha says a person who does not answer unilaterally a question that ought to be answered unilaterally, who does not answer analytically a question that ought to be answered analytically, who does not answer by raising a counterquestion a question that ought to be answered by raising a counterquestion, who does not set aside a question that ought to be set aside—such a person is indeed not fit to have a discussion, that is, not fit to carry on a meaningful conversation.[2]

In the Pāli discourses themselves, we do not find these questions illustrated with specific examples. Nonetheless, an example that we can give for the first is: "Are all conditioned phenomena impermanent?" From the Buddhist perspective, this is a question that should be given a unilateral answer in the affirmative: "Yes, all conditioned phenomena are impermanent." If the question is phrased: "Are all conditioned phenomena permanent?" even then the answer should be unilateral, but in the negative: "No, all conditioned phenomena are impermanent."

A good example for the second kind of question can be selected from the Pāli discourses themselves. When Subha, the young man, asked the Buddha for his opinion on whether it is the householder or the monk who succeeds in attaining what is right, just, and good, the Buddha replies: "Here (*ettha*), O young man, I give an analytical explanation (*vibhajjavāda*); I do not make here (*ettha*) a unilateral assertion (*ekaṃsavāda*)." For what determines the answer is not whether the person is a layman or a monk, but the practice of good conduct.[3] It will be noticed that in the Buddha's reply to Subha, the Buddha uses the adverbial form "here" (*ettha*). It means "in this respect," or to be more precise, "in relation to the question raised by Subha." The use of this adverbial form is of great significance in that it clearly indicates the specific context in which the Buddha gives the answer following the analytical method. If we were to overlook the context-indicating "here" (*ettha*), as has been done by some modern scholars, it would give the impression that the Buddha always follows the analytical method in preference to the unilateral method. But this is certainly not so.[4]

What is more, the misunderstanding of this situation has given rise to a widespread misconception that the Buddha always upheld the analytical method in preference to the unilateral method, and that therefore the Buddha was an upholder of the analytical method (*vibhajjavādī*).[5] The truth is that according to Buddhism a unilateral statement is no less valid or logical than an analytical statement just because it is unilateral. Likewise, an analytical statement is no less valid or logical than a unilateral statement just because it is analytical. What matters is not whether a given statement is unilateral or analytical, but the question in relation to which the statement is made.

As to the third kind of question, which ought to be answered by raising a counterquestion, an example can also be found in the Pāli discourses: "Is consciousness a person's soul?" the Buddhas was asked, "Or is consciousness one thing and the soul another?" In response, the Buddha raises the counterquestion: "What do you take to be the soul?"[6] The counterquestion is necessary because the notion of "soul" was interpreted in different ways among various religions and philosophies during the time of the Buddha.

It has been suggested that the third type of question appears to be only a subdivision of the second type.[7] This is not so, since the second kind of question can be answered without raising a counterquestion, whereas the third necessarily requires a counterquestion to clear up the ambiguities in the original question.

The Unanswered Questions

Before we come to the category of "unanswered questions" subsumed under the fourth kind of question, one that ought to be set aside, there are three issues that merit our attention. The first is obvious but sometimes ignored: the fact that these questions are never presented in the Buddhist texts as "unanswerable" or "inexpressible" (*avyākaraṇīya*). On the contrary, they are questions that have been left unanswered (*avyākata*). To call them unanswerable is, from the Buddhist perspective, to miss the point. It is tantamount to saying that they are perfectly legitimate questions, but that any answer to them transcends the limits of knowledge. When a question has been set aside, this means that the question is undetermined. Whether it is answerable or not, we do not know. What Buddhism has is not a category of "unanswerable questions" but the category of "unanswered questions."

A second issue is that if these questions have been declared undetermined, this does not mean that they have been rejected as false. To reject them as false is certainly to answer them and not to leave them unanswered. The correct position is brought into focus by the use of the words "unanswered" (*avyākata*), "set aside" (*ṭhapita*), and "rejected" (*paṭikkhitta*).[8] In this connection, the Pāli Buddhist commentarial exegesis says that "unanswered" means that which has not been answered "unilaterally, or analytically, or by raising a counterquestion."[9]

Finally, we come to the third issue, that if these questions have been declared undetermined, the theoretical views involved in them should not be understood as "indeterminate" in the sense of being neither true nor false, in other words, as neutral. "Indeterminate" is the meaning of the Pāli term *avyākata* when it is used in an ethical sense to mean what is neutral in moral contexts, that is, those acts that are kammically neither wholesome nor unwholesome.[10] The term *avyākata* is thus used in two different contexts. In a moral sense, it means kammically neutral. When it is used in regard to unanswered questions, it means not "indeterminate" but "undetermined," that is, as to whether they are true, false, or neither true nor false. When it comes to its truth value, we cannot predicate anything of what is left undetermined.

The four kinds of questions are in a Buddhist discourse introduced as: "There are these four kinds of explanations of questions."[11] The uncertainty that arises here is how the fourth kind of question, to which no answer is given, could also be considered as an explanation. The Abhidharmakośa raises this very same problem, and its answer is: "The very explanation that it is not a question to be explained is itself an explanation, for a question that should be set aside is, in fact, answered by setting it aside. How can one say that it is not an answer?"[12] This seems to be the reason why, as K. N. Jayatilleke has shown, in the *Mahāvyutpatti* this kind of question is introduced as "a question that should be explained by setting it aside" (*sthapanīya-vyākaraṇa*).[13]

Another factor that we need to remember is that, strictly speaking, it is not correct to say that the Buddha was silent on these questions. To say so implies that these questions belong to the realm of mysticism and that the Buddha thus adopted the attitude of a mystic in relation to such queries. The fact is that the Buddha very much responded to them. Although he did not give categorical answers to ten questions, he categorically stated the reasons for his not determining them as true or false. Moreover, the Buddha never resorted to silence as a means of communicating his teachings. Silence is just the opposite of communicating the doctrine, as clearly indicated by the words: "Either one engages in Dhamma talk or observes the noble silence" (*Dhammī vā kathā ariyo vā tuṇhībhāvo*).[14]

It is against this background that we need to understand why the Buddha has set aside certain questions unanswered.

The List of Unanswered Questions

1. Is the world eternal? (*sassato loko*)
2. Is the world not eternal? (*asassato loko*)
3. Is the world finite? (*antavā loko*)
4. Is the world infinite? (*anantavā loko*)
5. Is the soul the same as the body? (*taṃ jīvaṃ taṃ sarīraṃ*)
6. Is the soul one thing and the body another? (*aññaṃ jīvaṃ aññaṃ sarīraṃ*)
7. Does the tathāgata exist after death? (*hoti tathāgato parammaraṇā*)
8. Does the tathāgata not exist after death? (*na hoti tathāgato parammaraṇā*)
9. Does the tathāgata both exist and not exist after death? (*hoti ca na hoti ca tathāgato parammaraṇā*)
10. Does the tathāgata neither exist nor nonexist after death? (*neva hoti, na na hoti tathāgato parammaraṇā*).[15]

It is clear that the first four questions concern the nature of the universe that we inhabit. These questions refer to the problem of whether the universe is eternal or noneternal in terms of time and finite or infinite in terms of space. The next two questions deal with the issue of whether the soul and the physical body are identical or different. What they implicitly ask is whether we should accept the identity principle, which sees a unity between the psycho and the somatic, or the duality principle, which sees a difference between them. The last four questions relate to the postmortem survival of the tathāgata, the one who has realized emancipation. In this connection, the Pāli Buddhist exegesis says that here tathāgata means "soul" or "the living being" in the sense of a separate self-entity.[16] What this interpretation seems to mean is that those unenlightened persons who ask the last four questions mistakenly consider that there is an independent separate self-entity corresponding to the term "tathāgata."

It is very likely that these ten questions were a metaphysical questionnaire on some perennial philosophical problems that were there even before the rise of Buddhism, so much so that every religious and philosophical system was expected to provide answers to them. This fact should explain why these inquiries became the subject of many controversies among the many religious and philosophical systems during the time of the Buddha. It should also explain why the ten questions were put to the Buddha by the followers of other religions and sometimes by the Buddha's own disciples.

The Reasons for Raising the Ten Questions

From the Buddhist perspective, the reasons for raising the ten questions can be traced to what may be called the Buddhist psychology of ideologies: the diagnosis of the psychological wellsprings of all theoretical views. Thus, explaining why the Buddha, unlike other religious teachers, does not provide answers to these questions, Mahāmoggallāna says: "Unlike other religious teachers, the Buddha does not consider material form as self, or self as having material form, or material form in self, or self in material form." Mahāmoggallāna's statement, with appropriate changes, is repeated with respect to the other four aggregates as well.[17]

As noted in an earlier chapter, the "self" view is one of the three ways in which the ego-consciousness manifests itself. The "self" view affirms the presence of an abiding self in the five aggregates of the empiric individuality. This view is not the result of any deliberate reflection. It arises at an elementary reflective level out of latent tendencies (*anusaya*) leading to "I" making, "mine" making, and conceit (*ahaṃkāra-mamaṃkāra-mānānusaya*), and is ultimately due to the desire to have a permanent basis for individual existence. Although it arises at an elementary reflective level, the "self" view could subsequently lead to many speculative views concerning the nature of the world. Hence the Buddhist monk Isidatta tells Citta, the householder:

> Now, householder, as to those divers views that arise in the world . . . and as to these sixty-two views set forth in the *Brahmajāla* [*Sutta*], it is owing to the personality view ("self" view) that they arise, and if the personality view ("self" view) exists not, they do not exist.[18]

Thus, from the Buddhist perspective, all theoretical views, including those involved in the ten unanswered questions, are ultimately due to the "self" view. They all have the self as their point of view. As long as this view persists as our ideational framework, there is the ingression of the egocentric perspective into our perceptual experience. It is the ingression of the egocentric perspective into the sphere of the perceptual experience that results in what Buddhism calls "distortional thinking" (*maññanā*), the thinking that distorts the nature of actuality. This distortional thinking consists of our attributing properties not belonging to the objects of cognition. It is to this situation that the first discourse of the Majjhima Nikāya draws our attention. The first part of this discourse shows how the "uninstructed worldling" (*assutavā puthujjana*) responds to some twenty-four kinds of objects.

The objects are listed in such a way as to represent all that comes within the range of experience. They range from the four primary elements of matter to such abstract categories as "diversity" and "unity," the idea of "totality," and nibbāna as the supreme goal. What is more, in explaining the cognitive pattern of the "the uninstructed worldling" in relation to these objects, the discourse uses two verbs: one is "perceives" (*sañjānāti*) and the other is "conceives" (*maññati*). The first verb, as the commentary explains, refers to some kind of perverted perception (*saññā-vipallāsa*). The reason for this kind of response to the object is unwise attention (*ayoniso manasikāra*) to it, which, in turn, is due to the impact of the latent defilements, namely, greed, aversion, and delusion, which come to the surface of higher levels of awareness. The second verb refers to distortional thinking (*maññanā*) due to the insertion of the egocentric perspective into the objects of cognition.[19]

Thus, as long as what is referred to as the "self" view persists, so long will our pronouncements on the nature of reality be conditioned by the egocentric perspective. It is to this situation that Mahāmoggallāna draws our attention when he says that if the Buddha does not answer the ten unanswered questions it is because the Buddha is free from the "self" view. What this statement clearly implies is that once the "ego" notion is eliminated, the very validity of raising such questions also becomes invalidated. In other words, within the context of the Buddhist teaching relating to the nature of reality, these ten questions become inappropriate avenues of investigation.

The connection between the "self" view and the ten unanswered questions is clearly shown in the *Brahmajāla Sutta* of the Dīgha Nikāya. In its section on speculations about the past (*pubbanta-kappika*), we find four theories subsumed under "eternalism." Of them, three are based on retrocognitive experience of past lives and one on pure reasoning. The four theories assert in four different ways the eternal preexistence of not only the world but also both the self and the world together. We can accommodate here the theoretical view of the first unanswered question, namely, that the world is eternal. The second view, that the world is noneternal, finds no specific mention in the sutta, but is drawn by implication as the opposite of the first. In the *Pañcattaya Sutta* of the Majjhima-Nikāya, where we get a similar list of views, we do find the view that the world is noneternal specifically mentioned. Then in its section on the doctrines of the finitude and infinity of the world (*antānantavāda*), the *Brahmajāla Sutta* sets forth four doctrines regarding the extension of the world—whether the world is finite, infinite, both, or neither.

Whereas the first three are based on meditative experience, the fourth is based on reasoning. The first two views listed here correspond exactly to the theses involved in the third and fourth unanswered questions.

The next two questions, as to whether the soul and the body are identical or not, are also clearly based on the "self" view.

Then we come to the last four unanswered questions on the postmortem survival of the tathāgata, based on the fourfold predication: whether he exists, does not exist, both, or neither. Although the term "tathāgata" means the one who has realized emancipation, the Pāli Buddhist exegesis says that those who ask these questions do so by thinking that there is an independent "self" entity called "tathāgata." Thus, here too the four questions are based on the "self" view.

The fourfold predication, referred to above, has given rise to many comments by modern scholars. Louis de La Vallée-Poussin calls it "a four-branched dilemma" of Buddhist dialectic and believes that it violates the principle of contradiction. K. N. Jayatilleke, who made an in-depth study on the subject, seeks to validate the fourfold predication by showing that according to the Buddhist discourses, they are "the four possible positions or logical alternatives that a proposition can take."[20]

In this connection, we would like to make two observations. The first is that, as mentioned earlier, it is very likely that these four questions are part of a pre-Buddhist questionnaire on certain obtuse metaphysical problems. Therefore, in this particular context, the authorship of the fourfold predication cannot be attributed to Buddhism. The second observation is that what actually matters to Buddhism is not the manner of the predication, but the object of predication. The object of predication is the self, whose existence Buddhism categorically denies. Therefore, as far as Buddhism is concerned, it does not matter whether the fourfold predication is logically valid or not.

If we may adapt an illustration from the Abhidharmakośa, to ask whether the soul or self exists after death, or does not, or both, or neither is like asking whether the son of the barren woman exists after death, or does not, or both, or neither, for it is not logically possible for a barren woman to have a son. In the same way, it is not logically possible to speak of what happens to the soul or self after death. According to Buddhism, what exists is not the soul or self, but the notion of the "soul" or "self" (*atta-vāda*). Hence the four questions are meaningless.

Another reason why these four questions are meaningless stems from the use of the four verbal forms, namely, "exists," "does not exist," "both exists and does not exist," and "neither exists nor nonexists." The Buddhist doctrine of dependent arising transcends the binaryism of existence (*atthitā*) and nonexistence (*natthitā*). There are no static entities, either to exist or to nonexist. There is only becoming—a continual appearance of successive phenomena. As such, in the Buddhist context the notion of "exists" and "does not exist" does not arise.

The Reasons for Not Answering the Ten Questions

As to why the Buddha does not answer these questions, we can identify at least three main reasons. The first reason we can see even among the motives, discussed above, for raising these questions. If the "self" view is the reason for raising these questions, and if Buddhism does not recognize the "self" view, then from the Buddhist perspective the questions are meaningless and therefore do not warrant answers. Meaningless questions are not answerable either in the affirmative or in the negative. To make them answerable they need to be rephrased in a meaningful manner.

The second reason for not answering the ten questions comes into focus when the Buddhist monk Māluṅkyaputta seeks the answers to the questions from the Buddha. In reply, the Buddha tells him the answers are not relevant to understand the fact of suffering and its complete eradication, and illustrates his point with the parable of the poisoned arrow. Accordingly, the Buddha goes on to say that the answers to the questions "do not conduce to aversion, to dispassion, to cessation of suffering, to calming, to higher knowledge, to awakening, or to nibbāna."[21] The questions are left unanswered for pragmatic reasons: they have no relevance to realizing the ultimate goal of Buddhism. Whether the questions are answerable or not is another issue, which equally has no relevance to Buddhism as a religion.

A third and final reason why the Buddha leaves the ten questions unanswered comes into focus when the Buddha declares that each question is "a thicket of theoretical views, a wilderness of theoretical views, a contortion of theoretical views, a vacillation of theoretical views, and a bondage of theoretical views," to which the Buddha does not wish to enter.[22] The Buddha does not endorse either attachment or repugnance to any theoretical view. Both attitudes are due to greed and aversion and both lead to futile arguments and counterarguments.

At this juncture it is necessary to separate the first four unanswered questions from the rest. As mentioned earlier, they relate to whether the world is eternal or noneternal, finite or infinite. If Buddhism does not answer these four questions, there is another reason, besides the reasons given above, for not answering the ten questions. This concerns how Buddhism understands the term "world" as it occurs in the four questions. The last two questions, whether the world is finite or infinite in terms of space, show that those who raise these questions understand "world" in a physical sense as well. However, for Buddhism what corresponds to "world" in the four questions is samsara, the cycle of repeated births and deaths, in other words, the world of conditioned experience in its samsaric dimension.

Is saṃsāra, then, eternal or noneternal, finite or infinite? The answer comes from the Buddha's well-known statement: This saṃsāra has an unknown and undetermined end; a first beginning is not conceivable (*Anamataggo 'yaṃ saṃsāro, pubbā koṭi na paññāyati*).[23]

Let us first consider why saṃsāra is said to have no conceivable first beginning. Buddhism does not postulate an uncaused first cause as to the origin of the world. If "dependent arising" begins with ignorance, ignorance should not be understood as a cosmogonic principle to mean the first cause. The Buddha says: "The first beginning of ignorance is not known [such that we may say] before this there was no ignorance, at this point there arose ignorance . . . but that ignorance is causally conditioned can be known."[24]

Let us now consider why saṃsāra is said to have an unknown or undetermined end. This needs to be understood in light of the Buddhist teaching on nibbāna. As noted in the previous chapter, nibbāna is described as "the cessation of the world" (*loka-nirodha*) or "the end of the world" (*lokanta*). Both descriptions refer to the end of the saṃsāric process. Thus, although saṃsāra has no conceivable first beginning, it can certainly be brought to an end: not by all, but by those who realize nibbāna. If saṃsāra is not terminable, nibbāna, which is deliverance from suffering, is not possible. And since it is not possible to say who will attain nibbāna, the end of saṃsāra cannot be determined in a final manner, that is to say, in a manner embracing all living beings.

We have the story of the wanderer Uttiya, who came to the Buddha to get answers to the ten unanswered questions. When the Buddha gave his reasons for not answering them, Uttiya adopted a subtle ruse to get the Buddha committed in his answers, particularly to the two questions concerning whether the world is eternal or noneternal. Uttiya rephrased the question in this way: "On hearing the Buddha's teaching, will the whole world, or half of it, or a third of it arrive at nibbāna?" At these words, the Buddha was silent. Then Ānanda intervened and told Uttiya that he was repeating the same question in a different way, and that is precisely why the Buddha remained silent.[25]

From the Buddhist perspective, therefore, saṃsāra is neither eternal nor noneternal. If the saṃsāric process is eternal, no one will be able to attain nibbāna because what is eternal cannot be terminated. The pursuit of higher life to attain nibbāna would become meaningless. If the saṃsāric process is noneternal, everyone will attain nibbāna. Pursuit of the higher life to attain nibbāna would be abortive.

As to the next two questions about whether the world is finite or infinite in terms of space, all we need to say is that in the Buddhist context the two questions do not arise, for by "world" Buddhism means not the physical world, but the world of conditioned experience in its saṃsāric dimension.

The Wider Range of the Unanswered

As shown by his dialogues with contemporary religious teachers and philosophers, the Buddha's attitude to theoretical views is not one based on arguments to refute them as wrong. Rather, the Buddha's attitude is to keep himself aloof from such spurious arguments. What is called "the middle position" is another expression for "keeping equally aloof from" mutually exclusive theoretical views. In this particular sense, the range of the "unanswered" assumes a wider dimension to embrace the Buddha's response to all theoretical and speculative views.

Nowhere does this become so clear as in the Buddha's attitude to some sixty-two theoretical views enumerated in the first discourse of the Dīgha Nikāya. Here none of the sixty-two theoretical views is judged as true or false. All that we find is a psychological diagnosis of how these views arise and why they persist in the world at large, and, more important, how they can be transcended by identifying and eliminating their psychological wellsprings. It is a clear case of not answering any of the sixty-two theoretical views in terms of true or false. Thus they all become "unanswered," although of course they are not presented as questions.

This position becomes further clarified by the Buddhist doctrine of dependent arising. Dependent arising is called "the doctrine of the middle," since it adopts a middle position in relation to such theoretical views as "all exists" (extreme realism) versus "all does not exist" (extreme nihilism), "all is a unity" (radical monism) versus "all is a plurality" (radical pluralism), and so on. When these views were presented to the Buddha, he did not endorse as true or reject as false any of these mutually exclusive views by giving either a yes or a no answer. All that the Buddha says is that without "entering into either of the extremes" (*ubho ante anupagamma*), he teaches the Dhamma by the middle (*majjhena dhammaṃ deseti*). In this instance, "without entering into either extreme" means the same thing as "to teach Dhamma by the middle." Both in turn mean "to leave the question unanswered."

We find the wider scope of "the unanswered" more clearly articulated in a passage from the Sanskrit Sūtra Piṭaka cited in the *Abhidharmakośa-Vyākhyā* of Ācārya Yaśomitra. This passage is a dialogue between a brahmin and the Buddha:

> **The Brahmin:** "Master Gautama, is the one who acts the same as the one who experiences [the result]?"
> **The Buddha:** "Brāhmaṇa, this is undetermined (*avyākṛtam etad brāhmaṇa*)."
> **The Brahmin:** "[Then] is the one who acts different from the one who experiences [the result]?"
> **The Buddha:** "Brāhmaṇa, this is undetermined (*avyākṛtam etad brāhmaṇa*)."
> **The Brahmin:** "When asked whether the one who acts is the same as the one who experiences, you say that it is undetermined. When asked whether the one who acts is different from the one who experiences, you say that it is undetermined. What indeed is the meaning of what the Master Gautama has said?"
> **The Buddha:** "Brāhmaṇa, when one asserts that the one who acts is the same as the one who experiences, this amounts to eternalism. When one asserts that the one who acts is different from the one who experiences, this amounts to annihilationism. Without entering these two extremes, the tathāgata teaches the doctrine through the middle way" (*Etāvaṃtāv anugamya tathāgato madhyayā pratipadā dharmaṃ deśayatī ti*).[26]

It will be noticed that in this passage the term "undetermined" or "unanswered" (*avyākṛta*) is used by the Buddha in responding to the questions raised by the brahmin. As seen from the latter part of the dialogue, here "unanswered" means: "without entering these two extremes the tathāgata teaches the doctrine through the middle way."

The passage shows that unlike the Pāli suttas, in the corresponding Sanskrit *sūtras* "unanswered" or "undetermined" is said to have been used by the Buddha not only in responding to the well-known ten questions but also in responding to other non-Buddhist theoretical views. Yet as regards meaning there is no difference between what the Pali and Sanskrit discourses say. What this semantic analysis really shows is the wider range of "what is unanswered." It is not limited to the well-known ten unanswered questions. Rather, "the unanswered" refers to the way the Buddha responded to all theoretical and speculative views.

The method adopted for this purpose is to examine the logical and practical consequences of a given theoretical view, in the event of its being accepted. We find this approach well illustrated in the dialogue between a brahmaṇa and the Buddha quoted above. In other words, to examine the logical and practical consequences of a given theoretical view is tantamount to asking whether its acceptance leads to situations that obstruct the path to emancipation. The best example is how the Buddha keeps himself equally aloof from the two views assumed by the two unanswered questions, namely: Are the soul and the body the same? Is the soul one thing and the body another? Referring to these two views, the Buddha says:

> Verily, if one holds the view that the self (soul) is identical with the body, in that case, there can be no holy life. If one holds the view that the self (soul) is one thing and the body another, in that case, too, there can be no holy life. Avoiding both extremes the tathāgata teaches the doctrine that lies in the middle.[27]

It will be noticed that neither of the two mutually exclusive views is judged as wrong. All that the Buddha says is that he keeps himself equally aloof from both by adopting "the doctrine that lies in the middle." This is the criterion adopted by the Buddha with respect to all other theoretical views and ideologies. It is in this sense that we maintain that the scope of "the unanswered" is very wide indeed, much wider than the mere scope of the ten unanswered questions.

The False Theoretical View

Although the Buddha keeps himself aloof from many theoretical views, it is with respect to one kind of theoretical view that he uses the term "wrong" or "false" (*micchā*). This view is as follows:

> There is nothing given, nothing offered, nothing sacrificed; no fruit or result of good and bad actions; no this world, no other world; no mother, no father; no beings who are reborn spontaneously; no good and virtuous recluses and brahmins in the world

who have themselves realized by direct knowledge and declare this world and the other world.[28]

The wrong view, described above, has four main ingredients: (1) denial of the distinction between what is and what ought to be, (2) denial of moral causation, (3) denial of postmortem survival, and (4) denial of the possibility of spiritual life. If the Buddha describes this view as "distorted" and "false," it is because it leads to the collapse of the moral foundation of society, thereby destroying the possibility for the practice of all religious life (*brahmacariyavāsa*), whether it is Buddhist or not. The wrong view has the following four subdivisions: materialistic annihilationism (*ucchedavāda*) that reduces everything to matter, moral nonconsequentialism that denies any correlation between the act and its results (*akiriyavāda*), moral noncausationism (*ahetukavāda*) that asserts that everything happens fortuitously, and fatalism that denies the effects of all human effort (*aviriyavāda*).[29] Therefore the Buddha unequivocally states that he sees no single factor so responsible for the arising of unwholesome states of mind as wrong view. Again he says that there is no single factor so responsible for the suffering of living beings as wrong view.[30]

We would like to conclude this chapter by commenting on some modern interpretations as to why the Buddha left some ten questions unanswered. We find four main interpretations. The first proposes that the Buddha did not know the answers to them and therefore observed silence. This interpretation is an attempt to understand the Buddha's silence in light of skepticism or naïve agnosticism. The second interpretation is that the Buddha knew the answers, but since they were not relevant to gaining final emancipation, the Buddha abstained from answering them. This is an attempt to understand the Buddha's silence in light of pragmatism. The third is that solutions to these questions go beyond the grasp of the intellect, in other words, they transcend the limits of knowledge and, as such, are not answerable. This is an attempt to understand the Buddha's silence within the framework of rational agnosticism. According to another interpretation, whereas the first four questions transcend the limits of knowledge, the next six questions are logically meaningless.[31]

These different interpretations bring into focus three different positions: (1) The Buddha did not know the answers. (2) The Buddha knew the answers. (3) The questions transcend the limits of knowledge and are therefore unanswerable. In light of what we have observed as to why the questions were not answered, these three interpretations are totally unacceptable and hence totally unwarranted. The fact is that in the context of Buddhist teachings, all the questions are inappropriate and consequently meaningless. As a result, the question whether they are answerable or not does not arise.

One could argue that the interpretation based on pragmatic reasons is acceptable, since the Buddha himself says that he does not want to answer these questions, as they are not relevant to realizing the final emancipation. Yet there is a big difference between what the Buddha says and what the modern interpretation claims. According to the modern interpretation, the Buddha knew the answers to the questions, but for pragmatic reasons withheld the answers to them. On the other hand, if the Buddha says that he has left these questions unanswered because they are not relevant, that does not mean that he knew the answers to them. What the Buddha knew was not the answers to the questions but how and why they arise as meaningless questions. Therefore, if the Buddha has left them unanswered, it is because they do not justify answers either in the affirmative or in the negative, for in the context of Buddhist teachings, the ten unanswered questions are ten unwarranted questions.

Furthermore, as we have already mentioned, the category "what is unanswered" has a wider scope: It is not limited to the ten well-known questions but includes as well the position the Buddha adopted in relation to some other theoretical and speculative views. So if the modern interpretations as to why the Buddha left some questions unanswered are valid, these interpretations should be valid with respect to other theoretical positions for which the Buddha did not give definitive answers either in the affirmative or in the negative.

12

THE BUDDHIST ATTITUDE TO THE IDEA OF "GOD"

THE IDEA of a "personal deity," a creator god conceived to be eternal and omnipotent, does not find a place in the teachings of the Buddha. Nor does this idea find a place in any of the subsequent schools of Buddhist thought that come under the three main Buddhist traditions on the continent of Asia, namely, Theravāda in the south, Mahāyāna in the east, and Vajrayāna in the north.

Issara is the term used in the Pāli discourses to refer to what certain other religious teachers conceived of as god, the divine creator. From the Buddhist perspective, the idea of an "everlasting god" or an "immortal soul" comes under "spiritual eternalism." As we saw in the first chapter, from its very beginning Buddhism dissociated itself from the notion of "eternalism." Thus, in the Buddhist worldview, the very idea of a "creator god," conceived to be eternal, does not arise. Furthermore, the fundamental doctrines relating to the Buddhist view of existence, nonself and dependent arising, rule out the very possibility of introducing the "god" concept into Buddhist teachings.

Nevertheless, in the teachings of the Buddha we find explicitly stated arguments against a theistic view of existence. The reason for these arguments is the prevalence during the time of the Buddha of the idea of a "creator god" among certain religious teachers.

One reason adduced in support of the "god" idea is that all higher knowledge should necessarily come from a higher source, a divine being who is omniscient. Thus Pokkharasāti, a brahmin teacher who lived during the time of the Buddha, is represented as saying: "Those recluses and brahmins who claim 'an adequate spiritual kind of knowledge and vision' (*alam-ariya-ñāṇa-dassana-visesa*) are making an assertion that is ridiculous, worthless, empty, and vain. For how can a *mere human being* (*manussa-bhūto*) have such knowledge."[1] This claim, in other words, implies that a religion should be based only on divine revelation.

The Buddhist Epistemological Argument

A religion is not said to be false by the Buddha just because it is based on divine revelation. What the Buddha says is that what is claimed to be revealed can have a twofold result, in the sense that it could be either true or false. Thus, even if a person hears something on the most profound revelation, that utterance could be empty, hollow, and false, whereas what he does not hear on the most profound revelation could be factual, true, and not otherwise. It is hence not proper for an intelligent person, a person who wants to safeguard the truth, to assert categorically: This alone is true and anything else is false. The Buddha goes on to say that if a person wants to safeguard the truth, he should then say: This is what I have heard (from revelation). Yet that person should refrain from committing himself to the categorical assertion: This alone is true and anything else is false.[2] The most salutary attitude in this regard is to suspend judgment. Whether a conclusion based on revelation is true or false has to be determined by factors other than its claim to be based on the most reliable revelation.

It is also observed that a religion based on revelation is not satisfactory (*anassāsika*), for what is revealed can lend itself to four interpretations:

It is well remembered (well transmitted), and true.
It is well remembered (well transmitted), and false.
It is ill remembered (badly transmitted), and true.
It is ill remembered (badly transmitted), and false.[3]

In view of these possibilities, what is claimed to be revealed is not trustworthy. Even if its origins are true, there is no guarantee that the message has been accurately transmitted by those who transmitted it. Lack of caution and circumspection or lapse of memory, for instance, could easily distort what is claimed to be divinely revealed.

The Buddhist Argument Based on Moral Grounds

That everything is due to creation on the part of god (*sabbaṃ issara-nimmāṇa-hetu*) is one of the three sectarian views mentioned in the Buddhist discourses.[4] From the Buddhist perspective, the belief in a creator god cannot provide a proper foundation for the theory and practice of moral life (*kammavāda*). It is of course true that a theistic theory recognizes the need to practice moral life. Nonetheless, as Buddhism argues, it fails to justify the efficacy of moral acts (*kiriyavāda*) and the role of human effort in the practice of moral life (*viriyavāda*).[5]

The cogency of this Buddhist argument is evident in an encounter the Buddha had with certain ascetics and brahmins who claimed to believe in divine creation:

> There are some ascetics and brahmins who maintain and believe that whatever a man experiences, be it pleasant, unpleasant, or neutral, all that is caused by God's act of creation. I went to them and questioned them [whether they held such a view], and when they affirmed it, I said: "If that is so, venerable sirs, then people commit murder, theft, and unchaste deeds owing to God's act of creation; they indulge in lying, slanderous, harsh, and idle talk owing to God's act of creation; they are covetous, full of hate, and hold wrong views owing to God's act of creation. Those who fall back on God's act of creation as the decisive factor will lack the impulse and effort for doing this and not doing that. Since for them, in truth and fact, [the necessity for] action or inaction does not obtain."[6]

Here, as the Buddha argues, a theory of divine creation is totally unacceptable because of two reasons: It fails to establish a causal correlation between acts and their consequences. It equally fails to justify the necessity and desirability of human effort in pursuing the moral life. The view that everything is due to the fiat of a creator god amounts to theistic determinism, just as the view that everything is due to past kamma leads to kammic determinism.

The Mahābodhi Jātaka (V. 238) contends that the idea of "divine creation" implies that man is not morally responsible for his actions:

> If God designed the life of the entire world—the glory and the misery, the good and the evil acts—man is but an instrument (*niddesakārī*) of his will and God [alone] is responsible.

Ācārya Nāgārjuna, the founder of the Madhyamaka school of Buddhism, makes the following assertive statement:

> We know the gods are false and have no concrete being,
> therefore the wise man believes them not.
> The fate of the world depends on causes and conditions,
> therefore the wise man may not rely on gods.

The Buddhist Argument Based on the Existence of Evil

The Mahābodhi Jātaka (VI. 208) argues:

> If Brahmā is the lord of the whole world and creator of the multitude of beings, then why has he ordained misfortune in the world without making the whole world happy? For what purpose has he made the world full of injustice, deceit, falsehood, and conceit? Or is the lord of beings evil in that he ordained injustice when there could have been justice?

Should Higher Knowledge Come from an Omniscient God?

As mentioned, one reason adduced by a Brahman in support of a theistic view of existence is that all higher knowledge should come from an omniscient divine being, not from "a mere human being." Buddhism adopts the opposite position. To underpin this position there is a story recorded in a Buddhist discourse.

The story begins with a Buddhist monk who lived during the time of the Buddha. One day he came to be disturbed by a serious metaphysical problem: Where do the four great elements of matter cease without any remainder? In modern terms this problem translates as: Where does matter come to complete end? The monk believed that no human being could answer his question, so he thought of putting it to heavenly beings. Since that monk had already developed considerable mental concentration, the way to the heavenly realms appeared before him. He first came to the lowest heavenly realm, though the denizens there could not provide the answer to his question. So the monk went from heaven to heaven, still failing to receive the answer to his query. Finally, he made his way to the brahma world and put the question to the Great Brahmā: "Friend, where do the four great elements of matter cease without remainder?" Then the Great Brahmā said: "Monk, I am Brahmā, Great Brahmā, the Conqueror, the Unconquered, the All-Seeing, All-Powerful, the Lord, the Maker and Creator, the Ruler, Appointer and Orderer, Father of All That Have Been and Shall Be."

For the second and third time the monk repeated the question, yet he again received the same evasive reply. When the monk insisted on receiving an unequivocal answer, the Great Brahmā took him by the arm, led him to a corner, and said: "Monk, these heavenly beings believe there is nothing Brahmā does not see, there is nothing he does not know, there is nothing he is unaware of. That is why I did not speak in front of them. But, monk, I myself don't know where the four great elements of matter cease without any remainder. You did a mistake in bypassing the Buddha in your search for an answer to this question."

So the monk came to the world of human beings and put his question to the Buddha. The Buddha said: "You should not ask where the four great elements of matter cease without remainder. Instead the question should be rephrased: '*Where do earth, water, fire, and air no footing find?*' And the answer is: 'Where consciousness is signless, boundless, all-luminous. That's where earth, water, fire, and air find no footing.'"[7]

Obviously the purpose of this story is to show that the Great Brahmā is ignorant, although he is considered all-knowing. The main message intended to be conveyed is that higher knowledge comes not from God, as believed by some, but from an enlightened human being (*manussa-bhūta*). The source of knowledge is just the opposite of what the brahmins assert. This story also highlights the belief that if there is anything to be called "divinity," it is but exalted humanity. An enlightened human being who is free from passion, aversion, and delusion is superior to all gods, including the Great Brahmā, whom the brahmins considered the creator of the world.

The Parable of the Staircase

According to the Buddha, the attempt to find union with the Great Brahmā, whose existence cannot be properly verified, is like making a staircase without knowing where it is leading to. Thus, addressing Vāseṭṭha, a brahmin student, the Buddha says:

> Vāseṭṭha, it is just as if a man were to build a staircase for a palace at a crossroads. People might say: "This staircase for a palace—do you know whether the palace will face east or west, north or south, whether it will be high, low, or of medium height?" And he would say: "No." And they might say: "Well then, you don't know or see what kind of a palace you are building the staircase for?" And he would say: "No." Does not the talk of that man turn out to be stupid?
>
> Certainly, reverend Gotama.[8]

God as the Ineffable Highest Splendor

As can be seen from the following dialogue between the Buddha and Udāyin, some brahmin teachers conceived god as an ineffable splendor:

> **The Buddha:** "Well then, Udāyi, what is your own teacher's doctrine?"
> **Udāyi:** "Our own teacher's doctrine, venerable sir, says thus: 'This is the highest splendor.'"
> **The Buddha:** "But what is that highest splendor, Udāyi, of which your teacher's doctrine speaks?"
> **Udāyi:** "It is, venerable sir, a splendor greater and loftier than which there is none. That is the highest splendor."
> **The Buddha:** "But, Udāyi, what is that splendor, greater and loftier than which there is none?"
> **Udāyi:** "It is, venerable sir, that highest splendor, greater and loftier than which there is none."
> **The Buddha:** "For a long time, Udāyi, you can continue in this way, saying, 'A splendor greater and loftier than which there is none, that

is the highest splendor.' But still you will not have explained that splendor.

"Suppose a man were to say: 'I love and desire the most beautiful woman in this land.' And then he is asked: 'Good man, that most beautiful woman whom you love and desire, do you know whether she is a lady from the nobility or from a brahmin family or from the trader class or worker class?' And he replies, 'No.'—'Then, good man, do you know her name and that of her clan? Or whether she is tall, short, or of middle height, whether she is dark, brunette, or golden-skinned, or in what village or town or city she dwells?' And he replies: 'No.' And then he is asked: 'Hence, good man, you love and desire what you neither know nor see?' And he answers: 'Yes.' What do you think, Udāyi, that being so, would not that man's talk amount to nonsense?"

Udāyi: "Certainly, venerable sir, that being so, that man's talk would amount to nonsense."

The Buddha: "But in the same way, you Udāyi, say, 'A splendor, greater and loftier than which there is none, that is the highest splendor,' and yet you have not explained that splendor."[9]

Devas as Heavenly Beings

Although Buddhism does not believe in a creator god, it recognizes a large number of heavenly beings, beings that inhabit the myriad planes of existence in Buddhist cosmology. Their recognition does not in any way contradict Buddhist teachings:

1. None of these heavenly beings are portrayed as omniscient, omnipresent, and omnipotent. If the Great Brahmā believes that he is the creator of the world, it is a delusion on his part.
2. Any kind of heavenly existence is within saṃsāra, the cycle of births and deaths. Therefore, no heavenly being is free from the three signs of sentient existence, namely, impermanence, suffering, and nonsubstantiality. Prolonged heavenly life does not mean eternal life. From the Buddhist perspective, even divine pleasures are suffering, for, according to the Buddhist definition of the term, "suffering" means any kind of conditioned experience, whether it is extremely pleasant or otherwise.

3. The final goal of Buddhism, which is nibbāna, is the complete elimination of passion, aversion, and delusion, all while living as a human being, not birth in heaven. The Buddha says that if a Buddhist monk practices the higher life expecting to be born in heaven, he is aspiring to a lower goal.[10]
4. In fact, as the Buddha himself says, the heavenly beings themselves fancy that to be born as human beings is to go to heaven (*Manussattaṃ kho bhikkhu, devānaṃ sugati-gamana-saṅkhātaṃ*).[11] For Buddhism true heaven is not up above, but here below in the terrestrial world of human beings.
5. Prayers to gods have no role to play in the Buddhist path to emancipation.

On the Futility of Prayers

Union with Brahmā, the Creator God, is the religious goal of the brahmins. However, there was no unanimity among them as to the proper path to this goal. One day two brahmins, Vāseṭṭha and Bhāradvāja, referred this matter to the Buddha. Then the Buddha told Vāseṭṭha:

> Vāseṭṭha, it is just as if this River Aciravatī were brimful of water so that a crow could drink out of it, and a man should come along wishing to cross over, to get to the other side, to get across, and, standing on this bank, were to call out: "Come here, other bank, come here!" What do you think, Vāseṭṭha? Would the other bank of the River Aciravatī come over to this side on account of that man's calling, begging, requesting, or wheedling?
>
> No, Reverend Gotama.
>
> Well now, Vāseṭṭha, those brahmins learned in the Three Vedas who persistently neglect what a brahmin should do, and persistently do what a brahmin should not do, declare: "We call on Indra, Soma, Varuṇa, Isāna, Pajāpati, Brahmā, Mahiddhi, Yama." But that such brahmins who persistently neglect what a brahmin should do, . . . will, as a consequence of their calling, begging, requesting, or wheedling, attain after death, at the breaking-up of the body, to union with Brahmā—that is just not possible.[12]

The Notion of "Godhead" as the Ultimate Ground of Existence

Sometimes the notion of "God" is interpreted not as a personal god but as a kind of ultimate reality considered to be the ultimate ground of existence. The best example is the Upanisadic (Vedantic) teaching relating to Brahman, the cosmic soul as the ultimate ground of being.

It is worth noting that Buddhism does not distinguish between two levels of reality, one metaphysical, the other empirical. The metaphysical reality is normally interpreted either as a personal god or as an impersonal godhead.

What connects the two levels of reality is the soul. Since Buddhism rejects the notion of a "soul," the notion of a "metaphysical background" to the world of experience similarly finds no place in Buddhism.

Can nibbāna be considered Buddhism's counterpart to the idea of an "ultimate ground of being"? In our chapter on nibbāna it was observed that nibbānic experience means deconstruction (*vi-saṃkhāra*) of consciousness, resulting from the destruction of passion, aversion, and delusion. Accordingly, nibbānic experience is not projected against a metaphysical background: nibbāna is not the primordial cause or the ultimate ground of existence.

All that needs to be said here is that the Buddha's teaching on nonself, or nonsubstantiality, completely excludes the possibility of an impersonal godhead in whichever way it is described. Nonself means the absence of a self-entity both in its microcosmic and macrocosmic sense.

Concluding Remarks

In the course of this chapter we saw that the idea of "God," whether it is understood in a personal or in an impersonal sense, does not have its counterpart in the Buddha's teachings. What we have in Buddhism is not theology but anthropology, for the main thrust of the Buddha's teachings is not on a search for metaphysical first principles or final consummations of the universe. Rather, it is a search for the meaning of human life. As a religion, Buddhism begins with what is immediately given, our immediate experience or the conscious reality—which nobody can deny. The four noble truths constituting the essence of Buddhism do in fact begin with the fact of suffering as our immediate indubitable experience. In conquering suffering we have to fall back on our own resources without depending on grace and divine intervention. Most important, unlike in theistic religions, in Buddhism the final emancipation is to be sought and found within this world, as a human being, and not in an escape from it to a divine realm.

> Seek not rebirth afar in future states.
> Pray, what could heaven itself advantage you!
> Now, in this present world, and in the state
> in which you find yourselves, be conquerors![13]

APPENDIX

Buddhism and the Issue of Religious Fundamentalism

The term "religious fundamentalism" embraces all religious phenomena and movements that emerge as a reaction against some kind of perceived danger, as, for instance, the marginalization of religion due to the onset of science and technology. According to *Fundamentalisms Comprehended*,[1] some of the basic ingredients of religious fundamentalism are:

- Ultraorthodoxy: the recognition of the absolute inerrancy of the religious scriptures.
- Ultraorthopraxis: the attempt to practice religious life, based almost on a literal, rather than on a hermeneutical, interpretation of the rules and regulations laid down in the religious scriptures.
- Exclusivism.
- Militant piety.
- Fanaticism.

Exclusivism as the Root Cause of Fundamentalism

There can be many reasons for the emergence and prevalence of religious fundamentalism. Nevertheless, we can identify exclusivism as its root cause. Other kinds of fundamentalism, as, for instance, those arising in relation to one's own race, nationality, ethnicity, or political ideology, also have exclusivism as their root cause.

How the Buddha Defines Exclusivism

The most precise, and therefore the most acceptable, definition of exclusivism can be found in the teachings of the Buddha. It is the attitude of mind that manifests in relation to one's own view that "this alone is true, all else is false" (*Idaṃ eva saccaṃ; moghaṃ aññaṃ*).[2] This kind of dogmatic and exclusivist assertion is due to what is called *sandiṭṭhi-rāga*, that is, "infatuation with the rightness of one's own view or dogma or ideology."[3] Another Pāli expression with a similar connotation is *idaṃ-saccābhinivesa*.[4] It means "adherence to one's own view and asserting that this [alone] is the truth." All such categorical assertions with respect to one's own religion or ideology lead to what Buddhism calls *diṭṭhi-parāmāsa*, "tenaciously grasping views."[5]

The Danger of Attachment to Views Whether They Are Right or Wrong

An attitude of mind, driven by exclusivism, can easily provide fertile ground for bigotry and intolerance, indoctrination and unethical conversion, militant piety and persecution, interpersonal conflicts and acts of terrorism. From the Buddhist perspective, dogmatic attachment to views and ideologies, whether they are true or false, is very much more detrimental and fraught with danger than our inordinate attachment to material things. A good example is today's fast-growing "industry" of suicide bombing. Interreligious and intrareligious wars, often referred to by the misnomer "holy wars," are another case in point.

How Buddhism Looks at Views

For Buddhism, a view is only a means to an end, a guide for goal-oriented action. In his well-known discourse on the Parable of the Raft (*Kullūpamā*), the Buddha says that his teachings are not for the purpose of grasping (*gahaṇatthāya*), but for the purpose of crossing over (*nittharaṇatthāya*): to cross over from the hither shore of saṃsāra to the thither shore of nibbāna.[6] The Dhamma taught by the Buddha has only relative value, relative to the realization of the goal. As one Chinese Buddhist saying goes, the Dhamma is like a finger pointing to the moon. If we focus our attention only on the finger we cannot see the moon. Nor can we see the moon without looking at the finger.

Buddhism and Pluralism

The Dhamma is not actuality as such but a description of actuality, and therefore it can be presented in many ways, adopting many perspectives. It can also be communicated through many dialects and languages. What this brings into focus is best described as pluralism. Pluralism could be understood as the direct opposite of totalitarianism, the attempt to reduce everything into an unalterable, monolithic structure, where no alternative possibilities are permitted. We can even argue that pluralism is the direct opposite of fundamentalism as well. Where there is pluralism, there cannot be fundamentalism; where there is fundamentalism, there is no room for pluralism. In Buddhism, we can see many instances of pluralism, from its cosmic perspectives to its social dimensions.

Buddhist Cosmic Pluralism

The Buddhist view of the world or universe is not confined to our earthly existence. Nowhere does Buddhism assert that Earth is the center of the universe. From its very beginning Buddhism recognized the vastness of space and the immensity of time. In one Buddhist discourse, we read:

> As far as these suns and moons revolve shedding their light in space, so far extends the thousandfold world system. In it are a thousand suns, a thousand moons, thousands of earths, and thousands of heavenly worlds. This is said to be the thousandfold minor world system. A thousand times such a thousandfold minor world system is the twice-a-thousand middling world system. A thousand times such a twice-a-thousand middling world system is the thrice-a-thousand major world system.[7]

These world systems are, however, never static. They are either in the process of expansion (*vivaṭṭamāna*) or in the process of contraction (*saṃvaṭṭamāna*). These cosmic processes take immensely long periods of time. They are measured in terms of eons (*kappa*).[8]

Pluralism and the Concept of "Buddha"

The Buddha did not attribute his teachings to a divine source, nor did he claim to be a reformer of an earlier teaching. Therefore, the best way to describe the Buddha is to describe him as a discoverer. From the Buddhist perspective, therefore, what really matters is not the historicity of the discoverer (the Buddha) but the veracity and validity of the discovery (the Dhamma). The veracity and validity of the Dhamma does not depend on the historicity of the Buddha, just as the validity of scientific discoveries does not depend on the historicity of those who discovered them. If the Buddha is a discoverer, this also means that the Buddhahood is not the monopoly of one individual. This is precisely why Buddhism admits that there had been many buddhas in the remote past and there will be many buddhas in the distant future. When we consider the immensity of time and the vastness of space with billions of galactic systems within it, and the possibility of many kinds of living beings inhabiting them, to speak of only one Buddha for all time and all space is, to say the least, extremely parochial.

Buddhist Doctrinal Pluralism

What the Buddha taught has given rise to a colossal number of doctrines and doctrinal interpretations, which we find incorporated in three main Buddhist traditions: Theravāda in South Asia, Vajrayāna in North Asia, and Mahāyāna in East Asia. The presence of many doctrinal interpretations does not necessarily mean that they have deviated from the original teachings. Rather, they could be understood in light of the saying that what is true can be restated in different ways. It is also instructive for us to remember that the criterion of what is and what is not the Dhamma is not textual but pragmatic: what leads to the cessation of passion, aversion, and delusion is the Dhamma, what leads away from it is not the Dhamma.

Buddhist Scriptural Pluralism

Buddhist scriptural pluralism is equally colossal. There are four Buddhist canons: Pāli Buddhist, Chinese Buddhist, Tibetan Buddhist, and Mongolian Buddhist. They are not translations into four different languages of one and the same Buddhist canon, although of course they have many commonalities as well as differences.

Buddhist Cultural Pluralism

When it comes to religious culture, Buddhism could be the most pluralistic religion in the world. To whichever country Buddhism was introduced, Buddhism did not level down its cultural diversity to create a monoculture. The Buddhist culture of China is different from the Buddhist culture of Japan, and both are different from the Buddhist culture of Thailand or of Myanmar or Sri Lanka. Because Buddhism promotes cultural pluralism, it does not become a culture-bound religion. Just as a bird can fly from place to place, leaving behind its cage, even so Buddhism can fly from one place to another, say from Hong Kong to America, leaving behind its cultural baggage.

Buddhist Social Pluralism

We find many instances of pluralism in the Buddhist attitude to society as well. As a religion, Buddhism does not interfere with and impose unnecessary restrictions on people's ways of living. We never hear of Buddhist dress, Buddhist food, or Buddhist medicine laid down as valid for all times and climes, for these are things that change from place to place and from time to time, depending on the progress of our knowledge.

Pluralism is true for marriage too. There are many forms of marriage, such as monogamy, polygamy, polyandry, and so on. In the modern world, the legally recognized practice is mostly monogamy. Nevertheless, nowhere does Buddhism say that other forms of marriage are immoral. The form of the marriage could change from time to time, from place to place. If it changes, there is no problem for Buddhism. For Buddhism marriage is only a social institution. It is something entirely mundane, not a religious "sacrament." Nor does Buddhism say that marriage is an indissoluble bond. Therefore, if two married partners are incompatible, they can certainly divorce, provided, of course, they follow the laws of the country as enacted for such separations.

Buddhism has no prohibitions against birth control. If a married couple decides to practice contraception to prevent children being born, that is entirely their private business. They are not committing any act that is morally evil. Nor will the Buddhist saṅgha, whether Theravāda, Mahāyāna, or Vajrayāna, ever promulgate an edict condemning and prohibiting such acts.

Abortion is of course a different matter. Since abortion involves the taking of life, it goes against the first precept. However, in our opinion abortion can be condoned in cases of serious health hazards if abortion is the lesser evil. It is instructive for us to remember two things: One is that according to Buddhism what really matters is the intention or volition (*cetanā*). It is intention or volition that the Buddha has identified as kamma. The second is that in following morality, Buddhists are not expected to do so by absolutely grasping moral precepts (*aparāmaṭṭhaṃ*).[9]

Pluralism in the Buddhist Monastic Order

We can find pluralism in the Buddhist saṅgha organization as well. The saṅgha is not a pyramid-like organization exhibiting an ascending hierarchical order presided over by a supreme head. It is not centralized, but decentralized. The principle of organization is not perpendicular and vertical, but parallel and horizontal. This structure allows for diversity within the saṅgha community. It is this characteristic that makes it strongly resilient.

The Unity and Oneness of Humankind

Where Buddhism avoids pluralism is only perhaps in its emphasis on the unity and oneness of humankind. The Buddha categorically rejected the brahmanical social hierarchy, which was based on four castes. Among several Buddhist arguments against the caste system, one of the most persuasive is the biological (*jātimaya*). The argument begins by saying that different kinds of species, such as ants, worms, birds, and four-footed animals, have biological differences. But when it comes to human beings we cannot notice such biological differences:

> "Not as regards their hair," says the Buddha, "not as regards their head, ears, mouth, nose, lips, or brows; nor as regards their neck, shoulders, belly, back, hip, breast, anus, or genitals; nor as regards their hands, feet, palms, nails, and calves are there any biological (*jātimaya*) differences between two human beings."[10]

The Biological Argument in Another Form

Addressing a brahmin called Assalāyana, who believed in the superiority of the brāhmaṇa caste, the Buddha questions him:

> "What do you think, Assalāyana? Suppose a mare were to be mated with a male donkey, and a foal were to be born as the result. Should the foal be called a horse after the mother or a donkey after the father?"
>
> Assalāyana answers: "It is a mule, Master Gotama, since it does not belong to either kind."[11]

Here too we find the biological argument. If the mule is biologically different from the mare and the donkey, this is because it is the offspring of the mare and the donkey, who are also biologically different. However, if a so-called high-caste brāhmaṇa woman were to marry a so-called low-caste man, and if they were to beget a child, surely the child would not be biologically different from the two parents who begot him.

The Biological Argument by Aśvaghoṣa

This biological argument was also presented by Aśvaghoṣa, the Buddhist sage poet, in his *Vajrasuci* (first century CE):

> The doctrine of the four castes is altogether false. All men are of one caste. Wonderful! You affirm that all men proceeded from one, that is, Brahma the Creator God; how then can there be a fourfold inseparable diversity among them. If I have four sons by one wife, the four sons, having one father and one mother, must all be all essentially alike. Know too that distinctions of race among beings are broadly marked by differences of conformations

> and organizations. Thus the foot of the elephant is very different from that of the horse; that of the tiger unlike that of the deer; and so of the rest, and by that single diagnosis we learn that those animals belong to very different races. But I never heard that the foot of a Ksatriya (a person from the warrior caste) is different from that of a brahmin (a person from the priestly caste) or that of a sudra (a person from the menial caste). All men are formed alike, and are clearly of one race.[12]

Prejudices Based on Race (Jāti) and Caste (Gotta)

The recognition of the unity and oneness of humankind is the foundation for the practice of all spiritual life. Those who are "bound by racial prejudices" (*jāti-vāda-vinibbaddhā*) as well as those who are "bound by caste prejudices" (*gotta-vāda-vinibbaddhā*), says the Buddha, "have strayed far from the way of salvation" (*ārakā anuttarāya vijjā-caraṇa-sampadāya*). The outcast as described by the Buddha is not one who is born in a particular caste, but "one who hardens his heart by virtue of his birth in a particular race (*jāti-tthaddho*), or by virtue of his wealth (*dhana-tthaddho*) or caste (*gotta-tthaddho*), and despises his neighbor (*saṃ ñātiṃ atimaññeti*)."[13]

The Buddhist Attitude to Other Religions

The Buddha refers to all other religious teachers as *Kammavādino*, that is, those who uphold the moral life, those who maintain that society should have a moral foundation. Accordingly, the Buddha recognized in no uncertain terms the right of all religions to exist, not only in different times and places but, more important, in the same time and place as well. In this connection, we would like to draw the reader's attention to two instances only, although there are many more.

The first we find in the Upāli discourse of the Sutta Piṭaka. As recorded here, one day Upāli, a well-known disciple of Nigaṇṭha Nātaputta, the founder of the Jain religion, had a long debate with the Buddha on the subject of kamma. At the end of the debate Upāli was convinced that the Buddha was right. So he told the Buddha that he wanted to become a disciple of the Buddha. Then the Buddha told him: "You have been a longstanding disciple of Nigaṇṭha Nātaputta. Therefore, it is proper for such well-known people like you to investigate thoroughly before you make a decision." Eventually, however, Upāli became a disciple of the Buddha. Then the Buddha told him: "Householder, your family has long supported Nigaṇṭha Nātaputta. You should therefore continue to provide him and his followers with alms and other material benefits when they come to your home."[14]

The second instance we can find in the Buddha's well-known admonition to Sigāla the householder. In this discourse, the Buddha tells Sigāla that it is his duty to minister to all samaṇas and brāhmaṇas in five ways: "by lovable deeds, by lovable words, by lovable thoughts, by keeping open house for them, and by supplying their material needs."[15] What is important to remember is that the words *samaṇas* and *brāhmaṇas* mean all religious teachers and practitioners, whether they are Buddhist or otherwise.

The Four Kinds of Religion

When it comes to other religions, the Buddha mentions four kinds:

1. A religion based on divine revelation or tradition (*anussava*).
2. A religion based on the claimed omniscience of its founder (*sabbaññutā*).
3. A religion based on logical and metaphysical speculation (*takka-vīmaṃsa*).
4. A religion based on pragmatism, with a skeptical or agnostic foundation (*amarāvikkhepa*).

What is most instructive is that the Buddha does not say that any of these four religions is "false" (*micchā-diṭṭhi*). As a matter of fact, the Buddha refers to all four religions as *brahma-cariyavāsa* (practice of higher life), a term used in referring to Buddhism as well. However, according to the Buddha's assessment, none of these religions are satisfactory or consoling (*anassāsika*).[16]

Buddhist Psychology of Ideologies

This attitude of the Buddha in relation to other religions has to be understood in light of what we would like to introduce here as the "Buddhist psychology of ideologies." The rationale behind this kind of psychology is that our desires and expectations have a direct impact on what we choose to believe in. We find this idea clearly articulated in the well-known Buddhist formula of dependent arising, where one of the causal statements is "with desire as condition is clinging" (*taṇhā-paccayā upādānaṃ*). This clinging is described as fourfold, namely, clinging to sense pleasures (*kāmūpādāna*), to rites and rituals (*sīlabbatūpādāna*), to metaphysical views (*diṭṭhūpādāna*), and to soul theories (*attavādupādāna*). For our present purpose, we need be concerned only with the latter two. What both mean is that if we believe in metaphysical as well as soul (substance) theories it is because we are impelled to believe in them by our own desires. Accordingly, when it comes to ideological positions, Buddhism seeks to diagnose their origin by delving deep into their psychological wellsprings.

How Buddhism Sets Itself Aloof from Other Religious Views

It is in the context of the Buddhist psychology of ideologies that we need to understand how the Buddha responds to non-Buddhist theoretical views. Nowhere does this become as evident as in the very first discourse of the Pāli Buddhist canon, where we find enumerated some sixty-two religious and philosophical views current at the time. None of these views are rejected as false. Instead what the Buddha discusses is how these views arise and prevail entirely owing to psychological reasons, and more important, how these views can be transcended by eliminating their psychological mainsprings.[17] This, in brief, is how Buddhism sets itself aloof from other religious views without condemning any of them as false.

Then Is Not the Dhamma Taught by the Buddha Also a View?

Yes, of course, the Dhamma too is a view. But it is a view to eliminate all views, including the Dhamma itself as a view. This is the precise message conveyed to us by the Buddha's comparison of his Dhamma to a raft, a raft to go from the hither shore of saṃsāra to the thither shore of nibbāna. Accordingly, the ultimate goal of Buddhism is not to *have a view*, but *to view things as they actually are*. When Vacchagotta, the wandering philosopher, asked the Buddha: "Venerable Good Gotama, do you have any view?" the Buddha replied: "I have not come to any view (*diṭṭhiñ ca anupagataṃ*), but I have viewed (*diṭṭhañ ca tathāgatena*)." When one has seen things as they actually are (*yathābhūta-ñāṇa*), then all views come to an end. What we call a "view" is a perspective or a particular way of looking. "A particular way of looking" is not to look at things as they actually are.

Can There Be Emancipation or Salvation outside Buddhism?

In answering this question, we need to mention again that the Buddha is the one who discovers the truth but does not have a monopoly on the truth. This leaves open the possibility for others to discover the truth. The Buddhist idea of an "individual buddha" (*pacceka-buddha*), one who discovers the truth for oneself, is a clear admission of this fact. In the Suttanipāta of the Pāli Buddhist canon, the Buddha says: "I do not declare that all other samaṇas and brāhmaṇas are sunk in birth and decay (*Nāhaṃ sabbe samaṇa-brāhmaṇase jātijarāya nivutā ti brūmi*)."[18] *Samaṇa-Brāhmaṇa* is the expression used by the Buddha to mean all religious teachers and practitioners, not necessarily the followers of the Buddha. This is a clear assertion, on the part of the Buddha, of the possibility of salvation or emancipation outside Buddhism.

However, this statement should not be understood as a blanket certificate issued by the Buddha to validate all other religions. The possibility of salvation outside Buddhism does not mean that Buddhism values all religions alike and considers them equally true. What the statement clearly demonstrates is that what the Buddha had discovered and realized, others too can discover and realize for themselves. No more, no less.

Buddhism and Inclusivism

Nowhere does Buddhism assert that what is good and noble is confined to Buddhism. We find this saying in a Pāli discourse and in a Mahāyāna work: "Whatever is said by the Buddha is well said; whatever is well said is said by the Buddha."[19] The first part of this saying is clear enough not to require clarification; the second part is rather intriguing. What it means is that if there is anything well said, no matter by whom, no matter when, no matter where, if it accords with what the Buddha taught, it is also said by the Buddha. Accordingly, if there is anything well said in the sacred scriptures of all other religions, or for that matter even in nonreligious secular works, all that can be subsumed under the "word of the Buddha." Obviously the extension is only to what is well said, not to what is ill said.

In concluding this appendix on Buddhism and the issue of religious fundamentalism, we would like to refer to two edicts issued by the Buddhist King Asoka of ancient India. These two edicts, as the reader will notice, shed much light on how harmony and concord between different religions can be established.

Harmony between Religions

> Beloved-of-the-Gods, King Piyadasi [King Asoka], honors both ascetics and the householders of all religions, and he honors them with gifts and honors of various kinds. But Beloved-of-the-Gods, King Piyadasi, does not value gifts and honors as much as he values this—that there should be growth in the essentials of all religions. Growth in essentials can be done in different ways, but all of them have as their root restraint in speech, that is, not praising one's own religion or condemning the religions of others without good cause. And if there is cause for criticism, it should be done in a mild way. But it is better to honor other religions for this reason. By so doing one's own religion benefits, and so do other religions, whereas doing otherwise harms one's own religion and the religions of others. Whoever praises his own religion because of excessive devotion, and condemns others with the thought "Let me glorify my own religion," only harms his own religion. Therefore, cordial contact between religions is good. One should listen to and respect the doctrines professed by others. Beloved-of-the-Gods, King Piyadasi, desires that all should be well-learned in the good doctrines of other religions.[20]
>
> [Edict issued in 256 before the Common Era]

Conquest by Dhamma: The Highest Conquest

> Now it is conquest by Dhamma that Beloved-of-the-Gods considers to be the best conquest, and the conquest by Dhamma has been won here, on the borders, even 600 yojanas away, where the Greek King Antiochos rules, beyond there where the four kings named Ptolemy, Antigonos, Magas, and Alexander rule, likewise

in the south among the Cholas, the Pandyas, and as far as Tamraparni [Sri Lanka]. Here in the king's domain among the Greeks, the Kambojas [Persians], the Nabhakas, the Nabhapamkits, the Bhojas, the Pitinikas, the Andhras, and the Palidas, everywhere people are following Beloved-of-the-God's instructions in Dhamma. Even where Beloved-of-the-God's envoys have not been, these people too, having heard of the practice of Dhamma and the ordinances and instructions in Dhamma given by Beloved-of-the-Gods, are following it and will continue to do so. This conquest has been won everywhere, and it gives me great joy—the joy that only conquest by Dhamma can give.[21]

[Edict issued in 250 before the Common Era].

NOTES

Chapter 1. Some Preliminary Observations

1. On this observation, see Gombrich, "The Significance of Former Buddhas in The Theravāda Tradition," 62. As Gombrich further observes: "If we compare Buddhism to other world religions, we may be struck by the conscious and explicit originality of its founder."
2. S. II 25: *Uppādā vā Tathāgatānaṃ anuppādā vā Tathāgatānaṃ ṭhitā va sā dhātu dhammaṭṭhitatā dhammaniyāmatā idappaccayatā. Taṃ Tathāgato abhisambujjhati abhisameti; abhisambujjhitvā abhisametvā ācikkhati deseti paññapeti paṭṭhapeti vivarati vibhajati uttānīkaroti passathā ti c'āha.*
3. G.S. I 94.
4. D. II 156.
5. A. BJE. I 46–47. See *Culla Vedalla Sutta* in M., which contains answers given by the nun Dhammadinnā to questions raised by the lay disciple Visākha. When Visākha reported the entire conversation he had with the nun Dhammadinnā to the Buddha, the Buddha said: "The nun Dhammadinnā is wise and has great wisdom. Had you asked me the meaning of this, I would have explained it to you in the same way that the nun Dhammadinnā had explained it."
6. MLDB 882 (M. III 11).
7. See M. I: *Bahuvedanīya Sutta*; also S. IV 424–25.
8. Ibid.

9. Ibid.
10. S. BJE. V (1), 212.
11. S. IV 359–61.
12. Besides the normal definition, we find two more: *Katamañ ca bhikkhave dukkhaṃ ariya-saccaṃ? Pañcuppādanakkhandhā ti'ssa vacanīyaṃ* (S. BJE V-2, 276), and *Katamañ ca bhikkhave dukkhaṃ ariya-saccaṃ? Cha ajjhattikāni āyatanānīti'ssa vacanīyaṃ* (S. BJE V-2, 278). Individual existence can be represented either by the five aggregates of grasping or by the six internal sense bases. Therefore, that "life itself is suffering" (see chap. 6) can be stated in two ways: suffering means the five aggregates of grasping, or suffering means the six internal sense bases.
13. M.V., 266: *Paññattiṃ anatikkamma—paramattho pakāsito.*
14. VsmṬ. 225; PV. v. 1066.
15. Vin. III 150. 16; A. II 60.
16. A. II 60.
17. Ibid. There are four other persons, the Buddha says, who misrepresent what he has taught: one who is hateful (*duṭṭho*) and overcome with hate (*dosantaro*), one who is faithful (*saddho*) but with wrong grasping of the Dhamma (*duggahitena*), one who declares what the Buddha has not declared as declared by him, one who declares what the Buddha has declared as not declared by him.
18. KvuA. 89–90: *Na sā* [*dhamma-niyāmatā = paṭiccasamuppādo*] *aññatra avijjādīhi visuṃ ekā atthi. Avijjādīnaṃ pana paccayānaṃ yev'etaṃ nāmaṃ. Uppanne'pi hi Tathāgate anuppanne'pi avijjāto saṅkhārā sambhavanti, saṅkhārādīhi ca viññāṇādīni.* The opposite view that seeks to reify the principle of dependent arising is attributed to Pubbaseliyas and Mahīsāsakas. As recorded in Kvu. 584–85, some Buddhist schools maintained that "there is an immutable something called thusness in the very nature of things, material or otherwise," which is unconditioned. Thus distinct from matter, there is materiality of matter (*rūpassa rūpatā*), distinct from feeling, there is feelingness of feeling (*vedanāya vedanatā*), and so forth.
19. KvuA. 135; Abhvk. 288.
20. Abhvk. 156.
21. VsmṬ. 510: See the use of the genitive expression: *cittassa uppāda* (consciousness's origination), which is explained as: "It originates, therefore it is called origination. The consciousness itself is the origination (*uppajjatī ti uppādo; cittam eva uppādo cittuppādo*)." The two terms in the genitive

expression do not correspond to two distinct entities; they refer to one and the same phenomenon. The Sarvāstivādins, on the other hand, argue that if no distinction is admitted between the characteristic (*lakṣaṇa*) and the characterized (*lakṣya*), both will be identical. If origination, for instance, is not different from what originates, then the use of the genitive expression, for example, "origination of color," cannot be justified, for this will mean the same thing as "color of color." Here Ācārya Vasubandhu points out that this way of interpreting will entail interminable problems. In order to justify the notion of "nonsubstantiality" (*anātmatva*), for example, it will be necessary to postulate the independent existence of an entity called "nonsubstantiality" corresponding to it. To justify the notions of "number," "extension," "individuality," "conjunction," "disjunction," and "existence," one will have to admit a number of independently existing entities corresponding to them. There are as many originations as there are things originating. When we want to single out a particular origination, we use the genitive expression "the origination of color" or "the origination of sensation." However, the origination of color is not something different from the originating color, nor is the origination of sensation something different from the originating sensation.

22. SA. I 51.
23. KvuA. 103.
24. D. I 202.
25. See, e.g., D. II 217; S. I 9; A. I 158.
26. D. II 100; S. V 153; Mln. 144.
27. A. Tika-Nipāta: *Tathāgata-ppavedito bhikkhave dhamma-vinayo vivaṭo virocati, no paṭicchanno.*
28. Vin. BJE. III 42.
29. CDB. 1348–49. (S. BJE. IV 590–91).
30. D. III 226; S. II 58; Vbh. 329.
31. CDB. 1349.
32. The widespread practice of rendering the term *punabbhava* as "rebirth" is misleading. *Punabbhava* means not "rebirth" but "rebecoming"; it is an instance of dependent arising (*paticca-samuppada*), not the transmission of an entity from one birth to another. The Pāli term that should correspond to "rebirth" is *punar-uppatti*, which term does not occur either in the Pāli canon or in the postcanonical exegetical literature.
33. A. BJE. I 336–38; 338–39.
34. See chapter 10 on *nibbāna*.

35. For example, the sublime quality of loving kindness (*mettā*) is the same as nonaversion when it is elevated to the highest level as a positive factor. See Bhikkhu Bodhi, *A Comprehensive Manual of Abidhamma*, 86.
36. M. I 65.

Chapter 2. The Birth of Buddhism

1. CDB. 544, 947.
2. See, e.g., M. I 65.
3. See, e.g., D. I 13, III 108; S. II 20, III 99.
4. D. I 46: *Tasmāt' iha tvaṃ Ānanda imaṃ dhammapariyāyaṃ atthajālan'ti'pi naṃ dhārehi. Dhammajālan'ti'pi naṃ dhārehi. Brahmajālan'ti'pi naṃ dhārehi. Diṭṭhijālan'ti'pi naṃ dhārehi. Anuttaro saṅgāmavijayo'ti'pi naṃ dhārehī ti.*
5. M. I 427, 486.
6. Ibid.
7. D. I (*Brahmajāla Sutta*): *ayaṃ attā rūpī cātummahābhūtiko.*
8. DB. 73–74 (D. I 57).
9. See, e.g., S. III 49.
10. MLDB. 160 (M. I 65).
11. See, e.g., D. III 113; S. IV 330.
12. Ibid.
13. D: *Sāmaññaphala Sutta.*
14. The Pāli term used to refer to the skeptics is *amarāvikkhepikā*, which has been translated as "eel-wrigglers." *Amarā* means a species of fish that constantly emerge and dive down in the water so that it is difficult to get hold of them. In the same way a skeptic is said to resort to evasive statements. See *Brahmajāla Sutta*, which refers to four kinds of skepticism based on four different grounds.
15. Vin. BJE. III 20 (PTS. translation).
16. Ibid.
17. See *Sandaka Sutta* in M.
18. Ibid.
19. M. III 232.
20. See, e.g., D. III 212, 216; S. V 432.
21. Nyanaponika Thera, *The Vision of Dhamma*, 269.
22. Ibid.

23. D. I 28; S. II 223; A. III 440.
24. Iti. 76.

Chapter 3. Dependent Arising

1. M. I 264; Ud. 2.
2. At S. II 26, "dependent arising" is said to have four characteristics: thusness (*tathatā*), not nonthusness (*avitathatā*), not otherwiseness (*anaññathatā*), and specific conditionality (*idappaccayatā*). Buddhist exegesis clarifies these as follows: The first means that those conditions alone, neither more nor less, bring about this or that event. The second means that when the conditions come together, there is no failure even for a moment to produce the events. The third refers to the invariable relationship that subsists between the cause and the effect, in the sense that no event different from the effect arises with the help of other events or conditions. The fourth refers to the arising of phenomena from specific conditions, as, for example, the arising of decay and death, with birth as its specific condition.
3. See, e.g., *utu-pariṇāma* to mean "change of season" (A. II 87, III 131, V 110); *sammā pariṇāmaṃ gacchati* to mean "alteration of food" or "digestion" (M. I 188; S. I 168; A. III 30).
4. See, e.g., A. II 177, III 32, V 59; Vbh. 379.
5. D. III 216.
6. S. BJE. III 28.
7. The Sāṃkhya is referred to in the Pāli Buddhist exegesis as *Kāpilā*, "the followers of Kapila," the founder of the system, and also as *Pakativādino*, "the exponents of primordial nature," because in their view *prakṛti* (Pāli: *pakati*) is the ultimate causal nexus of the world of nonself.
8. PsmA. 140; VsmṬ. 546.
9. VsmṬ. 301.
10. Ibid., 138: *yathā-paccayaṃ pavattamānānaṃ sabhāva-dhammānaṃ natthi kā ci vasavattitā.*
11. DhsA. 460.
12. S. BJE. IV 88.
13. CDB. 140.
14. S. II 77.
15. Ibid.
16. Ibid., II 19.

17. Ibid., II 20–21.
18. *Path of Purification*, 639.
19. A. III 440; S. II 223.
20. S. BJE. II 32.
21. D. I 31–32
22. S. II 20–21.
23. Ibid., III 53.
24. Vsm. XVII 66–67.
25. S. II 20–21.
26. Ibid. BJE. IV 480.
27. A. V 113.
28. M. I 265.
29. S. IV 68.
30. This distinction, although not in the Pāli suttas, is clearly mentioned in Vbh. 137.

Chapter 4. Nonself and the Putative Overself

1. Among such interpreters are Radhakrishnan, *Indian Philosophy*, vol. 1; Rhys Davids, *The Birth of Indian Psychology and Its Development in Buddhism*; Grimm, *The Doctrine of the Buddha*; Perez-Remon, *Self and Non-Self in Early Buddhism*; Horner and Coomaraswamy, *The Living Thoughts of Gotama Buddha*; Bhattacharya, *L'Atman-Brahman dans le Bouddhisme ancien*.
2. S. II 156.
3. Ibid., III 147.
4. A. II 52; Netti. 85.
5. See, e.g., Vin. I 33, 41, 57.
6. A. IV 137.
7. See, e.g., S. I 188, II 53.
8. M. III 282. (trans. Wijesekera, *Three Signata*)
9. See *Cūla Saccaka Sutta* in M.
10. S. III 66.
11. VsmṬ. 138.
12. S. III 24; S. IV 130, 141.
13. Ven. Ñāṇamoli Thera, "Anattā according to the Theravāda," 46. Slight modifications for clarity are my own here and in subsequent excerpts from published translations.
14. M. I 191.

15. Ibid.
16. See, e.g., D. III 228; M. I 261.
17. M. I 433.
18. Based on the *Madhupiṇḍaka Sutta* of M. For an exquisite disquisition on this subject, see Ven. Bhikkhu Ñāṇananda, *Concept and Reality in Early Buddhist Thought.*
19. Based on ibid., 85.
20. Ibid., 90–91 (M. I 136–37).
21. S. II 60.
22. M. III 18.
23. S. IV 54.
24. Sn. v. 1124.
25. Cf. A. II 34: *Yāvatā, bhikkhave, dhammā saṅkhatā vā asaṅkhatā vā virāgo tesaṃ aggam akkhāyati yadidaṃ . . . nirodho nibbānaṃ.*
26. S. IV, *Atthatta Sutta* in *Abyākata-Saṃyutta.*
27. Oldenberg, *Buddha, His Life, His Doctrine, His Order,* 110.
28. Radhakrishnan, *Indian Philosophy,* 1: 676.
29. S. IV, *Atthattha Sutta* in *Abyākata-Saṃyutta.*
30. Ibid., BJE. V (I) 278.
31. *Bodhicaryāvatāra,* IX 60.
32. Cf. S. III 81: *pañcakkhandhe abhiññeyya pariññeyya.*
33. Nyanaponika Thera, *Buddhism and the God-Idea, Selected Texts,* 12.
34. See *Anupada Sutta* in M.
35. See Nyanaponika Thera, *The Vision of Dhamma,* 295.
36. See chapter 10 on *nibbāna.*
37. M. I 64–65.
38. Ñāṇamoli Thera, *The Lion's Roar,* 1.
39. AKvy. 697.
40. VbhA. 49–50.
41. Conze, *Buddhism,* 18.

Chapter 5. Analysis of Mind

1. CDB. 130 (S. I 39).
2. Nyanaponika Thera, *Satipaṭṭhāna,* 3.
3. M. I 256.
4. S. III 67–68, trans. Nyanatiloka Mahāthera, *The Word of the Buddha.*
5. M. I 259.

6. ADVṬ., 5: *cittaṃ ārammaṇikaṃ nāma*; 4: *sati hi nissaya-samanantara-paccaye na vinā ārammaṇena cittaṃ uppajjatī ti tassa tā lakkhaṇā vuttā. Etena nirālambanavādimataṃ paṭikkhittaṃ hoti.*
7. CDB. 890 (S. III 53).
8. See, e.g., S. II 3–4.
9. Ibid.
10. CDB. 596.
11. S. II 95.
12. D. I 21.
13. See, e.g., S. II 248, III 231.
14. Cf. AKB: *mūla-sattva-dravya.*
15. See, e.g., D. III 211; A. V 50.
16. Cf. Dhp. v. 36: *Cittaṃ rakkhetha medhāvī, cittaṃ guttaṃ sukhāvahaṃ.*
17. M: *Cūla Vedalla Sutta.*
18. See Dhs. 2.
19. M. I 112.
20. *Mahāvedalla Sutta* in M.
21. DhsA. 110–11.
22. Nyanaponika Thera, *Abhidhamma Studies*, 119–23.
23. S. BJE. III 150.
24. A. II 157; Mln. 61.
25. AKvy. 305: *adhyucyate'nenety adhivacanaṃ. vāṅ nāmni pravartate. nāmārthaṃ dyotayatīty adhivacanaṃ nāma /.* AKB. 244: *manaḥsaṃsparśaḥ ṣaṣṭhah so'dhivacanasaṃsparśa ity ucyate / kiṃ kāraṇaṃ adhivacanam ucyate nāma / tat kilāsyādhikamālambanamayo'd hivacana'saṃsparśa iti / yathoktaṃ 'cakṣur-vijñānena nīlaṃ vijānāti no tu nīlaṃ manovijñānena nīlaṃ vijānāti nīlam iti ca vijānātī' ti /.*
26. AKB. 244: *apare punar āhuḥ / vacanam adhikṛtyārthesu manovijñānasya pravṛttir na pañcānām / atas tad evādhivacanam / tena samprayuktaḥ sparśo'dhivacanasaṃsparśar ity eka āśrayaprabhāvito dvitīyaḥ saṃprayogaprabhāvitaḥ /.*
27. M. I 190.
28. Stcherbatsky, *The Central Conception of Buddhism and the Meaning of the Word "Dharma,"* 13.
29. M. I 298; see also DhsA. 221.
30. *Madhupiṇḍika Sutta* in M.
31. Bhikkhu Bodhi, *Comprehensive Manual of Abhidhamma*, 156.
32. S. III 67–68.

33. Ñāṇananda, *Concept and Reality in Early Buddhist Thought*, 6.
34. M. I 301.
35. Ibid., I 65.
36. In the Theravāda Abhidhamma two more mental factors, namely, mental one-pointedness (*ekaggatā*) and psychic life faculty (*arūpa-jīvitindriya*), are added to this category and they are introduced as the universal concomitants of consciousness (*sabba-citta-sādhāraṇa*). In the Sarvāstivāda Abhidharma, on the other hand, the number is increased to ten: *vedanā* (feeling), *cetanā* (volition), *saṃjñā* (perception), *chanda* (predilection/inclination), *sparśa* (contact), *prajñā* (understanding), *smṛti* (mindfulness), *manaskāra* (mental application), *adhimokṣa/adhimukti* (determination), and *samādhi* (concentration). These are called *mahābhūmika-dharmas.*
37. S. II 114.
38. S. XII 65 (trans. Ven. Bhikkhu Bodhi).
39. D. II 69.
40. See, e.g., Sugunasiri, "The Whole Body, Not Heart, as Seat of Consciousness: The Buddha's View," 409–30.
41. Tikapaṭṭhāna (Conditional Relations). 4: *Yaṃ rūpaṃ nissāya mano-dhātu ca mano-viññāṇa-dhātu ca vattanti, taṃ rūpaṃ mano-dhātuyā ca mano-viññāṇa-dhātuyā ca taṃ-sampayuttakānañ ca dhammānaṃ nissaya-paccayena paccayo.*
42. Vsm. 596–97.
43. Harvey, "The Mind-Body Relationship in Pali Buddhism: A Philosophical Investigation," 29–41 (M. I 276).
44. M. I 95.
45. Dhp. v. 204.
46. See, e.g., D. I 67; M. II 187.
47. Cf. The eight bases of indolence (*kusītavatthu*) in A. IV 332–33.
48. *Theragāthā*, 15.
49. This explains why the three factors of materiality come under matter conditioned by nutriment (*āhāra-samuṭṭhāna*), temperature (*utu-samuṭṭhāna*), and consciousness (*citta-samuṭṭhāna*).
50. DhsA. 151; Vsm. 465–66.

Chapter 6. Diagnosis of the Human Condition

1. M. I 90.
2. Since we have clarified the wide philosophical implications of the Pāli term

dukkha, we will continue to use the term "suffering" as its rendering into English.

3. S. IV 383.
4. M. I 190–91.
5. D. I 110; M. I 379.
6. Ibid.
7. DB. I 273 (S. I 62; A. II 48).
8. Sharma, *Spokes of the Wheel*, 122.
9. Vin. BJE. III 22.
10. S. BJE. II 32.
11. Vin. BJE. III 22.
12. Dhp. v. 204.
13. See, e.g., M. III 18–19.
14. D. III 216.
15. S. V 430, 435; Psm. II 104.
16. David-Neel, *Buddhism, Its Doctrines and Its Methods*, 82–83.
17. M. I 429.
18. Ibid., 431.

Chapter 7. Theory of Moral Life

1. A. I 16.
2. Sn. v. 895; M. II 171; Dhs. 1498.
3. CNd. 176.
4. S. V 144; Psm. II 63; Vsm. 605.
5. D. I 115; S. II 33; A. I 62.
6. D. I 115; S. II 33; A. I 287; Vin. I 71.
7. D. I 53.
8. D. I 115; A. I 62; Vin. I 71.
9. A. BJE. I 310.
10. Ibid.
11. A. III 337–38.
12. *A Buddhist Manual of Psychological Ethics* (*Dhammasaṅgaṇi*), 15–16.
13. DhsA. 121. Among the many expressions used for human effort are *ārambha-dhātu* (initiative), *nikkama-dhātu* (exertion), *purisatthāma* (human vigour), *purisa-viriya* (human energy), and *purisa-parakkama* (human effort).
14. A. III 415.

15. A. III 410.
16. A. IV 9.
17. Ibid.
18. M. I 116: *yaññad'eva, bhikkhave, bhikku bahulaṃ anuvitakketi anuvicāreti tathā tathā nati hoti cetaso.*
19. DhsA. 250; Abhvk. 132.
20. Nyanaponika Thera, *Abhidhamma Studies*, 69; Nyanaponika Thera, *Vision of Dhamma*, 117.
21. DhsA. 60.
22. DhsA. 63: *ārogyaṭṭhena anavajjaṭṭhena kosalla-sambhūtaṭṭhena ca kusalaṃ.*
23. Dhp. v. 276.
24. Sn. v. 336.
25. S. BJE. IV 436–37.
26. MLDB. 837 (M. II 14).
27. DA. II 432; DhsA. 272.
28. A. I 249.
29. CDB. 1343–44.
30. Malalasekera, *The Buddha and His Teachings*, 32.
31. Ibid.
32. A. BJE. II 414 (PTS translation).
33. A. II 95.
34. M. I 45.
35. Ibid., I 236.
36. S. V 169.
37. CDB. 1648.
38. D. II 400.
39. MLDB. 649.
40. Ibid.
41. A. II 68.
42. M. I 25.
43. S. IV 163.
44. M. III 29.

Chapter 8. Practice of Moral Life

1. A. BJE. I 134.
2. S. II 168, III 239; A. I 271.

3. M. I 40; A. III 154, IV 284; Vin. I 179.
4. M. III 71.
5. Vin. I 10; D. II 312. *Saṅkappa* is defined at DhsA. 124 as *abhiniropaṇā*, i.e., fixing one's mind on.
6. M. I 179, 268.
7. Ibid., I 396.
8. Dhp. v. 281.
9. M. I 179, 180.
10. D. I 9.
11. A. BJE. II 94.
12. M. I 466.
13. Cf. Vbh. 383; Kvu. XIV 6; DhsA. IV 3; Vsm. 11, 17.
14. A. BJE. V 86.
15. Dhp. v. 129.
16. S. V 354.
17. M. I 342; S. IV 172, 188.
18. A. I 147; Vsm. 14.
19. A. BJE. III 412.
20. D. II 80; S. II 70.
21. A. I 51: *Dve 'me bhikkhave sukkā dhammā lokaṃ pālenti.*
22. MLDB. 524 (M. I 416).
23. See *Apaṇṇaka Sutta* in M.

Chapter 9. Pursuit of Happiness

1. See M. I 342; S. IV 172, 188.
2. Sn. v. 296.
3. S. III 56
4. DhsA. 63: *ārogyaṭṭhena anavajjaṭṭhena kosalla-sambhūtaṭṭhena ca kusalaṃ.*
5. See *Satipaṭṭhāna Sutta* in M.
6. See ADS. (Cittasaṅgaha-vibhāga); Bhikkhu Bodhi, *Comprehensive Manual of Abhidhamma*, 32.
7. A. 7: 60; trans. Ven. Ñāṇamoli Thera, in Nyanaponika Mahathera, *The Four Sublime States.*
8. *Metta Sutta* in Sn.
9. A. BJE. VI 644.
10. Ibid. VI 14–15.

11. Dhp. vs. 227, 228 (trans. Ven. Sri Acharya); Buddharakkhita, *Dhammapada*, 77.
12. Dhp. v. 203.
13. D. III 58–59.
14. Ibid., I 136–37.
15. Ibid., III 65.
16. Dhp. v. 204.
17. GS. (*Aṅguttara Nikāya*), IV 187.
18. Mahathera, *Everyman's Ethics*, 14.
19. LDB 466 (*Sigālovāda Sutta* in D.).
20. Mahathera, *Everyman's Ethics*, 5.
21. BJE I 244.
22. S. I 81.
23. Mahathera, *Everyman's Ethics*, 8.
24. S. I 81.
25. Mahathera, *Everyman's Ethics*, 9.
26. Ibid., 11–12.
27. M. I 507.
28. Ibid., III 230.
29. Ibid., III 321.
30. Dhp. v. 290.
31. *Theragāthā*, 160.
32. M. I 246.
33. A. IV 64.
34. M. I 144.
35. M. II 223.
36. Ibid., II 121.
37. CDB. 1860 (S. BJE. V (2) 298).
38. *Theragāthā*, 63: Elder Pakkha: *sukhen'anvāgataṃ sukhaṃ*.
39. *Theragāthā*, 220: Elder Aṅganikabhāradvaja: *sukhena sukhaṃ laddhaṃ*.
40. Bhikkhu Bodhi, *Transcendental Dependent Arising*, 4. Ven. Bhikkhu Bodhi's book is an exquisite disquisition on this subject.

Chapter 10. Nibbāna

1. M. I 139.
2. D. III 217; S. IV 19.
3. A. V 9; S. V 9.
4. Vin. I 8, II 156; S. I 141.

5. S. IV 544.
6. Sn. v. 799.
7. S. II 173, III 31.
8. A. II 232.
9. D. III 102.
10. M. II 29.
11. M. I 10: *Nibbānassa sacchikiriyā ñāyassa adhigamo.*
12. D. III 230; M I 10; S. III 26.
13. S. V 144; Psm. II 63.
14. S. III 83–84.
15. A. II 52; Netti. 85.
16. A. IV 68.
17. M. I 487.
18. MA. II 144.
19. S. I 62.
20. Ibid., I 72.
21. See chapter 3 on dependent arising.
22. A. II 49.
23. S. IV 2.
24. M. I 487–88.
25. S. BJE. V 98. The Buddha says that if a monk does not appropriate the six bases of contact as "this belongs to me," "this I am," and "this is my self," then his six bases of contact become *pahīna* (abandoned). Thus the term *pahīna* is used not in a literal but in a psychological sense.
26. See S. BJE. V 30, 32, 64.
27. Ibid., IV 381.
28. Ibid., II 17.
29. Ibid., III 140.
30. Udāna 80.
31. ItiA. 129.
32. Cf. D. III 275: *Yaṃ kho pana kiñci bhūtaṃ saṅkhataṃ paṭiccasamuppannaṃ nirodho tassa nissaraṇaṃ.*
33. S. IV 21.
34. CDB. 915.
35. Dhp. v. 154.
36. S. IV 27.
37. S. BJE. IV 130.
38. See chapter 5 on analysis of mind.

39. MLDB. 202 (M. I 111).
40. Ibid., 1204, n. 229.
41. A. BJE. II 312.
42. Ibid.
43. M. I 32.
44. Ibid., I 400.
45. A. BJE. V 476.
46. S. BJE. III 12.
47. Vin. BJE. III 12.
48. Ibid., III 14.
49. D. III 230.
50. S. II 239; M. I 205.
51. S. II 78.
52. Saṅgharakshita, *A Survey of Buddhism*, 110.
53. Iti. 38.
54. D. BJE. II 210: *Yañ ca piṇḍapātaṃ bhuñjitvā Tathāgato anupādisesāya nibbāna-dhātuyā parinibbāyati.* Also A. BJE. V 296: *Puna ca paraṃ Ānanda yadā Tathāgato anupādisesāya nibbāna-dhātuyā parinibbāyati.*
55. Iti. 38.
56. MLDB. 592–94. (M. I 487.)
57. See, e.g., Jayatilleke, *The Early Buddhist Theory of Knowledge*, 475.
58. S. IV 383.
59. Ibid., III 109–10.

Chapter 11. The Unanswered Questions

1. A. II 46.
2. Ibid., I 197.
3. M. II 197.
4. Another instance of the Buddha following the *vibhajjavāda* method is recorded in A. X 94: "Sir, the Blessed One blames what is blamable, praises what is praiseworthy. Sir, by blaming what is blamable and praising what is praiseworthy, the Blessed One speaks after analyzing. Here (*ettha*), the Blessed One does not speak categorically."
5. See, e.g., Mahāthera, *Buddhist Dictionary*, *vibhajjavāda*. Grimm, *Doctrine of the Buddha*, 49: "The teaching of the Buddha is therefore a religion of reason; moreover, in the canon it is characterized directly by the epithet *vibhajjavāda*, a word which is translated in Childers' Pali Dictionary as

'religion of logic or reason.'" Wintenitz, *A History of Indian Literature*, 2: 62. Law, *A History of Pali Literature*, xii. PTSD, see *vibhajati*. Rahula, *History of Buddhism in Ceylon*, 50 n. 2. Jayawickrama, *The Inception of Discipline and the Vinaya Nidāna*, 22.

6. D. I 185.
7. See, e.g., Jayatilleke, *Early Buddhist Theory of Knowledge*, 286.
8. M. I 426.
9. AA. 121.
10. See, e.g., Dhs. 45.
11. A. IV 359.
12. AKB. 402.
13. Jayatilleke, *Early Buddhist Theory of Knowledge*, 282 (*Mahāvyutpatti*, 83, p. 29).
14. A. IV 359.
15. M. I 427; I 485.
16. AA. II 308–9.
17. S. IV 398.
18. Ibid., IV 526.
19. M. I 1ff.; see Bhikkhu Bodhi, *Discourse on the Root of Existence*, 1ff.
20. Jayatilleke, *Early Buddhist Theory of Knowledge*, 475.
21. M. I 432.
22. Ibid., I 486.
23. S. BJE. II 276–77.
24. A. V 113.
25. Ibid., BJE. VI 346–47.
26. AKvy. 465.
27. S. II 156.
28. M. I 515.
29. Ibid., I 515.
30. A. I 16.
31. Beckh, *Buddhismus*, vol. 1, *Einleitung, der Buddha*, 120ff. Keith, *Buddhist Philosophy in India and Ceylon*, 63ff. Poussin, *L'Abhidharmakośa de Vasubandhu*, vol. 4, *Quatrième chapitre*, 68ff. Murti, *Central Philosophy of Buddhism*, 36ff. Jayatilleke, *Early Buddhist Theory of Knowledge*, 470ff.

Chapter 12. The Buddhist Attitude to the Idea of "God"

1. M. II 200–201.
2. Ibid., II 170–71: Divine revelation can be subsumed under the term *anussava*.

The Buddha's argument against divine revelation applies equally to belief based on (a) faith (*saddhā*), (b) one's own liking (*ruci*), (c) superficial reflection (*ākāra-parivitakka*), and (d) approval of a theory thought about (*diṭṭhinijjhānakkhanti*).

3. See *Caṅki Sutta* in M.
4. A. BJE. I 310.
5. Ibid. I 310–11.
6. Ibid.
7. See *Kevaḍḍha Sutta* in M.
8. LDB. 190.
9. Translation from Ven. Nyanaponika's *Buddhism and the God Idea* (M. II 62), 10–11.
10. Among the five shackles in the heart that prevent a monk from attaining nibbāna, one is his aspiration to be born in heaven: "Again, a bhikkhu lives the holy life aspiring to some order of gods thus: 'By this virtue or observance or asceticism or holy life, I shall become a [great] god or some [lesser] god,' and thus his mind does not incline to ardor, devotion, perseverance, and striving. As his mind does not incline to ardor, . . . this is the fifth shackle in the heart that he has not severed." MLDB. 195.
11. Iti. 76.
12. LDB. 190–91.
13. A verse attributed to the Buddha in Milinda Pañha, *The Questions of King Milinda*, 328.

Appendix

1. Marty and Appleby, *Fundamentalisms Comprehended.*
2. M. II 170.
3. Sn. v. 891.
4. D. III 230; S. V 59; Dhs. 1135; Vbh. 374.
5. Dhs. 1498.
6. *Alagaddūpama Sutta* in M.
7. A. I 227–28, IV 59–60.
8. S. II 181.
9. S. I 49.
10. *Vāseṭṭha Sutta* in M. and Sn.
11. *Assalāyana Sutta* in M.
12. Quoted from Wilson, *Indian Caste*, 302–3.

13. Sn. 104.
14. *Upāli Sutta* in M.
15. D. III 192.
16. *Sandaka Sutta* in M.
17. M. I 261.
18. *Brahmajāla Sutta* in D.
19. *Aggivacchagotta Sutta* in M: "*Atthi pana bhoto Gotamassa kiñci diṭṭhigatan ti? Diṭṭhigatan ti kho Vaccha apanītaṃ etaṃ Tathāgatassa. Diṭṭhaṃ h'etaṃ Vaccha Tathāgatena: iti rūpaṃ, iti rūpassa samudayo, iti rūpassa atthaṅgamo. Iti vedanā . . . iti saññā . . . iti saṅkhārā . . . iti viññāṇaṃ . . .*" 24 Sn. v. 1082.
20. *Uttara Sutta* in A and Bodhicaryāvatāra-pañjikā.
21. Translation by Dhammika, "The Edicts of King Asoka," 386–87.

ABBREVIATIONS

A.	Aṅguttara Nikāya
AA.	Aṅguttara Nikāya Aṭṭhakathā
Abhvk.	Abhidhammattha Vikāsinī
ADVṬ.	Abhidhammattha Sangaha-Vibhāvinī-Ṭīkā
AKB.	Abhidharmakośa Bhāṣya
AKvy.	Abhidharmakośa Vyākhyā (Sphuṭārthā) of Yaśomitra
CDB.	Connected Discourses of the Buddha
CNd.	Culla-Niddesa
Dhp.	Dhammapada
D.	Dīgha Nikāya
DA.	Dīgha Nikāya Aṭṭhakathā
Dhs.	Dhammasaṅgaṇi
DhsA.	Dhammasaṅgaṇi Aṭṭhakathā
G.S.	Gradual Sayings
Iti.	Itivuttaka
Kvu.	Kathāvatthu
KvuA.	Kathāvatthu Aṭṭhakathā
M.	Majjhima Nikāya
MA.	Majjhima Nikāya Aṭṭhakathā
MLDB.	Middle Length Discourses of the Buddha
Mln.	Milinda Pañha
M.V.	Mohavicchedanī
Peṭ.	Peṭakopadesa

Psm.	Paṭisambhidāmagga
PTS.	Pali Text Society, London, Oxford
PTSD.	Pali-English Dictionary of the Pali Text Society
PV.	Paramattha-Vinicchaya
S.	Saṃyutta Nikāya
SA.	Saṃyutta Nikāya Aṭṭhakathā
Sn.	Suttanipāta
Ud.	Udāna
UdA.	Udāna Aṭṭhakathā
Vbh.	Vibhanga
Vin.	Vinaya
Vsm.	Visuddhimagga
VsmṬ.	Visuddhimagga Ṭīkā

BIBLIOGRAPHY

Primary Sources

Abhidhammattha Vikāsinī. Edited by A. P. Buddhadatta. Colombo, 1961.

Abhidharmakośa Bhāṣyam of Vasubandhu. Edited by P. Pradhan. Patna, 1975.

Abhidharmakośa Vyākhyā (Sphuṭārthā) of Yaśomitra. Edited by U. Wogihara. Tokyo, 1932–1936.

Aṅguttara Nikāya I–V. Edited by R. Morris, E. Hardy, C. A. F. Rhys Davids. Pāli Text Society, reprinted 1999.

Aṅguttara Nikāya Aṭṭhakathā (Manorathapūraṇī) I–V. Edited by M. Walleser and H. Kopp. Pāli Text Society, reprinted 1973–77.

Dhammasaṅgaṇi. Edited by E. Muller. Pāli Text Society, reprinted 2001.

Dhammasaṅgaṇi Aṭṭhakathā (Atthasālinī). Edited by E. Muller. Pāli Text Society, reprinted 1979.

Dīgha Nikāya I–III. Edited by T. W. Rhys Davids and J. E. Carpenter. Pāli Text Society, reprinted 1995–2001.

Dīgha Nikāya Aṭṭhakathā (Sumaṅgalavilāsinī) I–III. Edited by T. W. Rhys Davids, J. E. Carpenter, and W. Stede. Pāli Text Society, reprinted 1968–71.

Itivuttaka. Edited by E. Windisch. Pāli Text Society, reprinted 1975.

Kathāvatthu I–II. Edited by A. C. Taylor. Pāli Text Society, reprinted 1999.

Kathāvatthuppakaraṇa Aṭṭhakathā. Edited by N. A. Jayawickrama. Pāli Text Society, 1979.

Mahāniddesa I–II. Edited by Louis de La Vallée-Poussin and E. J. Thomas. Pāli Text Society, reprinted 2001.

Majjhima Nikāya, I–III. Edited by V. Trenkner, R. Chalmers, and Mrs. Rhys Davids. Pāli Text Society, reprinted 2002–4.

Majjhima Nikāya Aṭṭhakathā (*Papañcasūdanī*) I–IV. Edited by J. H. Woods, D. Kosambi, and I. B. Horner. Pāli Text Society, reprinted 1976–77.

Milinda Pañha. Edited by V. Trenckner. Pali Text Society, reprinted 1997.

Mohavicchedanī. Edited by A. P. Buddhadatta and A. K. Warder. Pāli Text Society, 1961.

Nettippakaraṇa. Edited by E. Hardy. Pāli Text Society, reprinted 1995.

Paramatthavinicchaya. Edited by A. P. Buddhadatta. *Journal of the Pāli Text Society*, 1918.

Paṭisambhidāmagga I–II. Edited by A. C. Taylor. Pāli Text Society, reprinted 2003.

Peṭakopadesa. Edited by Arabinda Barua. Pāli Text Society, reprinted 1982.

Saṃyutta Nikāya I–V. Edited by L. Feer and Mrs. Rhys Davids. Pāli Text Society, reprinted 1994–2001.

Saṃyutta Nikāya Aṭṭhakathā (*Sāratthappakāsinī*) I–III. Edited by F. L. Woodward. Pāli Text Society, reprinted 1977.

Suttanipāta. Edited by D. Anderson and H. Smith. Pāli Text Society, reprinted 1997.

*Theragāth*ā. Edited by H. Oldenberg. Pali Text Society 1883, reprinted 1997.

Tikapaṭṭhāna (with commentary) I–II. Edited by Mrs. Rhys Davids. Pali Text Society, 1921–23.

Udāna. Edited by P. Steinthal. Pāli Text Society, 1948.

Udāna Aṭṭhakathā (*Paramatthadīpanī*). Edited by F. L. Woodward. Pāli Text Society, reprinted 1977.

Vibhanga. Edited by C. A. F. Rhys Davids. Pali Text Society, reprinted 2003.

Visuddhimagga I–II. Edited by C. A. F. Rhys Davids. Pāli Text Society, reprinted 1975.

Visuddhimagga Ṭīkā (*Paramatthamañjūsā*). Edited by M. Dhammānanda. Colombo, 1928.

Primary Sources Translated

A Buddhist Manual of Psychological Ethics (*Dhammasaṅgaṇi*). Translated by Mrs. Rhys Davids. Oriental Translation Fund, New Series 12. London, 1923.

The Connected Discourses of the Buddha (*Saṃyutta Nikāya*). Translated by Bhikkhu Bodhi. Wisdom Publications, Boston, 2000.

Dialogues of the Buddha (*Dīgha Nikāya*) I–III. Translated by T. W. Rhys Davids. Sacred Books of the Buddhists II–IV. London, 1899–1912.

The Expositor (*Dhammasaṅgaṇi Aṭṭhakathā*) I–II. Translated by Maung Tin. Edited by Mrs. Rhys Davids. Pāli Text Society, 1920–21.

The Guide according to Kaccāna Thera (*Nettippakaraṇa*). Translated by Bhikkhu Ñāṇamoli. Pāli Text Society, 2008.

The Long Discourses of the Buddha (*Dīgha Nikāya*). Translated by Maurice Walshe. Boston: Wisdom Publications, 1987.

The Middle Length Discourses of the Buddha (*Majjhima Nikāya*). Translated by Bhikkhu Ñāṇamoli and Bhikkhu Bodhi. Boston: Wisdom Publications, 2001.

The Path of Discrimination (*Paṭisambhidāmagga*). Translated by Bhikkhu Ñāṇamoli. Pāli Text Society, 1992.

The Path of Purification (*Visuddhimagga*). Translated by Bhikkhu Ñāṇamoli. Colombo, 1956.

Points of Controversy or Subjects of Discourse (*Kathāvatthu*). Translated by S. Z. Aung and Mrs. Rhys Davids. Pāli Text Society, 1915.

Suttanipāta: Text and Translation. N. A. Jayawickrama, Postgraduate Institute of Pāli and Buddhist Studies, University of Kelaniya, Colombo, 2001.

Secondary Sources

Abraham Vélez de Cea. "Emptiness in the Pāli Suttas and the Question of Nāgārjuna's Orthodoxy." *Philosophy East and West* 55, no. 4 (2005): 501–28.

Anālayo. *From Craving to Liberation: Excursions into the Thought-World of the Pāli Discourses*. New York: The Buddhist Association of the United States, 2009.

———. *From Grasping to Emptiness: Excursions into the Thought-World of the Pāli Discourses*. New York: The Buddhist Association of the United States, 2010.

Beckh, H. *Buddhismus*, vol. 1, *Einleitung, der Buddha*. Berlin: Göshen, 1919.

Bhattacharya, K. *L'Atman-Brahman dans le Bouddhisme ancien*. Paris: École Française d'Extreme-Orient, 1973.

Bodhi, Bhikkhu, ed. *A Comprehensive Manual of Abhidhamma: The Abhidhammattha Sangaha of Ācariya Anuruddha*. Pāli translation by Mahāthera Nārada, revised by Bhikkhu Bodhi. 4th ed. Kandy: Buddhist Publication Society, 2016. BPS Pariyatti edition, 2000. PDF eBook, 2012: https://store.pariyatti.org/Comprehensive-Manual-of-Abhidhamma-A-PDF-eBook_p_4362.html (accessed November 7, 2016).

———. *The Discourse on the All-Embracing Net of Views: The Brahmajāla Sutta and Its Commentaries*. Kandy: Buddhist Publication Society, 1978.

———. *The Discourse on the Fruits of Recluseship: The Sāmaññaphala Sutta and Its Commentaries*. Kandy: Buddhist Publication Society, 1989.

———. *The Discourse on the Root of Existence: The Mūlapariyāya Sutta and Its Commentaries*. Kandy: Buddhist Publication Society, 1976.

———. *The Great Discourse on Causation: The Mahānidāna Sutta and Its Commentaries*. Kandy: Buddhist Publication Society, reprinted 2000.

———. *The Noble Eightfold Path: The Way to the End of Suffering*. Kandy: Buddhist Publication Society, reprinted 2010;

———. *Transcendental Dependent Arising: An Exposition of the Upanisā Sutta*. The Wheel Publication nos. 277–78. Kandy: Buddhist Publication Society, 1980.

Buddharakkhita, Sri Acharya. *Dhammapada: A Practical Guide to Right Living*. Singapore: Suki Hotu Dhamma, 1990.

Burns, Douglas M. *Nirvana, Nihilism and Satori*. Kandy: Buddhist Publication Society, 1968.

Collins, Steven. *Selfless Persons: Imagery and Thought in Theravada Buddhism*. Cambridge: Cambridge University Press, 1982.

Conze, Edward. *Buddhism: Its Essence and Development*. Oxford: Cassirer, 1951.

———. *Buddhist Thought in India: Three Phases of Buddhist Philosophy*. London: George Allen & Unwin, 1962.

David-Neel, Alexandra. *Buddhism, Its Doctrine and Its Methods*. New York: St. Martin's Press, 1978.

Dhammika, S. "The Edicts of King Asoka." *Collected Wheel Publications* 25, nos. 377–93. Kandy: Buddhist Publication Society, 1991.

Gethin, Rupert. *The Buddhist Path to Awakening: A Study of the Bodhi-Pakkhiyā Dhammā*. Leiden: E. J. Brill, 1992.

———. *The Foundations of Buddhism*. Oxford: Oxford University Press, 1998.

Gombrich, Richard. *How Buddhism Began: The Conditioned Genesis of the Early Teachings*. London: Athlone, 1996.

———. "Recovering the Buddha's Message." *The Buddhist Forum* 1 (1990): 5–20.

———. "The Significance of Former Buddhas in the Theravāda Tradition." In *Buddhist Studies in Honour of Walpola Rahula*. London, 1980.

———. *What the Buddha Thought*. London: Equinox Publishing, 2009.

Grimm, George. *The Doctrine of the Buddha: The Religion of Reason and Meditation*. Translated by Bhikkhu Sīlācāra. 2nd ed. Berlin: Akademie Verlag, 1958.

Hamilton, Sue. *Identity and Experience: The Constitution of the Human Being according to Early Buddhism*. London: Luzac Oriental, 1996.

Harvey, Peter. "The Mind-Body Relationship in Pāli Buddhism: A Philosophical Investigation," *Asian Philosophy* 3, no. 1 (1993): 29–41.

———. *The Selfless Mind: Personality, Consciousness, and Nirvana in Early Buddhism*. Richmond, England: Curzon Press, 1995.

Horner, I. B., and A. K. Coomaraswamy. *The Living Thoughts of Gotama Buddha*. London: Cassell, 1948.

Jayatilleke, K. N. *The Early Buddhist Theory of Knowledge*. London: George Allen & Unwin, 1963.

Jayawickrama, N. A. *The Inception of Discipline and the Vinaya Nidāna: Being a Translation and Edition of the "Bāhiranidāna" of Buddaghosa's "Samantapāsādikā," the Vinaya Commentary*. London: The Pali Text Society, 1962.

Kalupahana, D. J. *Ethics in Early Buddhism*. Honolulu: University of Hawai'i Press, 1995.

———. *The Principles of Buddhist Psychology*. Albany: State University of New York Press, 1987.

Karunaratna, W. S. *Buddhist Psychology: Citta, Cetasika, Cetanā, Consciousness, Encyclopaedia of Buddhism.* Extract No. 4. Colombo, 1995.

———. *The Buddhist Theory of Causality.* Colombo, 1974.

Keith, A. B. *Buddhist Philosophy in India and Ceylon.* Oxford: Clarendon Press, 1923.

Law, B. C. *A History of Pāli Literature.* 2 vols. London: Kegan Paul, 1933.

Mahāthera, Narada. *Everyman's Ethics: Four Discources of the Buddha.* Kandy: Buddhist Publication Society, 1985.

Mahāthera, Nyanatiloka, trans. *The Word of the Buddha.* Kandy: Buddhist Publication Society, 1927.

Malalasekera, G. P. *The Buddha and His Teachings.* Colombo: Lanka Bauddha Mandalaya, 1957.

Marty, Martin E., and R. Scott Appleby, eds. *Fundamentalisms Comprehended: An Anthology of Articles.* Chicago: University of Chicago Press, 2004.

Murti, T. R. V. *Central Philosophy of Buddhism: A Study of the Mādhyamika System.* London: George Allen & Unwin, 1955.

Ñāṇamoli, Bhikkhu. *The Life of the Buddha according to the Pali Canon.* Kandy: Buddhist Publication Society, 1972.

Ñāṇamoli Thera. "*Anattā* according to the Theravāda." In *The Three Basic Facts of Existence: III—Egolessness (Anattā), Collected Essays,* edited by Nyanaponika Thera, 45–55. The Wheel Publication nos. 202–4. Kandy: Buddhist Publication Society, 1974. http://www.bps.lk/olib/wh/wh202.pdf (accessed November 7, 2016).

———. *The Lion's Roar: Two Discourses of the Buddha.* Kandy: Buddhist Publication Society, 1993.

Ñāṇananda, Bhikkhu. *Concept and Reality in Early Buddhist Thought.* Kandy: Buddhist Publication Society, 1997.

———. *The Magic of the Mind: An Exposition of the Kālakārāma Sutta.* Kandy: Buddhist Publication Society, reprinted 1997.

Ñāṇavīra, Thera. *Clearing the Path: Writings of Ñāṇavīra Thera (1960–1965).* vols. 1–2. Dehiwale: Buddhist Culture Centre, 2001–2.

———. *The Tragic, the Comic and the Personal: Selected Letters of Ñāṇavīra Thera.* Edited by Samanera Bodhesako. Kandy: Buddhist Publication Society, 1987.

Norman, K. R. *Collected Papers.* vol. 2. Oxford: Pāli Text Society, 1991.

Nyanaponika Mahathera. *The Four Sublime States.* The Wheel Publication no. 6. Kandy: Buddhist Publication Society, 1958.

Nyanaponika Thera. *Abhidhamma Studies: Buddhist Explorations of Consciousness and Time*. Edited with an introduction by Bhikkhu Bodhi. Kandy: Buddhist Publication Society, 1965, 1985; Boston: Wisdom Publications, 1998, 2015.

———, ed. *Buddhism and the God-Idea*. Kandy: Buddhist Publication Society, 1970. BPS online edition, 2008: http://www.bps.lk/olib/wh/wh047.pdf (accessed November 4, 2016).

———. *Satipaṭṭhāna: The Heart of Buddhist Meditation: A Handbook of Mental Training based on the Buddha's Way of Mindfulness*. London: Rider, 1962; Kandy: Buddhist Publication Society, 1992.

———. *The Vision of Dhamma: Buddhist Writings of Nyanaponika Thera*. Edited by Bhikkhu Bodhi. Kandy: Buddhist Publication Society, 1994.

Nyanatiloka, Mahāthera. *Buddhist Dictionary: Manual of Buddhist Terms and Doctrines*. Colombo, 1956.

———. *Fundamentals of Buddhism*. Kandy: Buddhist Publication Society, 1994.

———. *The Word of the Buddha*. Kandy: Buddhist Publication Society, 1927.

Oldenberg, Hermann. *Buddha, His Life, His Doctrine, His Order*. Translated by William Hoey. Delhi: Low Price Publication, 2011.

Perez-Remon, J. *Self and Non-Self in Early Buddhism*. The Hague: Mouton Publishers, 1980.

Poussin, Louis de La Vallée. *L'Abhidharmakośa de Vasubandhu*, vol. 4, *Quatrième chapitre*. Paris: Paul Geuthner, 1923–25.

Premasiri, P. D. *Ethics in Buddhism, Encyclopaedia of Buddhism*. Extract No. 1. Colombo, 2002.

Radhakrishnan, S. *Indian Philosophy*. vol. 1. London, 1958.

Rahula, Walpola. *History of Buddhism in Ceylon: The Anuradhapura Period, 3d Century BC–10th Century AD*. Colombo: M. D. Gunasena, 1966.

———. *What the Buddha Taught*. London: The Gordon Fraser Gallery, 1959.

Rhys Davids, C. A. F. *The Birth of Indian Psychology and Its Development in Buddhism*. London, 1936

———. *Buddhist Psychology*. London, 1914.

Saṅgharakshita, Bhikshu. *A Survey of Buddhism*. Boulder, CO: Shambhala Publications, 1980.

Sarachchandra, E. R. *Buddhist Psychology of Perception*. Colombo, 1958.

Sharma, Arvind. *Spokes of the Wheel: Studies in Buddha's Dhamma*. New Delhi: Books & Books, 1985.

Stcherbatsky, Th. *The Central Conception of Buddhism and the Meaning of the Word "Dharma."* Prize Publication Fund, vol. 7. London: Royal Asiatic Society, 1923.

Sugunasiri, S. H. J. "The Whole Body, Not Heart, as Seat of Consciousness: The Buddha's View." *Philosophy East and West* 45, no. 3 (1995): 409–30.

Tilakaratne, Asanga. *Nirvana and Ineffability: A Study of the Buddhist Theory of Reality and Language*. Colombo: Postgraduate Institute of Pali and Buddhist Studies, University of Kelaniya, 1993.

Warder, A. K. *Indian Buddhism*. Delhi: Motilal Banarsidass, 1980.

Watanabe, F. *Philosophy and Its Development in the Nikāyas and Abhidhamma*. Delhi: Motilal Banarsidass, 1983.

Wijesekara, O. H. de A. *Buddhist and Vedic Studies*. Delhi: Motilal Banarsidass, 1994.

———. *Three Signata: Anicca, Dukkha, Anatta*. Kandy: Buddhist Publication Society, 1982.

Wilson, John. *Indian Caste*. London: Blackwood, 1877.

Wintenitz, Maurice. *A History of Indian Literature*, vol. 2, *Buddhist and Jain Literature*. Delhi: Motilal Banarsidass, 1998.

INDEX

ABOUT THE AUTHOR

Y. KARUNADASA, PHD (University of London), PhD Honoris Causa (Mahamakut Buddhist University, Bangkok, Thailand), DLitt Honoris Causa (University of Kelaniya, Sri Lanka), is professor emeritus at the University of Kelaniya and a former director of its Postgraduate Institute of Pāli and Buddhist Studies. He was a Commonwealth Academic Staff Fellow (1974–1975) and visiting professor (1993) at SOAS University of London, a Distinguished Numata Chair Professor at the University of Calgary (2001), and a Tung Lin Kok Yuen Visiting Professor at the University of Toronto (2008). Currently he is the MaMa Charitable Foundation Visiting Professor at the University of Hong Kong. Among his published works are *The Theravāda Abhidhamma: Its Inquiry into the Nature of Conditioned Reality* and *The Buddhist Analysis of Matter.*

WHAT TO READ NEXT FROM WISDOM PUBLICATIONS

Rebirth in Early Buddhism and Current Research
Bhikkhu Anālayo

"A detailed study of the much-debated Buddhist doctrine of rebirth. *Rebirth in Early Buddhism* and Current Research illuminates a complex topic with great clarity and understanding."—Joseph Goldstein, author of *Mindfulness: A Practical Guide to Awakening*

Manual of Insight
Mahāsi Sayadaw
Forewords by Joseph Goldstein and Daniel Goleman

"The teachings of Mahāsi Sayadaw formed the essential context in which I learned, practiced, and studied meditation. That context is beautifully expressed in this book. I believe, as a Western laywoman who has been able to access the liberating teachings of the Buddha in a direct and pure form, I owe an inexpressible debt to Mahāsi Sayadaw's scholarship, understanding, and courage of transmission. It is a great gift to have this translation available."—Sharon Salzberg, author of *Lovingkindness*

Abihdhamma Studies
Buddhist Explorations of Consciousness and Time
Nyanaponika Thera and Bhikkhu Bodhi

"One of the most profound and lucid interpreters of Buddhist psychology in our time."—Daniel Goleman, author of *Emotional Intelligence*

About Wisdom Publications

Wisdom Publications is the leading publisher of classic and contemporary Buddhist books and practical works on mindfulness. To learn more about us or to explore our other books, please visit our website at wisdompubs.org or contact us at the address below.

Wisdom Publications
199 Elm Street
Somerville, MA 02144 USA

We are a 501(c)(3) organization, and donations in support of our mission are tax deductible.

Wisdom Publications is affiliated with the Foundation for the Preservation of the Mahayana Tradition (FPMT).